Scripta Series in Geography

Series Editors:

Richard E. Lonsdale, University of Nebraska
Antony R. Orme, University of California
Theodore Shabad, Columbia University
James O. Wheeler, University of Georgia

Other titles in the series:

The American Metropolitan System:

Present and Future

Edited by Stanley D. Brunn

University of Kentucky

and James O. Wheeler

University of Georgia

 V. H. Winston & Sons

 **Edward Arnold**

First published 1980 by
Edward Arnold (Publishers) Ltd.
41 Bedford Square, London WC1B 3DQ
and published simultaneously in the United States of America by Halsted Press, a division of
John Wiley & Sons Inc.

British Library Cataloguing in Publication Data

Brunn/Wheeler
    The American metropolitan system. – (Scripta series in geography).
    1. Metropolitan areas – United States
    I. Brunn, Stanley D   II. Wheeler, James O
    301.36'4'0973   HT334.U5

    ISBN 0-7131-6297-X

Library of Congress Cataloging in Publication Data

Brunn, Stanley D.
    The american metropolitan systems.

    (Scripta Series in geography)
    "A Halsted Press book"

    Includes index.
    1. Metropolitan areas – United States – Addresses, essays, lectures.
    2. Suburbs – United States – Addresses, essays, lectures.
    3. Urban economics – United States – Addresses, essays, lecture.
    4. Cities and towns – United States – Growth – Address, essays, lectures.
    5. Urban renewal – United States – Addresses, essays, lectures.
    I. Wheeler, James O., Joint Author   II. Title   III. Series.
    HT123.B77   307.7'6'0973   80-36824

    ISBN 0-470-27018-7

Typeset in the United States of America by
Marie Maddalena of V. H. Winston & Sons
Printed in Canada by The Hunter Rose Company Limited, Toronto.

Contents

Preface vi

Chapter 1 New Dynamics of Growth in the American Metropolitan System 1
Philip D. Phillips and Stanley D. Brunn

Chapter 2 Revitalization Trends in Downtown-Area Neighborhoods 21
Roman A. Cybriwsky

Chapter 3 Suburbanization in the 1970s: Interpreting Population, Socioeconomic, and Employment Trends 37
Peter O. Muller

Chapter 4 Exurban Areas and Exurban Migration 51
Curtis C. Roseman

Chapter 5 Spatial and Behavioral Aspects of the Counterstream Migration of Blacks to the South 59
James H. Johnson, Jr. and Stanley D. Brunn

Chapter 6 Geopolitical Fragmentation and the Pattern of Growth and Need: Defining the Cleavage between Sunbelt and Frostbelt Metropolises 77
Donald J. Zeigler and Stanley D. Brunn

Chapter 7 Lending Practices and Policies Affecting the American Metropolitan System 93
Joe T. Darden

Chapter 8 Regional and Structural Shifts in the American Economy since 1960 111
Thomas A. Clark

Chapter 9 Science and Technology in the American Metropolitan System 127
Edward J. Malecki

Chapter 10 Usages of Communication Technology and Urban Growth 145
Susan R. Brooker-Gross

Chapter 11 The Changing Patterns of Industrial Corporate Control in the Metropolitan United States 161
John D. Stephens and Brian P. Holly

Chapter 12 Energy and Its Effect on Regional Metropolitan Growth in the United States 181
Frank J. Calzonetti

Chapter 13 Alternative Prospects for America's Urban Future 201
Stephen S. Birdsall

Contributors 213

Index 214

Preface

A dominant thread woven into the fabric of contemporary urban geography in the United States is the coverage of topics and themes at a national level and within a systems context. The thread has become more noteworthy with the identification of topics and problems at the national scale and the importance of national policies to resolve them. The major thrust of this book is to identify some salient features and problems of contemporary and future American metropolitan systems. Each of the 13 chapters focuses on a specific urban topic, problem, or process from a national perspective.

Following the introductory chapter by Phillips and Brunn on the "Slow Growth Epoch," the remaining chapters are grouped into those dealing with population and policy changes, those treating economic and technologic changes, and a final chapter by Birdsall discussing alternative prospects for America's urban future. Five major topics are addressed. The first, which includes changes in the spatial form of the metropolis, treats inner city revitalization by Roman Cybriwsky, the diffusion of communication technology by Susan Brooker-Gross, and the immediate and long-term impacts of higher energy costs and diminished supplies by Frank Calzonetti. The second major topic considered is the changing economic functions of metropolitan areas; included are the statements on the increasing importance of service-performing industries by Tom Clark and the spatial structure of science and technology activities by Edward Malecki. The structure of national economic systems comprise the third major theme; John Stephens and Brian Holly dissect the changing spatial structure of industrial corporate head offices since 1955. The fourth topic discussed is population. Roman Cybriwsky's study, cited above, examines the extent of inner city revitalization, Peter Muller the evolution of suburbia or "the outer city," Curt Roseman the post-1970 nonmetropolitan growth, and James Johnson the extent and geographic structure of the black counterstream migration from North to South. The final topic dealt with is policy; two chapters have that theme as a primary focus. These are Joe Darden's examination of various lending practices (redlining) and Don Zeigler's analysis of the extent and causes of geopolitical fragmentation. Policy issues are also covered by Calzonetti, Malecki, Clark, and Cybriwsky, among others.

The 13 chapters identify a number of urban and metropolitan problems, some at the national scale and others at regional scales. Sunbelt-Frostbelt contrasts are referred to by a number of authors in regard to population change, energy, geopolitical fragmentation, and the post-industrial economies. Other problems discussed relate to individual behavior, e.g., the implications of communication technology on commuting, the impact of higher energy prices on personal travel, the lure of amenity environments, and the effects of revitalization attempts on the poor, minority, and elderly. Most authors suggest, in one way or other, that there are a number of economic and social transformations occurring within the American metropolitan system. Some suggest that the changes are already in evidence, such as the post-industrial economies, the impact of Federal assistance programs, and the effects of higher energy prices, whereas for others the diffusion of high-speed communication technology and the impacts of slower population and economic growth are yet to affect large numbers of people. Whatever the scale and extent of the changes, the impacts are likely to be apparent through all points and regions within the nation's economic and social systems.

The growth of urban geography as a systematic area within the discipline has flowered during the 1960s and 1970s. More theses and dissertations have been' completed on urban topics during these two decades than in all previous decades together. Likewise, the number of articles and book chapters has increased dramatically. Specialists have emerged with interests in a wide variety of economic, social, political, and environmental topics. In view of the increasing importance of metropolitan areas and systems in American life, it seemed to us as editors that the thoughts and writings of a number of young geographers, who are focusing on national issues, need to be conveyed to the profession and related disciplines. For these reasons a conscious attempt was made in our survey of contemporary American urban geography to solicit previously unpublished manuscripts that address selected topics within a national context. We feel the result of our effort is successful. All of the authors, except three, earned their Ph.D. degrees in the 1970s. It is those geographers trained in the 1970s who are helping to formulate the content of urban geography in the 1980s and 1990s. It is our hope as editors that the many ideas and topics conveyed throughout this book will stimulate undergraduate and graduate students in urban geography classes into thinking about the many still unstudied geographies of the American metropolitan system.

A number of individuals deserve thanks for their assistance in the preparation of this book. Deserving special thanks for the cartography is Jill Eilertsen of the Center for Cartographic Research and Spatial Analysis, Michigan State University. Mike Lipsey, also of the Center for Cartographic Research and Spatial Analysis, is recognized for his supervision of the cartography for this book. For their valued assistance in the typing, reproduction, and proofing the manuscript, we thank Mildred Bell, Yvonne Pommerville, June Sims, Kathy Smith, and Pat Wall, all of the Department of Geography at the University of Georgia. For assistance in the early stages of the editorial process, we thank Claire Stevenson, M.A. candidate, and for help toward the end of the editorial work we appreciate the aid of Sam O. Park, Ph.D. candidate, both in the Department of Geography at the University of Georgia. For assistance in compiling the index, we thank Dr. Sharon Price-Bonham of the University of Georgia.

We acknowledge the use of some figures in Chapter 1, reproduced with permission, which previously appeared in *Geographical Review*, Vol. 68 (1978) and in the *Journal of Geography*, Vol. 77 (1978). The Department of Geography, Michigan State University, is acknowledged for underwriting the cartographic costs for the book and the Department of Geography at the University of Geography for photographic reproduction of the figures. We also thank the authors for their willingness to meet our deadlines. Finally, we thank Victor Winston for his encouragement throughout the duration of this project.

Stanley D. Brunn
James O. Wheeler

Chapter 1

New Dynamics of Growth in the American Metropolitan System

Philip D. Phillips and Stanley D. Brunn

Population and economic changes begun in the 1960s and more evident in the 1970s suggest the U.S. is entering a new epoch. That epoch is identified by distinctive demographic, technological, energy, and transportation-communication features. The term "Slow Growth" is used to describe both the slower rates of natural increase and growing scarcity of energy resources, both which affect spatial patterns and processes operating within the American metropolitan system. Likewise the population growth of nonmetropolitan areas since 1970 and the impact of computer and telecommunication systems are having a pronounced effect on the form and structure that metropolitan areas are assuming.

The rates of natural increase in metropolitan areas, and especially the largest, in the Frostbelt are approaching a state of zero population growth. Sunbelt cities and states, on the other hand, are growing not only because of amenity environments but due to lower energy costs and growing markets to satisfy a post-industrial economy. The policy impacts of slow growth in metropolitan areas are especially important in regard to increased competition for federal funds to deal with an aging housing stock and infrastructure. Slow population growth will also affect the nation's economic growth, opportunities for innovations, entry into the job market, styles of management, and interregional and intrametropolitan competition for industries. Post-industrial societies will have to become cognizant of both the positive and negative effects of slow growth and slow growth cities to resolve problems that surface.

This chapter presents an overview of the changes that have differentiated growth patterns of metropolitan America in the 1970s from the patterns of previous decades.

The overview is presented in five major sections: (1) an introduction discussing the general framework of epochs of metropolitan evolution; (2) a presentation of the dimensions of change in the 1970s; (3) an analysis of why population trends in the 1970s have been different than in the preceding decades; (4) an inquiry into the effects these changes have had on metropolitan America; and (5) speculation as to the longer-term impacts the trends of the 1970s will have if they continue into the 1980s.

EPOCHS OF METROPOLITAN EVOLUTION:
A FRAMEWORK FOR CHANGE

In the 1970s the dynamics of the American metropolitan system changed dramatically from the patterns of the 1950s and 1960s. The rate of metropolitan population growth slowed; metropolitan to nonmetropolitan migration became dominant; energy abundance gave way to energy scarcity; the Frostbelt was overshadowed by the Sunbelt; and the transportation of goods gave way, in part, to the communication of ideas. The trends of the 1970s did not, however, represent an abrupt break with the past, but rather the culmination of changes long in the making. For example, net migration into metropolitan areas slowed greatly from the 1950s to the 1960s, but it was only in the 1970s that the balance reversed and net migration out of metropolitan areas became a reality.

The changes in the underlying dynamics of metropolitan America occurring in the 1970s were not unprecedented. Four major epochs in the evolution of the American metropolitan system prior to 1970 have been outlined:[1] the Sail Wagon Epoch, 1790 to 1830; the Iron Horse Epoch, 1830 to 1870; the Steel Rail Epoch, 1870 to 1920; and the Auto-Air-Amenity Epoch, from 1920 to 1970 (Fig. 1). Each of these epochs was characterized by a set of distinctive economic/technological, demographic, and geographic patterns and dynamics that affected the regional and internal structure of metropolitan growth. Cities grew, and declined, during each epoch in response to the dominant technologies, especially in energy, transportation, and communication.

Cities reflect the technologies and socioeconomic characteristics of the eras in which they emerged. The passage between epochs is a transition period of significant technological, economic, and social change. As a new epoch finds expression in the metropolitan system, parts of cities, and some entire metropolitan centers and regions, retain the physical structure of the past and become "inhabited ruins."[2] The transition between epochs also makes the trends of the past poor predictors of the shape of the future.

The changes occurring in the American metropolitan system during the 1970s indicate that a major new epoch is beginning to unfold. This new epoch is a distinct departure from the previous Auto-Air-Amenity Epoch. Because the most significant technical, social, and economic forces underlying this new epoch are slower growth and scarcity, we have chosen to call it the "Slow Growth" Epoch.

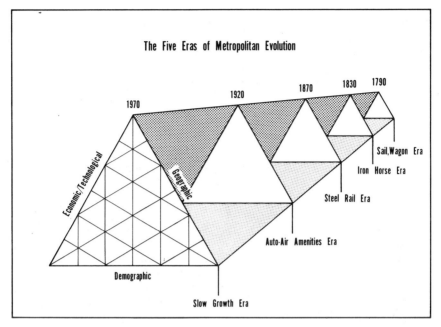

Fig. 1. The five eras of metropolitan evolution.

THE DIMENSIONS OF SLOW GROWTH

The overall population of America's metropolitan areas has undergone a remarkable deceleration that has been little noticed until recently. The growth rate of all Standard Metropolitan Statistical Areas (SMSAs) was 2.6% per year in the 1950s, but sagged to 1.7% per year in the 1960s, and fell to only 0.8% per year from 1970 to 1975. Thus, the American metropolitan system appears to be rapidly nearing a state of zero population growth.

Within the metropolitan system, the growth that has occurred in the 1970s has been much more concentrated than formerly in certain size classes of SMSAs and in certain regions of the country. Population growth in the first half of the 1970 to 1980 decade was concentrated in small- and medium-sized SMSAs much more than was growth in the 1960s (Table 1). In the 1960s, SMSAs with under 500,000 residents grew less rapidly than the average for all SMSAs; however, in the 1970s slower than average growth has occurred only in SMSAs with over 2 million inhabitants. Indeed, SMSAs with over 2 million population showed an overall absolute population decline from 1970 to 1975. SMSAs with under 250,000 population actually grew more rapidly in the 1970s than they had in the 1960s.

Regional patterns of metropolitan population growth have undergone marked changes from the 1960s to the 1970s (Table 2). Only one standard Census region,

Table 1. Annual Rate of U.S. Metropolitan Population Change by Size Class

Size class	Annual percentage change		Change, 1960–1970 to 1970–1975
	1960–1970	1970–1975	
2,000,000 and over	1.2	−0.1	−1.3
1,000,000 to 1,999,999	2.7	1.5	−1.2
500,000 to 999,999	1.8	1.1	−0.7
250,000 to 499,999	1.8	1.3	−0.5
Under 250,000	1.4	1.5	0.1
All areas	1.7	0.8	−0.9

Source: 1970 U.S. Census of Population and U.S. Census Current Population Reports, Series P-25, No. 709 (Washington, D.C., 1977).

the Mountain states (especially Colorado), had more rapid metropolitan growth in the 1970s than the 1960s. This more rapid population growth appears to result both from the perception of the Mountain states as relatively "unspoiled" natural areas and, paradoxically, from growing exploitation of coal and oil resources in the area. The most rapid decrease in metropolitan population growth rates between the 1960s and the 1970s occurred in the Pacific, East North Centeral, West North Central, and Middle Atlantic Census regions, with all of these areas experiencing at least a 1% per year decline in growth rates.

The impact of reduced metropolitan population growth rates was most severe in the Middle Atlantic and North Central states, where this reduction resulted in virtually no growth because previous rates of growth were modest. Metropolitan areas of the Middle Atlantic states actually showed a small absolute population loss in the 1970s. The Pacific states, notably California and Washington, showed a large drop in annual population growth rates from the 1960s to the 1970s, but the effect was not so dramatic because rates in the 1960s had been high. The relatively modest decrease in population growth rates from the 1960s to the 1970s in metropolitan areas in the South produced a comparative "boom" for this region. The South became the fastest growing of the four major Census regions in the 1970s, not because its rate of growth increased, but rather only because its rate of growth slowed less rapidly than other regions.

Growth rates of individual metropolitan centers indicate several changes in trends between the 1960s and 1970s (Figs. 2 and 3). In the 1960s absolute population decline was rare for SMSAs and was confined almost entirely to Appalachia. By the 1970s, absolute population decline was much more widespread—a total of 36 SMSAs showed absolute population declines from 1970 to 1975. Most of the larger areas that suffered declines were in the North Central and Northeast Census regions. Rates of increase slowed rapidly for many Pacific Coast cities, especially Los Angeles and Seattle, but remained high for cities in Florida, the desert Southwest

Table 2. Annual Rate of U.S. Metropolitan Population Change by Region

Region	Annual percentage change		Change 1960-1970 to 1970-1975
	1960-1970	1970-1975	
Northeast	0.9	−0.0	−0.9
New England	1.2	0.4	−0.8
Middle Atlantic	0.8	−0.2	−1.0
North Central	1.3	0.2	−1.1
East North Central	1.3	0.2	−1.1
West North Central	1.4	0.4	−1.0
South	2.2	1.8	−0.4
South Atlantic	2.6	2.0	−0.6
East South Central	1.1	1.1	−0.0
West South Central	2.1	1.8	−0.3
West	2.8	1.4	−1.4
Mountain	3.4	3.5	0.1
Pacific	2.7	1.0	−1.7
United States	1.7	0.8	−0.9

Source: 1970 U.S. Census of Population and U.S. Census Current Population Reports, Series P-25, No. 709 (Washington, D.C., 1977).

(Arizona and New Mexico), and along the Rocky Mountain Front in Colorado. A number of small metropolitan areas did not follow general trends as a result of specific local factors. Military cutbacks produced population decline in Columbus, Georgia (Fort Benning) while Clarksville-Hopkinsville, Tennessee-Kentucky (Fort Campbell) and El Paso, Texas (Fort Bliss) grew rapidly. University towns, such as Champaign-Urbana, Illinois (the University of Illinois), which had grown rapidly in the 1950s and 1960s as university enrollments swelled, grew slowly or declined in the 1970s as university enrollments stabilized or declined.

THE CAUSES OF SLOW GROWTH

Increasingly well-developed technologies of birth control, including acceptance of the birth control pill, sterilization, and abortion, have contributed to a rapid decline in crude birth rates per 1,000 population for the nation as a whole from 25.0 in 1955 to 19.4 in 1965 and 14.9 in 1974, while death rates remained virtually unchanged (Fig. 4). This decline in fertility has produced a decline in the intrinsic rate of natural increase from +12.1% per decade in 1965 to -5.0% in 1974. Only the demographic momentum of the post-World War II baby boom and net in-migration, both legal and illegal, from foreign countries have maintained even the modest rate of national population increase.

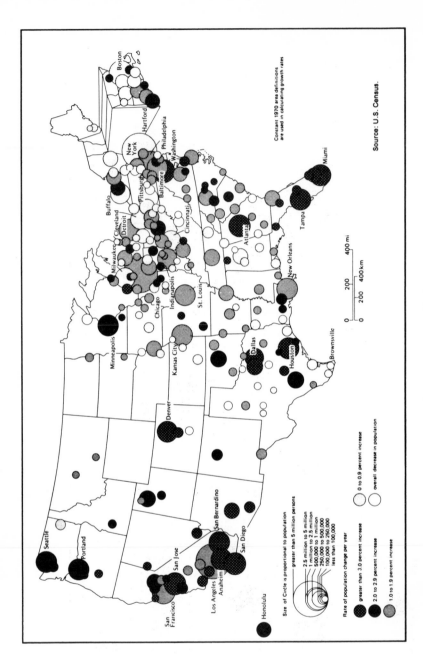

Fig. 2. Population change is SMSAs, 1960–1970.

6

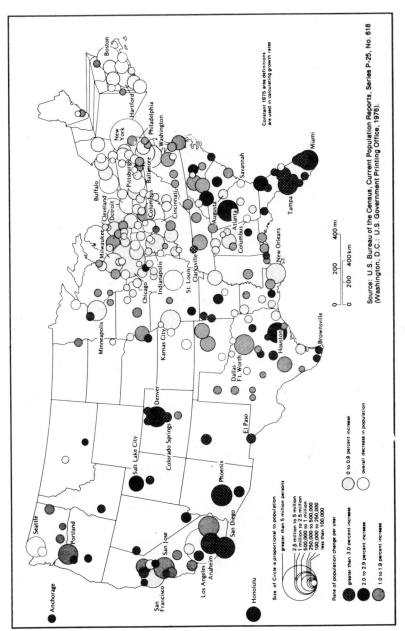

Fig. 3. Population change in SMSAs, 1970–1974.

7

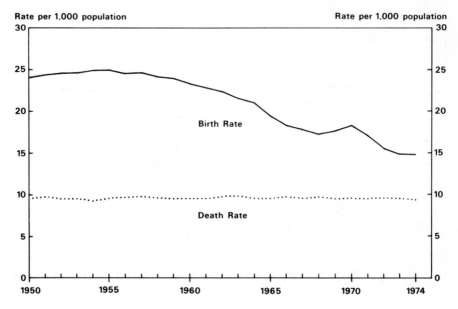

Fig. 4. Birth and death rates: 1950–1974.

By 1973, almost 70% of all American couples were using some form of birth control, with 25.1% using pills, 16.4% using sterilization, and 28.2% using other means. Of the 30% of couples not using contraception, most were infertile as a result of pregnancy or natural sterility. Another factor that appears to have led to a substantial decline in birth rates is the legalization of abortion, first in New York in 1970 and then in the nation in 1973. By 1974 there were 283 legal abortions for every 1,000 live births in the U.S., and abortions actually exceeded live births in the District of Columbia. The decline in rates of natural increase has had an extremely significant impact on metropolitan areas, both because such areas make up about two-thirds of the total national population and because they generally have even lower rates of natural increase than the nation as a whole. Slower natural population increase is a major social and technological divide, though of a considerably different and less tangible nature than many previous changes, such as the development of the steel rail and internal combustion engine described by Borchert.

Increase in energy availability, like population, appears to have diminished, contributing to the new Slow Growth Epoch. The Ford Foundation's study of future energy availability concluded that continued growth of energy at rates approaching those in the past is unlikely without massive government subsidies and unrealistically low price assumptions. As traditional fossil fuel supplies have become less available, regional price imbalances favoring supply regions have developed. For example, electric bills for industrial use in 1976 were three or more times higher in some northern industrial states such as New York than in southern and western

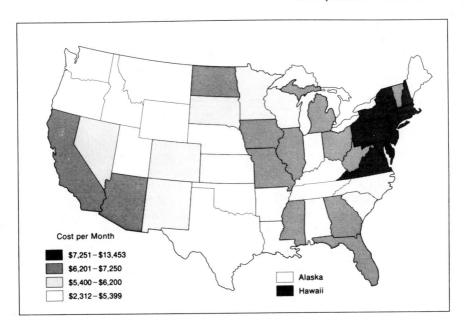

Fig. 5. Cost of electricity: industrial averages by state.

states such as Oklahoma or Wyoming (Fig. 5). Many authorities believe that this price differential is the real cause of the growth of industry and personal incomes in the Sunbelt and in western metropolitan areas.[3]

Not only has the availability of traditional coal, oil, and natural gas supplies in the Sunbelt and in rural areas placed them at a competitive advantage compared with the traditional Manufacturing Belt, but the future development of western subbituminous coal, oil shale, geothermal, and solar power will greatly favor these same areas. William H. Miernyk, in describing the "Decline of the Northern Perimeter," concluded that "as with most prolonged binges, the energy binge of the past quarter century is being followed by a hangover."[4] This hangover will probably be most unpleasant for large northeastern industrial cities with high energy costs.

A "rural renaissance" in the U.S. since 1970 has also slowed the growth of the urban system. The post-1970 shift of net migration to nonmetropolitan areas is in sharp contrast to historical trends. From 1790 to 1970 metropolitan America grew continually: and, with the possible exception of brief periods during the War of 1812 and the Great Depression of the 1930s, net migration was to metropolitan areas. This trend was so well ingrained that as recently as 1972 a report of the Commission on Population Growth and the American Future envisioned that most future population growth would occur in metropolitan areas. Yet from 1970 to 1974 nonmetropolitan areas grew at an annual rate of 1.3%, while metropolitan areas grew at a rate of only 0.8%, and three-quarters of all nonmetropolitan counties showed net in-migration.

Nonmetropolitan growth does not appear to be simply a spillover from metropolitan areas. Net in-migration is found not only in counties adjacent to SMSAs and in counties within commuting distance to SMSAs but also in remote rural counties, those with no urban place (town of 2,500 inhabitants or more), and no commuting to an SMSA. Nor is nonmetropolitan growth limited to a few regions. All of the 26 nonmetropolitan regions defined by Calvin Beale showed population growth from 1970 to 1974, and 24 of these areas had net in-migration. In contrast, in the 1960s only 5 of these 26 nonmetropolitan regions had net in-migration.[5]

Why are people moving to nonmetropolitan areas? To some extent this movement may represent a return to earlier home areas during the recession of the early 1970s and thus be similar to rural in-migration in the 1930s. Many other factors are involved, however. Increasing Social Security and other pension benefits allow greater numbers of retirees to move not only to cities in Florida and the Southwest but also to nonmetropolitan retirement areas in the Ozarks, the Texas hill country, the Sierra Nevadas, the Upper Great Lakes, and other areas. Greater incomes have allowed millions of other families to build second homes and vacation hideaways, overwhelmingly in nonmetropolitan areas. These second homes often become retirement or other permanent homes. Even as part-time residences, second homes spur construction industries, real estate sales, and local service economies in nonmetropolitan areas.

A good measure of the distribution of retirement and second home developments is provided by the distribution of land sales development sold on an interstate basis and reported to the U.S. Department of Housing and Urban Development (Fig. 6). The states with the largest numbers of developments are rural amenity and Sunbelt states, notably Florida and Arizona. Large numbers of developments are also found in the Ozark Mountain states (Arkansas and Missouri), in the southern Appalachians (North Carolina and Virginia), and in New England (especially New Hampshire). The Great Plains states and the urban-industrial states of the Northeast are conspicuous because of the small number of developments they have, especially in relation to their population. Although some of these interstate land sales developments are in metropolitan areas, many are in nonmetropolitan areas, and their location in sunshine, coastline, and topographic amenity areas clearly defines the type of area that Americans seek out in looking for the "good life."

Perhaps the most significant change affecting the metropolitan-nonmetropolitan migration balance has been the intensification and implimentation of a "rural mystique." While many Americans increasingly see the city as being crowded, dangerous, and dirty, the countryside and small towns are viewed as open, clean, and safe. This may be contrasted to the views of the early 20th century, when small-town America was seen as vacuous—a "Gopher Prairie," where, in the words of Sinclair Lewis, "dullness was made god." Guidebooks to "safe" small towns far from the corrupting influences of metropolitan areas have become best sellers. Telephones and the electronic media have broken down much of the isolation and provinciality of rural areas, while better transportation has made them more accessible. This has allowed increasing numbers of persons to enjoy the benefits of rural environments without their traditional shortcomings. Not only have retirees, vacationers, and the independently wealthy been attracted to rural areas, but small

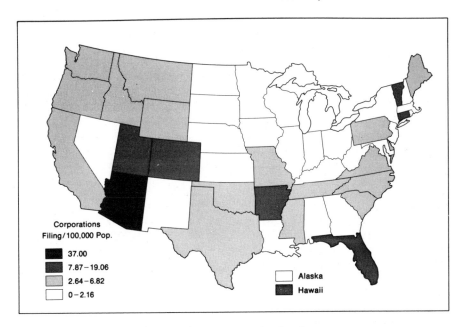

Fig. 6. Interstate land sales developers.

industries and artisans have been attracted as well, as have an undetermined number of footloose former metropolitan residents who have moved to small towns and rural areas to open general stores, gift shops, weekly newspapers, and the like.[6]

Recent out-migration from metropolitan areas may represent the beginning of what has been called a "post-city" age based on widely available, inexpensive electronic communications and data processing. Americans, unlike Europeans, have traditionally viewed cities not as cultural centers but as economic entities designed to facilitate communications and to pool labor. Thus, "no Frenchman can imagine France without Paris, but it is not so hard to imagine the United States without New York—millions of Americans engage in this fantasy every day."[7] Viewing the city in economic, and perhaps even social, terms, Ronald Abler could ask, "with complete time- and cost-space convergence, why even have cities?"[8]

The era of low-cost, widely available communications has been given many names by authorities as wide-ranging as Alvin Toffler and Zbigniew Brzezinski. Among those are post-industrialism, the super-industrial age, the age of discontinuity, the tectronic era, the communications era, and the electronic social transformation.

Whatever the name of the coming epoch, authorities agree that the erosion of geographic space will be one of its chief attributes. In a high communications technology society, many of the traditional pressures responsible for the growth of great metropolitan centers cease to exist.

The late 1960s and early 1970s have seen two major trends in communications technologies that have reduced urban centrality. The first has been the merger of the computer and telecommunications systems to transfer information and the development of time-sharing techniques bringing the capabilities of computers and the information in data banks to millions of locations. The second trend has been in the increasing capacity and wide diffusion of telecommunications. By the early 1970s, for instance, it was possible to transmit 108,000 simultaneous voice channels through one coaxial cable.

Communications scientists predict that in the next few decades the use of presently available communications techniques will increase vastly and that two-way cable transmission of television, facsimile mail and newspapers, and information retrieval between private homes and data banks will also become commonplace. As a result, office files, library information, and educational data will be readily and widely accessible, allowing people to work and learn at home and to live almost anywhere they wish. Whether or not future developments live up to the expectations of communications scientists, the move to substitute communications for transportation seems already to be under way. Between 1960 and 1973 the number of intercity ton miles of freight hauled grew by 68% and intercity passenger miles grew by 73%, while telephone conversations grew by 102% and cable-television subscribers by an amazing 1,023%. The rapid growth of cable television is indicated by an Atlanta television station, which is now received in 44 states via satellite-cable systems.

The form of settlement in a high communication "post-city" age remains in doubt. Jerome Pickard foresees an "urban splatter" along interstate highway corridors throughout the nation. Brian Berry, on the other hand, sees a "new frontier" for those of wealth in nonurban "rimland" environments of hills, water, and forests. He urges that we face this fact and "speed abandonment" of traditional cities so that we may achieve "an urban civilization without cities."[9] Others, however, do not foresee the end of the city and castigate those who do. Economist Wilbur Thompson, responding to Berry's predictions, said, "I believe that they [the cities] will come back for a reason that a good geographer like Brian Berry should appreciate: they have the best local site. Unfortunately, geographers do not study landscapes any more. They all have elaborate data processing equipment and run census data endlessly through their machines."[10] Whether we enter Berry's "post-city" age or Thompson's age of urban "comeback," it appears likely that improved communications technology will favor greatly lowered population densities and will allow realignment of development to high-amenity natural environments outside the bounds of traditional metropolitan areas.

SLOW GROWTH AND THE CHARACTER OF THE METROPOLITAN SYSTEM

Slower overall growth will cause the growth of regions and metropolitan centers to increasingly approach a zero-sum game. Traditionally, growth and decline have been measured relative to the elastic yardstick of ever-increasing national population and economic production. "Declining" regions and cities almost always grew in absolute population but at a slower rate than the nation as a whole; as a result they represented progressively declining proportions of the national population and economic output.

The effects of slower growth and a near-zero-sum game have become evident in recent years, first in manufacturing employment and more recently in total population. From 1967 to 1973 the South gained 802,000 jobs in manufacturing. The total growth of manufacturing employment in the U.S. during this period was only 644,000, however. As a result, the Northeast, and especially its metropolitan centers, became an absolute as well as a realtive loser, with a loss of 482,000 manufacturing jobs. Since 1970 interregional and intermetropolitan population change has also become more of a zero-sum game.

The reduced rate of natural population increase in the 1970s has been largely responsible for the radical increase in the number of SMSAs showing absolute population decline. Interregional and intermetropolitan economic shifts have always produced out-migration for some areas, but this has been more than balanced by a "cushion" of natural increase. In the 1960s natural increase was more than 1.6% per year for a large number of SMSAs and was less than 1.0% per year almost exclusively in cities of the Northeast and Florida with aged population structures (Fig. 7). By the 1970 to 1975 period, rates of population increase had slowed dramatically not only for the nation as a whole but also in almost every SMSA (Fig. 8). Only a few SMSAs of the Rio Grande Valley and in Mormon Utah maintained natural increase rates of more than 1.6% per year, and the vast majority of SMSAs had rate of increase of less than 1.0% per year. A good example of the effect of declining rates of natural increase on population change is provided by the Chicago SMSA, where the decline in natural increase made the difference between the observed 0.0% population change from 1970 to 1975 and the 2.0% increase that would have occurred from 1970 to 1975 if the natural increase rates of the 1960s had prevailed.

Slow growth and a near-zero-sum game in the metropolitan system will have a significant impact on interregional and intermetropolitan competition. Because absolute as well as relative losses will occur, competition for growth, especially in jobs, is likely to become more vicious. Recent "pirating" expeditions from the South and New England for New York firms is undoubtedly only a portent of more intense competition in the future. In efforts to woo industry and business many areas will be tempted to follow the same strategy as slowly growing cities in the past to accept lower wages, polluting industries, and the exploitation of human and natural resources by nonlocal corporations. Rather than being the boom envisioned by environmentalists, slow growth and no growth may be a short-term environmental nightmare.

Losers in the competition for corporate growth (and for governmental facilities as well) will demand compensatory aid from federal and state governments to prevent the absolute decline of their areas. As general population growth slows, it will become increasingly difficult to prevent some areas from declining if other areas are

14

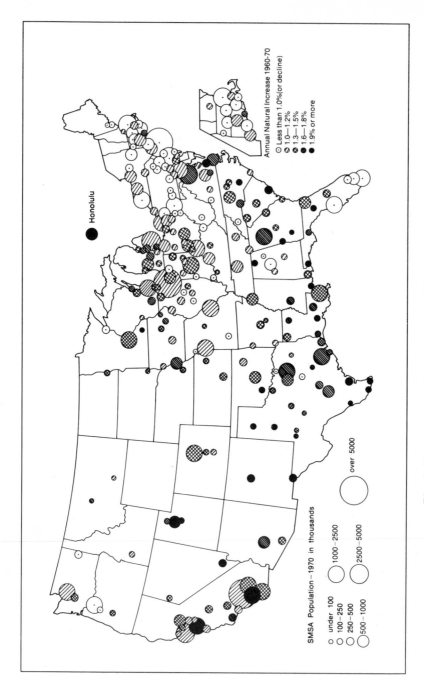

Fig. 7. Natural population increase in SMSAs, 1960–1970.

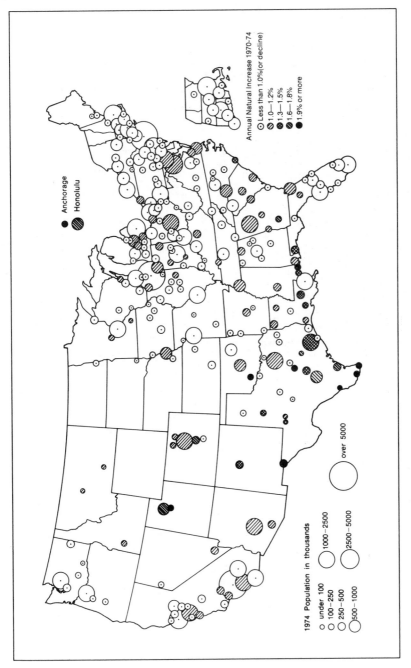

Fig. 8. Natural population increase in SMSAs, 1970–1974.

15

allowed to grow. Thus long-term forces toward a conservative welfare economy, in which efficiency is sacrificed to regional stability, will be set in motion. Control of growth and decline, if it occurs, could significantly diminish individual freedom of choice to live in preferred environments as inducements are established to artifically maintain the population of older manufacturing cities and regions at the expense of the Sunbelt.

Slower growth will also have a tremendous impact on the general economic and social character of metropolitan areas. Kenneth Boulding characterized the relationship between rates of population increase and employment hierarchies as follows:

> Hierarchies tend to have a triangular structure, with large numbers of people in lower levels and diminishing numbers in each echelon as one goes toward the top. If the age distribution is likewise triangular, then an individual who does not die first has a good chance of rising in the social hierarchy: that is, if he doesn't go out, he goes up. With the rectangular age distribution [found in no growth areas], however, a good many individuals go neither out not up. Then the question of what to do with older people who do not rise in the status or income hierarchies of society becomes very acute.[11]

Or, as Wilbur Thompson pithily observed, "Young professionals out West are pushing for no-growth so that the wait at the ski line is shorter. They will come to understand that under no-growth, the wait for promotion at the office is going to be longer—a hell of a lot longer."[12]

The experience of some of America's few previous no-growth cities, described by Edgar Rust in *No Growth: Impact on Metropolitan Areas*, fits this pattern. Cities such as Terre Haute, Indiana, have few young persons entering the job market because of heavy out-migration. As a result, corporate age profiles become top-heavy with executives who have remained in the same jobs for long periods of time, producing low levels of entrepreneurship and limited capacity for innovation. Nonlocal communications fields of such cities also tend to contract. Perhaps the most pernicious aspect of no-growth that Rust describes is the development of a deeply ingrained attitude of "risk-avoidance" by all institutions, including banks, churches, utility companies, and government agencies. These institutions learn that risk takers prosper in a growing area but perish in a stable area.[13] If American cities develop rectangular age profiles and reasonably stable populations as a result of lower rates of natural increase and net out-migration to nonmetropolitan areas, risk-avoidance may become the dominant style of management and aggressive entreprenuership and innovation may become less common.

Boulding is particularly gloomy in portraying the nature of an economy that is not growing. He suggests that a rapidly growing system is "cheerful," because the poor can become richer without the rich becoming poorer. A stable metropolitan area, in economic or population terms, generates more conflict and more often generates exploitation of people rather than resources by "mafia-type" social organizations.[14] Rust, in his investigation of previously nongrowing metropolitan areas, found greater inequalities of education, welfare, and public health there than in growing areas.[15] Thus it appears that no-growth metropolitan areas will have a strong tendency to develop high levels of social inequality and exploitation.

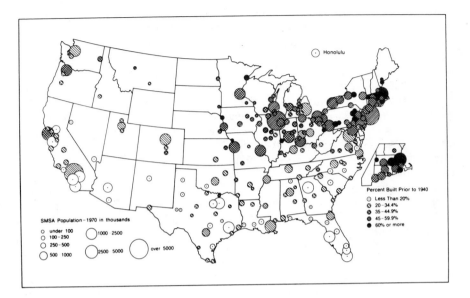

Fig. 9. Percentage of dwellings in SMSAs built before 1940.

Slower growth also implies an increasingly aged housing stock and infrastructure. Great regional disparities already exist in age of housing (Fig. 9). In almost no SMSAs of the Northeast and North Central region was less than 35% of the 1970 housing stock built before 1940, and in many of these SMSAs more than 60% of the housing was built before 1940. In contrast, in only a handful of cities in the South and West does more than 35% of the housing stock predate 1940, and in many cities pre-1940 housing is less than 20% of the total supply. Declining national population growth rates will produce fewer new families and less demand for housing. Employment in construction, both for residential and commercial purposes, will decline, with severe economic impacts. Moreover, much of the remaining construction will be not in new structures but in the repair, renovation, and restoration of existing structures. It is sobering to realize that the "boom" in the Sunbelt is only comparative, that the overall growth rate of metropolitan areas in the South in the 1970s is lower than the growth rates of metropolitan areas in the North Central states in the 1950s. By the year 2000 the housing stock of southern cities is likely to contain as high a proportion of housing more than 40 years old as northern cities had in 1970.

Slower growth will have some positive effects, however. In his study of previous no-growth and slow-growth cities, Rust found four major benefits of slower growth. Housing tends to be less expensive, more plentiful, and more often owner-occupied. Crime rates are markedly lower, even when the older age structure of nongrowth cities is accounted for. Stress diseases show a lower incidence in the apparently more placid and stress-free environment of nongrowing cities. Finally, nongrowth cities tend to exhibit stronger family, church, and ethnic ties and to more effectively transmit values from generation to generation. Rust concluded that "an overriding public objective ... should be to protect, enhance, and capitalize on the benefits of slow growth."[16] Edgar Hoover speculates that population stabilization can have many favorable impacts on metropolitan areas, including less demand for improved urban transport; slower flights of upper-income whites to the suburbs, less pressure on the environment and enhanced possibilities for housing rehabilitation and renovation, reduced racial strife, and improved school quality.[17] Likewise, Thompson suggests that central cities will have a greater ability to rebuild and renovate if they are freed of the need to house rapidly increasing populations of poor immigrants from rural areas.[18]

An international comparative study of 18 countries has revealed that the trends of slower metropolitan growth and net migration from more to less metropolitanized areas is widespread.[19] Of 18 highly or moderately developed industrial nations studied, 11 have shown a reversal of migration flows resulting in out-migration from national core areas to peripheral areas. This study also revealed that while significant short-term fluctuations in the number of persons moving to metropolitan regions could be correlated with economic conditions (with more in-migration to metropolitan regions in boom times), the long-term trend is generally toward dispersal. Thus, the Slow Growth Epoch is not peculiar to the American metropolitan scene, but rather appears to be occurring throughout the developed world.

AN UNCERTAIN PROSPECT

The nature of future slow-growth and no-growth cities is difficult to predict with certainty. Unlike no-growth cities of the past, which were islands of decline and out-migration in a growing system, no-growth cities of the future will be more similar to the system as a whole. The massive out-migration of the young that has characterized previous non-growing cities such as Terre Haute, Ind., and St. Joseph, Mo., will not be necessary to maintain slow or no population growth as rates of natural increase decline. Overcoming Americans' traditional love of newness and belief that growth is good may be the most difficult challenge of slower growth. Most chambers of commerce and civic organizations still actively seek population and economic growth for their area. Even those who call for no growth for the population of their own city or town rarely see it in the context of no growth in population, energy, or jobs for their entire region or the metropolitan system as a whole.

The embryonic Slow Growth Epoch described here is the product of many new societal trends. Overall, these trends are now poorly defined and understood, and many of them, if allowed for a prolonged period in the future, are contradictory and incompatible. The decline of the Manufacturing Belt and the growth of the Sunbelt can be documented, but how long these trends can continue before demands for equity in growth from declining areas become a strong political force is not clear. Already, groups such as the Northeast-Midwest Economic Advancement

Coalition have called for "a major economic stimulus of the sort only the federal government has the resources to provide."[20] In other words, it is time for Congress and the Executive branch to consider a Tennessee Valley Authority for the Northeast and Midwest."[21] Counter, pro-Sunbelt groups, such as the Southern Growth Policies Board, have been formed and claim that the South still needs help because the South still lags behind the nation in absolute terms. Claims and counterclaims between these groups led one observer to deplore the "U.S. North-South 'poor mouth' contest" in which both regions claim to be poorer and more beleaguered.[22]

The "post-city" age foreseen by many may not be compatible with higher costs for, and shortages of, energy. Although innovations in telecommunications allow decisions to be made in nontraditional rural settings, they cannot make the energy consumption levels of exurbanites as low as those of urbanites. Exurban residents consume more energy for transportation to purchase goods, for recreation, and for provision of vital services. Those who have chosen to live in exurban villages and in mountain hideaway homes will be faced with difficult, if not impossible, choices if energy prices continue to rise or if rationing of gasoline and other energy sources becomes widespread. These choices will be especially difficult for lower- and moderate-income households, which make up the bulk of the exurban population.[23] High energy use by exurbanites may also prompt government regulation of this type of development, severely curtailing the "post-city" age.

The nature of the Slow Growth Epoch that America appears to have entered will depend largely on compromises among the various contradictory forces that have produced it. Recently reversed trends in birth rates, metropolitan–nonmetropolitan migration, and energy availability may change again in unpredictable directions. Not only will trends clash, but society may not choose to follow new technologies to the fullest extent possible. The role of nontechnological ethical and moral constraints are exemplified by recent decisions of the U.S. Supreme Court limiting federal support of abortion to welfare mothers and the continuing strong "right-to-life" movement to end all abortions. Further evidence of ethical and practical limitations to technology is indicated by the fact that a computerized crime information network proposed by the FBI in the late 1960s has not been instituted in the late 1970s, not because of practical problems in collecting data and designing the system but because of fears that it would infringe on civil liberties.

The 1980s will reveal whether or not the trends of the 1970s will continue and reach fruition in an already recognized form, or if the 1970s were merely a transitional phase between the Auto-Air-Amenity Epoch and some as yet unguessed at new epoch. The transition periods between previous epochs were often marked by stop-gap technologies and "mini" epochs, such as the canal mania between the Sail-Wagon and Iron Horse epochs and the short-lived flowering of interurban railways between the Steel Rail and Auto-Air-Amenity epochs. The long-term future may bring a renaissance of the high density, mass transit oriented city because it is more energy efficient. If this happens, the nonmetropolitan boom in exurban housing and low density suburban "estates" may produce the ruins of the future—scattered dwellings remote from either places of employment or mass transit. The questions are provocative and complex, and sure answers will only come in hindsight several decades hence.

NOTES

[1] John R. Borchert, "American Metropolitan Evolution," *Geographical Review*, Vol. 57 (1967), pp. 301–32.

[2] Ibid., p. 329.

[3] A complete bibliography on these sources is found in Phillip D. Phillips, *No Growth and the Evolution of the American Metropolitan System* (Monticello, Illinois, Council of Planning Librarians, 1977) and Phillip D. Phillips and Stanley D. Brunn, "Slow Growth: A New Epoch of American Metropolitan Evolution," *Geographical Review*, Vol. 68 (1978), pp. 274–92.

[4] William H. Miernyk, "Decline of the Northern Perimeter," *Society*, Vol. 13 (1976), p. 26.

[5] Peter A. Morrison and Judith P. Wheeler, "Rural Renaissance in America?" *Population Bulletin*, Vol. 31 (1976), whole number 3.

[6] James E. Vance, Jr., "California and the Search for the Ideal," *Annals of the Association of American Geographers*, Vol. 62 (1972), pp. 185–210.

[7] Irving Kristol, "An Urban Civilization Without Cities," *Horizon*, Vol. 14 (1972), pp. 36–41.

[8] Ronald Abler, "Effects of Space-Adjusting Technology on the Human Geography of the Future," in Ronald Abler et al., *Human Geography in a Shrinking World* (North Scituate, Mass.: Duxbury Press, 1975), p. 35.

[9] Brian J. L. Berry, "Aging Metropolis in Decline," *Society*, Vol. 13 (1976), pp. 54–56.

[10] Wilbur Thompson, "Economic Processes and Employment Problems in Declining Metropolitan Areas," in George Sternlieb and James W. Hughes, eds., *Post-Industrial America: Metropolitan Decline and Interregional Job Shifts* (New Brunswick, N.J.: Center for Urban Policy Research, 1975), p. 196.

[11] Kenneth Boulding, "The Shadow of the Stationary State," *Daedalus*, Vol. 102 (1975), p. 94.

[12] Thompson, op. cit., note 10.

[13] Edgar Rust, *No Growth: Impacts on Metropolitan Areas* (Lexington, Mass.: Lexington Books, 1975).

[14] Boulding, op. cit., note 11, p. 95.

[15] Rust, op. cit., note 13, pp. 183–85.

[16] Ibid., pp. 221–22.

[17] Edgar M. Hoover, "Reduced Population Growth and the Problems of Urban Areas," in Sarah Mills Mazie, ed., *Population, Distribution, and Policy* (Washington, D.C.: U.S. Government Printing Office, 1972), pp. 457–542.

[18] Thompson, op. cit., note 10, p. 192.

[19] Daniel R. Vining, Jr., and Thomas Kontuly, "Population Dispersal from Major Metropolitan Regions: An International Comparison," *International Regional Science Review*, Vol. 3 (1978), pp. 49–73.

[20] "South Taking Funds Fight More Seriously," *New York Times*, Dec. 18, 1977.

[21] "The North-South 'Poor Mouth' Contest," *New York Times*, Jan. 14, 1978.

[22] Michael J. Harrington and Frank Horton, "Time to Help Out the North," *Chicago Daily News*, July 7, 1977.

[23] Phillip D. Phillips, *Exurban Commuters in the Kentucky Bluegrass Region* (Lexington, Ky.: Center for Real Estate and Land Use Analysis, 1976).

Chapter 2

Revitalization Trends in Downtown-Area Neighborhoods

Roman A. Cybriwsky

A process under way at a small scale in a growing number of cities in all regions is revitalization of neighborhoods in downtown areas. The scope and components of that social process are examined in this chapter. By drawing on the revitalization successes operating in several cities, one is able to identify the physical characteristics of areas designated for revitalization and the distinctive socioeconomic characteristics of those contributing to gentrification or upgrading efforts. Revitalization does not occur without problems that also need to be addressed: these include those poor, minority, and elderly who are displaced as well as the neighborhood conflicts that surface between old and new residents. The question we must ask, then, is "revitalization for whom?" This social face-lift of inner cities is not completely unexpected considering the family size, adult housing needs, and leisure emphasis for a post-industrial society. Downtown areas may come to have greater appeal with higher energy transportation costs. Changes of the scale and form of inner city neighborhoods need to be incorporated in our continuing examination of future urban spatial structure.

The downtown areas of many American cities have experienced a remarkable revitalization during the 1970s. In some cities this change has been massive, and has resulted in an almost total physical and social transformation of the central area. This has led some experts to proclaim that a major shift in the basic sociogeographic structure of American metropolitan areas is in the making. For example, the internationally respected city planner Edmund Bacon has recently argued that we are now witnessing a "swing of the pendulum" away from suburban life and in favor of central cities, and has predicted that big city downtowns will become increasingly desirable as places to work, shop, and, most importantly, to live.[1] James W. Rouse, the developer of new towns and suburban shopping malls, has put a similar prediction in stronger terms: In his opinion, inner city locations will be so much in demand by the turn of the century that "the suburb will be the obsolete place to live."[2] Such opinions are vastly different from those which dominated the 1950s and 1960s, when most experts wrote only of inner city neglect and decline, and declared that the future was in suburbia.

The bleakest prognosis was directed at neighborhoods in the urban core. It was expected that they would deteriorate with age, and that their debilitation would be hastened by such trends as the conversion of single units to multiple occupancy, increasing tax delinquencies and property abandonments, and the flight of business, industry, and residents to the suburbs. Only low-income groups would be left behind. Eventually, city neighborhoods would become slums and would be razed by renewal bulldozers. This downward spiral of neighborhood conditions is implicit in most social science models of inner city dynamics, as well as in almost all federal housing policy of recent decades.[3] In fact, neighborhood decay has been regarded to be so inevitable that such supposedly nondirectional terms as "neighborhood change" or "neighborhood transition" have come to imply something negative in American English.

However, recent experiences in a number of inner city areas indicate that neighborhoods may follow other courses as well. There are countless examples in cities all over the country of old neighborhoods which have undergone considerable revitalization, and which have begun to attract large numbers of new residents. Their rejuvenation was accomplished mainly by the private sector, with little or no assistance from publicly-funded renewal programs, and features substantial in-migration and housing renovation by middle- and upper-income persons. Examples of such newly rejuvenated neighborhoods include Society Hill and Queen Village in Philadelphia, the Capitol Hill in Washington, Park Slope in Brooklyn, German Village in Columbus (Ohio), and the Lafayette Square and Soulard districts in St. Louis.

A study of 105 revitalized neighborhoods in 30 of the nation's largest central cities by Philip Clay has distinguished two fundamental types of neighborhood revitalization, "incumbent upgrading" and "gentrification."[4] The first seems to occur most often in moderate-income communities with a strong sense of identity and active neighborhood associations. In such areas the revitalization is accomplished mainly by existing residents, joined by some newcomers of generally the same socioeconomic class. In gentrifying areas, the revitalization is done by outsiders, and is "more the result of individual effort than community or organizational initiative."[5] As the term gentrification suggests, new residents have higher socioeconomic status than long-term inhabitants.[6] Clay's research also points out that an important locational difference exists between upgraded and gentrified areas, the latter being almost always within the Central Business District or within a half mile of it.[7]

For the most part, revitalization of central city neighborhoods, whether by incumbent upgrading or gentrification, has been regarded as a welcome development. This is reflected in the optimistic tone of many newspaper and magazine articles on the subject.[8] This optimism is also evident in certain new federal and city housing policies which are patterned after this trend.[9] Among other benefits, private reinvestment in old neighborhoods is expected to stimulate new business in the city, help replenish the urban tax base, and foster the restoration and preservation of historic districts.

However, such gains for cities need to be balanced against certain problems which the gentrification type of revitalization seems to be creating. Specifically, the transformation of many run-down neighborhoods by higher socioeconomic groups has been so rapid and so complete that now only the wealthy can afford to live in them. Rents and property values have skyrocketed in many such areas far beyond the reach of low- and middle-income families, resulting in what has been called "in-town golden ghettos."[10] As the influx of well-off newcomers continues, long-term residents—often elderly persons on fixed incomes—are displaced from their homes. This displacement has caused some observers to voice doubts about the overall desirability of gentrification, and has caused serious questions to be raised about *for whom* cities are being rebuilt. In the words of Senator William Proxmire, whose Committee on Banking, Housing, and Urban Affairs recently heard testimony on this issue:[11]

> The save-the-neighborhood movement has come of age. Now it is time to ask: Save the neighborhood for whom? Will the increasing pace of neighborhood revitalization yield healthy, diverse communities, with a mix of race, age, and income? Or will it merely dislocate the old, the poor, and the black residents from older neighborhoods which are newly attractive to young professionals?

This essay provides an overview of neighborhood revitalization in the downtown areas of American cities during the 1970s. It focuses on gentrification and addresses four topics of particular importance: (1) the geographical extent of this type of revitalization among the nation's cities; (2) why this change is taking place; (3) who the people involved in gentrification are; and (4) some of the problems which have come to be associated with this change. In addressing these four questions, we will hope to provide a basis for at least partially anticipating patterns of future urban spatial structure.

A major difficulty which is encountered in these topics is that existing literature is incomplete and not based on much hard data. This situation exists largely because the changes in question are so recent, having gained momentum only after 1970.[12] As a result, such normally useful sources as the latest Census of Population and Housing (1970) and the Census of Business (1972) are outdated and offer little help.[13] Consequently, this analysis relies heavily on the few scattered sets of statistics which have been generated more recently in connection with specific case studies and other research projects, as well as on "softer" data contained in various reports on neighborhood change in selected cities. Because of these limitations, the reader will find that perhaps more questions are raised in this essay than are satisfactorily answered.[14] There are simply too many gaps in our understanding of gentrification for definitive conclusions at this time. However, it is hoped that the very raising of these questions will in itself be a useful exercise.

GEOGRAPHICAL EXTENT OF NEIGHBORHOOD REVITALIZATION

One of the questions that we know least about regarding downtown-neighborhood revitalization is its geographical extent at the national urban scale. We do not know exactly how many cities have been affected and to what degree, and we probably will not know with certainty until results of the 1980 census are in. However, there are at least three studies which provide early indications that revitalization is indeed widespread and that it is occurring in various types and sizes of cities in all parts of the country.

The first of these studies is an analysis by S. G. Lipton of socioeconomic trends in the cores of the 20 largest SMSAs.[15] It is based on a comparison of 1960 and 1970 census tract data, and, therefore, predates the start of revitalization in many neighborhoods. Nevertheless, the study shows that family income and educational attainment statistics, which were used by Lipton as surrogate measures for neighborhood revitalization, "improved" in or near the Central Business Districts of at least 10 of these places.[16] A second study is that by Philip Clay cited earlier. It was conducted during the spring and summer of 1977, and found at least some revitalization activity in each of 30 cities surveyed. Clay's report also points out that gentrification is not limited to the largest cities, but is "prevalent" in smaller communities as well.[17] The third research is a survey conducted in 1975 by the Urban Land Institute. It revealed that 70% of American cities with a population greater than 250,000 are experiencing "significant private market housing renovation in deteriorated areas," and that 60 separate neighborhoods in 20 of the largest cities were undergoing "major" revitalization activity.[18] Various scattered literature on the subject indicates that gentrification of downtown-area neighborhoods is important in at least the following diverse cities: New York City (Manhattan and Brooklyn), Philadelphia, San Francisco, Baltimore, Washington, Cincinnati, Columbus (Ohio), Albuquerque, New Haven, Seattle, Providence, New Orleans, Chicago, Charleston, Albany, Sacramento, St. Louis, Boston, Atlanta, and Jersey City.[19]

We also know little about the geographic extent of revitalization *within* cities. The only statistic available on this point is Clay's estimate that less than 5% of all central city neighborhoods have recently experienced gentrification.[20] However, it is clear that in some cities virtually the entire downtown area has been significantly changed by the revitalization process. Philadelphia is a case in point. Its Central Business District is ringed by neighborhoods in various stages of revitalization, including some newly fashionable ones which several years ago were referred to as slums.[21] Again, we will probably need to wait for 1980 census data before we know detailed information about the extent of neighborhood change in central cities and before cities can be compared.

REASONS FOR NEIGHBORHOOD REVITALIZATION

The neighborhood revitalization trend appears to have been stimulated by a large number of factors which have combined to make downtown-area living more desirable than in the recent past. A number of researchers have addressed themselves to identifying these factors, but our understanding of the trend is as yet too poor for definitive conclusions.[22] However, it is clear that the trend is based on broad changes in American society in general, and that its many causes are closely inter-related.

The complexity of the reasons which underlie neighborhood revitalization is illustrated in an unpublished paper on Vancouver, Canada, by David Ley.[23] It sets downtown-area revival into the context of modern North America society as inter-preted by sociologists Daniel Bell and Jurgen Habermas, and argues that renewed emphasis on the inner city is one of the geographical outcomes of the economy, politics, and culture of the post-industrial or advanced capitalist era. Specific factors which are said to underlie changing urban structure include expansion of the leisure classes, increased stress on the amenity ethic, and the growing impor-tance of consumption, rather than production, as a determinant of central city land use decisions.

Somewhat more specifically, other research on why revitalization is taking place points to certain demographic trends. Perhaps the most important of these is the increase in the number of persons in the prime house-buying range of 25 to 34. Between 1960 and 1978 the percentage of persons in the U.S. in this age category rose from 12.3 to 15.3.[24] This increase is the result of the post-World War II "baby-boom" and has created a large house-buying market.

A related and also important demographic change is an increase in adults-only households. In 1960 there were 19.4 million families in the U.S. with no children under 18. By 1970 this statistic had increased to 22.6 million, and in 1974 it was 25.3 million.[25] Similarly, the number of households consisting of unrelated in-dividuals and single persons has increased; there were 11.9 million such households in 1970 and 14.9 million in 1974.[26] Other demographic trends which are said to be important to neighborhood revitalization include increased numbers of divorced and separated individuals and heterosexual cohabitation.[27]

One of the implications of these statistics on inner city neighborhoods is that many people who are now in the housing market are seeking housing oriented solely to adult needs.[28] The absence of children negates many of the reasons why middle class Americans have preferred suburban living, and has caused many people who otherwise would not have done so to consider residence in the central city. The impact of this factor on metropolitan spatial structure has been docu-mented for Seattle, a city in which the number of households has been increasing at a time when total population is being lost. White, middle class families with children continue to leave the city for the suburbs, but the housing vacancies they leave behind are being filled by young, adults-only households which are being added to the population by the aging of the city's "baby-boom" children and by in-migration from beyond the metropolitan area.[29]

Many of the new young adults have entered professional, technical, and mana-gerial occupations. Between 1960 and 1970 the number of people in these cate-gories in the U.S. increased 7 million and their proportion among all categories of employment shifted from 19 to 25%.[30] As is evidenced by recent booms in office construction in various cities, including Philadelphia, Pittsburgh, Detroit, Milwaukee, Chicago, and Los Angeles, a significant fraction of new job opportunities in these fields has been in Central Business Districts.[31] As a result of these trends, demand has been stimulated for middle- and upper-income housing proximate to downtown workplaces.

The increased population of young adult households has been attracted disproportionately in inner city neighborhoods for a number of other reasons as well. One of the most commonly mentioned of these is a growing aversion by many people to suburban lifestyles in general and to the type of housing available in newer suburbs in particular. Interviews with new residents of downtown-area neighborhoods often reveal a preference for residence in racially and economically mixed communities and contempt for the assumed social homogenity of suburbia.[32] As Richard Fusch has argued, many Americans are unhappy with the perception that "everything has become the same in the suburbs," and increasing numbers of them have turned instead to the inner city. Here they can assert their identities and individualism with a "unique, old, restored house" in a mixed neighborhood.[33]

The difference in price between new suburban homes and those in old neighborhoods has also attracted young residents to the inner city. The value of most suburban housing has escalated beyond the reach of many first-time buyers. Continually rising construction and land development costs exacerbate the problem. As a result, "one of the few choices left open to this population is the inner city, where some substantial and architecturally, unique housing is available at relatively low cost."[34] Surveys of new residents in downtown neighborhoods support this contention. For example, a study in the Coliseum Square area of New Orleans has shown that 60% of recent home buyers indicated that price was a "very important" consideration in selecting their neighborhood, and that it was "important" to an additional 25%.[35] Similarly, 70% of recent migrants to the Virginia-Highlands section of Atlanta indicated that they were attracted to that neighborhood because it offered more housing space per dollar than suburban communities.[36]

Another frequent argument about why downtown-area revitalization is taking place concerns the rising cost and growing scarcity of fuel. As the energy situation in America worsens, close-in locations are expected to become increasingly advantageous, in part because reliance on the automobile will be lessened.[37] In fact, many new residents of downtown neighborhoods have indicated in surveys that walking-distance convenience to work was an important factor in their decision to locate where they live.[38] Furthermore, in old eastern cities where the housing stock consists mainly of row houses, it is expected that urban core locations will become increasingly attractive because such houses are more efficiently heated. However, experts disagree on the potential impact of energy considerations on residential location decisions. While some argue that the energy crisis can only favor central cities, others point to studies which suggest that Americans are not energy-price conscious, and simply pay higher costs for gasoline and home heating by cutting back in other areas.[39]

NEWCOMERS TO REVITALIZING NEIGHBORHOODS

The people most strongly identified with the neighborhood revitalization trend are often referred to as young professionals. This is an imprecise term, but is widely used, probably for want of a better one. It is meant to describe a population of in-migrants which is comprised mainly of "young, childless, white, highly educated and economically secure urbanites."[40]

Surveys of neighborhoods which have recently experienced revitalization support this generalization. For example, the study by Philip Clay cited earlier presents the following statistics for 57 "gentrified" neighborhoods: in 82% of these areas the predominant population is white; in 75% residents are mainly professionals or white-collar workers; and in 48% the population is comprised mainly of young families.[41] In addition, a study of 65 newly rejuvenated districts in 44 cities by The National Urban Coalition indicates that in more than 80% of these places, professionals and white-collar workers became the numerically dominant population after rehabilitation. This compares to a figure of only 30% before rehabilitation.[42]

Case studies of specific neighborhoods provide other data which describe newcomer populations. One such study was a survey conducted in the Queen Village section of Philadelphia. It indicates that 78% of new adult residents are in their 20s and 30s, and that 84% are engaged in professional and other white-collar occupations. Nearly 80% of the sample lived in households comprised of three or fewer persons, with the most common type of household being the childless husband and wife.[43] Bradley's analysis of newcomers to his Atlanta study area provides comparable statistics: 80% of adult householders were between the ages of 20 and 39; 69% had professional, technical, or managerial occupations; and 66% of households had no children under 18. In addition, his study reveals that newcomers are a highly educated population; 87% had some college background, at least 62% had finished college, and 33% has taken postgraduate courses.[44] The general affluence of newcomers is seen in the Coliseum Square area of New Orleans, where 90% of property owners who had purchased and renovated homes since 1971 had an annual family income in excess of $10,000, while 43% had incomes over $30,000.[45]

However, such statistics do not necessarily apply to all recently revitalized neighborhoods or to all cities where revitalization is taking place. For example, Christopher Winters, who has analyzed neighborhood trends in New York, Washington, Boston, and San Francisco, has expressed reservations about widespread usage of the "young professionals" designation. He argues that this term is accurate only to some extent, and that "it misses one of the most interesting aspects of neighborhoods undergoing rejuvenation."[46] Specifically, he asserts that in-migrants to rejuvenating neighborhoods tend to sort themselves out into different neighborhoods according to various lifestyle criteria, with the result that these areas vary greatly in population composition. Among the types of revitalizing districts that Winters identified are gay neighborhoods, artists' neighborhoods, and what he called "chic" neighborhoods. Another caution against generalizing too much about the inhabitants of revitalizing neighborhoods was presented by Shirley Laska and Daphne Spain. Their study of 12 such areas in New Orleans indicates that owner-renovators in that city are not mainly young singles and childless couples; 62% have children and 9% have four or more.[47]

Several studies suggest that the socioeconomic character of revitalizing neighborhoods varies with how far along a neighborhood is in the revitalization process. In the early stages, while the neighborhood is still run-down and inexpensive, the incoming population seems to consist of young singles and couples who are just getting started in the professions. In some cases, these "pioneers"—as the first newcomers to changing neighborhoods are often called—are artists. This was the case in the SoHo section of New York, where considerable loft space was made available by earlier declines in commerce and industry.[48] As the area improves, confidence in the neighborhood builds, property values rise sharply, and larger numbers of newcomers enter. Eventually, the neighborhood changes so much that it becomes accessible only to persons with high incomes. Society Hill in Philadelphia and Georgetown in Washington are but two examples of established revitalized neighborhoods where houses sell for well over $100,000.

One of the most important questions regarding who the newcomers to gentri-fying areas are concerns where they come from. It has been suggested that a sub-stantial proportion of these people are from the suburbs, and that their migration represents a "back-to-the-city" movement.[49] If this is the case, then inner city revitalization could be interpreted as the start of a massive reversal of the century-old decentralization trend in American metropolitan areas and would have funda-mental impacts on urban patterns in this country. But, if newcomers have non-suburban origins, then the trend should be intrepreted differently, possibly as something which is limited to only a select population group.

Data on this subject are as inconclusive as they have been on topics covered earlier, but have suggested to some researchers that the "back-to-the-city" move-ment is, in fact, primarily a "remain-in-the-city" *non*movement.[50] For example, the study by Laska and Spain found that only 9% of their sample listed the suburbs of that city as the previous place of residence. Eighty percent came from inner city addresses. Moreover, the research disclosed that most owner-renovators "have lived in the city not merely from young adulthood but even from childhood"; half of the sample grew up in inner city New Orleans and 10% in other inner cities.[51] Surveys in other urban areas show generally the same pattern. For instance, only 17% of new residents in Philadelphia's Queen Village came directly from suburban areas.[52] Similarly, 87% of migrants to the Virginia-Highlands neighborhood in Atlanta who were from the Atlanta area came from within the city itself.[53] So too, an ambitious study of migration to Washington, D.C., by George Grier and Eunice Grier revealed that only approximately one in six newcomer households to the District came from one of its major suburban jurisdictions. As might be expected for the nation's capital, most new residents came from locations outside the metropolitan area.[54]

However, there are at least two observations on the nature of these studies which should be made before conclusions about any suburban contribution to inner city revitalization are drawn. One is that most of the surveys discussed above apparently asked informants to identify only their *last* place of residence. It is possible, and indeed even likely, that a larger proportion of new residents in gen-trifying neighborhoods could be said to be from the suburbs if the research had traced respondents' migration histories back at least one more move. This pos-sibility is suggested by the Queen Village study, which found that a substantial number of newcomers moved to the neighborhood from the University of

Pennsylvania area (which is also in the inner city), and that before college many of these people lived in suburban locations.[55]

The second observation is that while only a small percentage of newcomers have moved directly from the suburbs, this figure might be growing. Several years ago, before the revitalization trend was important, the number of suburbs-to-inner city movers may have been virtually nil. It could well be that the 9 or 17% figures quoted earlier should be interpreted as impressive gains for central cities over a short period, rather than simply as small percentages.

Nevertheless, it appears that return migration from suburbia is, at present, only a small factor in the revitalization trend. People are simply not abandoning suburbs for inner city neighborhoods. Moreover, there are no data which indicate that suburbs-leavers are representative of suburban residents in general. Instead, the literature suggests that those new inner city residents who are from the suburbs are mainly young adults who have recently left their parents' homes.[56] What the data on the origins of newcomers do indicate, however, is that increasing numbers of Americans who could afford to do so are not choosing to locate in suburbia, and that "many cities are increasingly able to hold on to their population."[57] This in itself is significant regarding urban structure, because it seems to signal a slow-down of middle-class flight from cities.

PROBLEMS CAUSED BY GENTRIFICATION

The most serious problem associated with the resettlement of inner city neighborhoods by middle- and upper-income persons is the displacement of long-term residents. This problem has been widely publicized in the media, and has gained the attention of local officials and neighborhood leaders in cities across the country. In addition, it has come to the focus of considerable academic research and the main topic for discussion at various conferences on the impact of the revitalization movement.

This concern has developed, in part, because the emergence of the displacement problem brings into focus a fundamental conflict between commonly-held goals for the renewal of depressed cities on the one hand and social justice ideals on the other.[58] Revitalization of old neighborhoods by private market forces is regarded to be an effective and, in terms of public funds, generally inexpensive way of improving declining areas and rebuilding the city tax base. These gains have come, however, at the expense of substantial numbers of low-income people, who have often been forced to move from their homes by those same market forces. A disproportionate number of the victims have been elderly and/or minority persons.[59] Furthermore, the presence of sensitive moral issures are evident in that, for the most part, those revitalizing neighborhoods which are now so much in demand by middle- and upper-income people are some of the same places that the middle-class abandoned in its flight from central cities during earlier decades.

The causes of displacement are mainly economic. As demand by relatively well-off people for housing in inner city neighborhoods rises, rents and property values increase beyond the financial capabilities of many long-term residents. Renters tend to be displaced first, as landlords adjust prices to meet the increased demand, or as multiple-occupancy dwellings are converted to single, owner-occupancy. Many homeowners feel the pinch, because tax assessments generally go up following revitalization. The survey conducted by Clay showed that in 76% of the 57 gentrified neighborhoods he studied rents rose in excess of 50% after revitalization, and that house values increased by 50% or more in 74% of these places. Tax assessments increased in 71% of the 57 neighborhoods.[60] Paul Levy's study of Queen Village indicates that tax assessments in that neighborhood increased during the 1970s on the average by 200 to 300%, and in some cases by 600 to 700%.[61]

Some of the increase in housing costs in revitalizing neighborhoods is attributed to the actions of real estate developers and speculators. They often acquire properties beyond the edge of gentrifying neighborhoods and then resell them at higher prices. Frequently, no capital is invested in rehabilitation and windfall profits result. This activity is known as "flipping," and in some cases in Washington, D.C., has resulted in the doubling of prices within a month.[62]

In addition, the price of housing increases substantially following rehabilitation, making renovation a profitable business. For example, in 1977, in New York's Boerum Hill section, unrenovated houses purchased in the $20,000 to $40,000 range were selling for between $75,000 and $150,000 renovated, while $40,000 to $50,000 unrenovated three-flats in San Francisco's Mint Hill brought prices between $175,000 and $225,000 after renovation.[63] Even dilapidated shells sell for large sums in revitalizing neighborhoods; in Queen Village such structures were worth $200 or $300 in the 1960s but go for between $20,000 and $30,000 today.[64] Because such large gains can be made, the renovation of houses is in itself responsible for substantial displacement. This is seen in the Spring Garden section of Philadelphia, where Puerto Rican tenants are being evicted as the renovation-gentrification process moves through their neighborhood block after contiguous block.[65]

Virtually nothing is known about what happens to neighborhood residents after they have been displaced. Homeowners are probably more fortunate than renters, because most can turn a profit in selling their houses. However, a homeowner who is leaving a neighborhood because of inflated taxes—as is the case with elderly persons on fixed incomes—is probably in no position to assume a new mortgage.

Renters probably fare far worse. A study in Portland, Oregon, indicates that 46% of those displaced had difficulties affording their new rents.[66] Some evictees probably find living quarters in low-rent neighborhoods elsewhere in the city or in older, inner-ring suburban communities. The latter trend has been observed in Prince George's County, Maryland, outside Washington, D.C.[67] Many of the Puerto Rican evictees from Philadelphia's Spring Garden have moved to Kensington, a white, working-class neighborhood several miles away. Residents there now complain of block-busting tactics by real estate agents.[68] Elderly tenants are surely most strongly affected by the loss of a place to live; Philadelphia's Office of Adult Services reports that at least 40 displaced elderly persons—mostly from Queen Village and nearby neighborhoods—call each month asking for help in finding accommodations.[69]

Another problem which is often associated with revitalization is a decline in the quality of neighborhood life for established residents who remain. Many of the areas which are now receiving an influx of newcomer-gentrifiers are closely-knit, working-class communities in which residents are bound by ethnic and family ties. These areas have distinctive lifestyles which contrast markedly with those of new-comers and erode with population turnover. This is seen in Fairmount, a working-class ethnic community near downtown Philadelphia which has recently experienced significant gentrification. Many long-term residents complain about a loss of community in the area, and lament that "this place isn't like it used to be." As one lifelong Fairmounter put it: "I used to know all my neighbors, but now I don't know these new people. I don't have anything in common with them."[70]

Cultural differences between new and long-term residents often result in tensions. In Queen Village these have been manifested in arguments about restoring old houses to their original appearance. Many newcomers favor historical certification of their houses and have urged neighbors to do likewise. But, many long-term residents have resented being told how to keep their homes by "outsiders who only moved in yesterday." They are justifiably offended by suggestions that awnings, aluminum siding, and storm doors represent nothing more than "ignorant destruction of colonial architecture."[71]

Occasionally, tensions between new and old residents develop into overt conflict. This has happened in Spring Garden, where a backlash has emerged against newcomers. In one instance, a house belonging to a young teacher was firebombed on the day he was moving in, causing an estimated $20,000 to $30,000 damage. A 35-year-old Puerto Rican from an apartment on the same block was arrested and charged.[72] One of his friends, interviewed on the local television news, explained why he did it. A fairly close approximation of his words is:

> There used to be friends of ours in that house. But this white guy comes in and kicks them out. And he thinks he's improving the neighborhood. All of us [Puerto Ricans] are going to get thrown out, one by one. The man will just come one day and say "move."

Other problems in revitalizing neighborhoods are related to physical-environmental considerations. For example, in areas where there are large concentrations of newcomers in small rental units a critical shortage of on-street parking spaces has developed. Frequently, such areas also have significant increases in traffic, noise, and litter. In some cases, developers of vacant land have built shoddy houses, to capitalize as quickly as possible on the growing housing market, and have paid little heed to such matters as the capacity of sewer systems or problems with underground drainage. Furthermore, in some neighborhoods retailing establishments have become oriented more to tourists than to local residents, with the result that commercial streets have rapidly developed a honky-tonk character.[73]

CONCLUSION

This essay has reviewed literature on neighborhood revitalization in American cities during the 1970s. As has been noted throughout, data on the subject are generally inconclusive. The revitalization phenomenon is relatively new, and the research which has been cited here should be regarded mainly as first-step, exploratory research. Many of the studies discussed are based on small samples or have other methodological shortcomings, and, therefore, need to be interpreted carefully.[74] As a result, definitive statements and predictions about the future structure of American metropolitan areas would be premature.

Nevertheless, it is clear that an important change has been taking place during this decade in many inner city areas. Countless old neighborhoods in a variety of cities have been significantly upgraded, and many districts that were once thought of as slums have become attractive and fashionable places to live. At the very least, the revitalization trend indicates that the decline of many old areas has been reversed, and that a large subset of American population has become newly interested in inner city residence.

However, we can say very little with certainty about the overall benefits to cities of the revitalization phenomenon. To be sure, many formerly run-down areas have been improved physically and a significant number of historic cityscapes have been restored and preserved. But, many of the anticipated economic gains to cities have not been measured. For example, little is known about the net impact of revitalization on the urban financial situation. On the one hand, middle- and upper-income newcomers have benefited central cities economically more than lower-income inhabitants by paying more in real estate and other local taxes, stimulating more business activity, and demanding less in certain public services, such as welfare. But, on the other hand, newcomers have demanded other costly services, as, for example, in Queen Village, where residents requested more police protection, better trash collection, improved school curriculum, cobblestone streets, buried electrical wires, and new trees.[75] Thus, there is a need for a detailed economic cost-benefit analysis of the inner city population shift.

There is also a need to determine how long the revitalization trend might continue in American cities and how much territory it might eventually affect. The data cited in this essay suggest that the middle-class market for inner city housing is limited to young, well-educated, professional people. If this is indeed the case, then revitalization would wane as the baby-boom generation ages. However, there is no evidence that this is happening. In fact, there are some indications that the market is broadening to include substantial numbers of financially secure retirees who are being drawn to close-in locations by the cultural and entertainment facilities they offer. Nevertheless, the possibility does exist that the gentrification type of revitalization might have short duration and be limited almost exclusively to areas near Central Business Districts. In this event, the trends described here would not result in the major shift in metropolitan structure that some experts are anticipating.

This chapter has identified the displacement problem as the most serious of the negative outcomes of revitalization. While there is no good estimate of how many people have been affected by displacement, it is clear that the problem is widespread and that measures against it are necessary. A number of jurisdictions have recently adopted tax abatement legislation for elderly residents and Washington, D.C., has implemented an anti-speculation law. But, displacement has many causes and a combination of strategies against it are needed. As a report by the Community and Economic Development Task Force for the Urban Consortium has put it:[76]

> The challenge facing public officials is to maximize the obvious benefits of revitalization while minimizing, if not eliminating, the problems which it can also bring. The need is to be able to manage the revitalization process sufficiently so that the interests of established residents are adequately protected and their needs are properly met.

It is imperative that solutions to the displacement problem be found. Otherwise revitalization amounts to little more than a change in location of elite neighborhoods. Reinvestment in inner city areas by the middle-class is an important ingredient for the rebuilding of cities, and should be viewed as an opportunity "to promote strong communities which are racially, culturally and economically diverse."[77] If reinvestment continues to cause declines in neighborhood heterogeneity, however, then its net effect is only the subsitution of one set of urban problems with another.

NOTES

*The author would like to thank John C. Western for his helpful comments on an earlier draft.

[1] "The Prophet of Urban Civilization Spells Doom for Our Suburban Ideals," *Focus* (Philadelphia Business Newsweekly), March 22, 1978, p. 79.

[2] J. W. Rouse, "The Lure of an Urban Life-Style," *Conservation and New Economic Realities: Some Views of the Future*, Proceedings of a conference sponsored by The Conservation Foundation in San Francisco, Calif., on Nov. 18, 1977 (Washington, D.C.: The Conservation Foundation, 1978), p. 44.

[3] For example, see the models of neighborhood change in R. B. Andrews, *Urban Land Economics and Public Policy* (N.Y.: The Free Press); E. Hoover and R. Vernon, *Anatomy of a Metropolis* (N.Y.: Doubleday, 1959); and W. F. Smith, "Filtering and Neighborhood Change," in L. S. Bourne, ed., *Internal Structure of the City* (N.Y.: Oxford University Press, 1971), pp. 170-79.

[4] P. Clay, "Neighborhood Revitalization and Community Development: The Experience and the Promise," *Center for Community Economic Development Newsletter*, Aug.-Oct. 1978, pp. 1-9.

[5] Ibid., p. 3.

[6] The term gentrification comes to the United States from England. It is defined there as "the invasion of traditionally working class areas by middle and upper income groups" (C. Hamnett, "Improvement Grants as an Indicator of Gentrification in Inner London," *Area*, Vol. 5 (1973). p. 252).

[7] Clay, op. cit., note 4, p. 5.

[8] For example, see N. R. Pierce, "Nation's Cities Poised for a Stunning Comeback," *Washington Post*, July 3, 1977; H. Sutton, "American Falls in Love with Its Cities–Again," *Saturday Review*, Aug. 1978, pp. 16-21; "Downtown Is Looking Up," *Time*, July 5, 1976, pp. 60-67; and T. D. Allman, "The Urban Crisis Leaves Town," *Harper's*, Dec. 1978, pp. 41-56.

[9] C. T. Adams, "Federal Housing Policy and Neighborhood Change," paper presented at the annual meeting of the Association of American Geographers, New Orleans, Apr. 12, 1978.

34 Roman A. Cybriwsky

[10] P. O'Brien, "The Poor Are Being Driven Out," *Philadelphia Inquirer*, Dec. 17, 1978, p. 7-H.

[11] Neighborhood Diversity, transcript of hearings before the Committee on Banking, Housing, and Urban Affairs, U.S. Senate, on the Problems of Dislocation and Diversity in Communities Undergoing Neighborhood Revitalization Activity, July 7 and 8, 1977 (Washington, D.C.: The Conservation Foundation, 1977), p. 1.

[12] Meyers and G. Binder, *Neighborhood Conservation: Lessons from Three Cities* (Washington, D.C.: The Conservation Foundation, 1977), p. 1.

[13] Results of the 1977 Census of Business were not available as of this writing.

[14] The reader will be additionally frustrated by the fact that a large percentage of references in the notes are to be unpublished papers with limited circulation. In geography and other disciplines, research on neighborhood revitalization is just beginning, and the list of published material is short.

[15] S. G. Lipton, "Evidence of Central City Revival," *Journal of the American Institute of Planners*, Vol. 43 (1977), pp. 136–47.

[16] These 10 cities are New York, Washington, D.C., Boston, Philadelphia, Seattle, Minneapolis, Pittsburgh, Milwaukee, Los Angeles, and Baltimore.

[17] Clay, op. cit., note 4, p. 3.

[18] These figures are cited in Urban Consortium, *The Displacement Problem in Revitalized Urban Neighborhoods*, Report of the Community and Economic Development Task Force, Washington, D.C., Sept. 1977, p. 6.

[19] An excellent bibliography on neighborhood revitalization in most of these cities is B. London, *The Revitalization of Inner City Neighborhoods* (Monticello, Ill.: Vance Bibliographies. 1978).

[20] Clay, op. cit., note 4, pp. 3–4.

[21] Some sources on neighborhood change in downtown Philadelphia are R. A. Cybriwsky, "Social Aspects of Neighborhood Change," *Annals of the Association of American Geographers*, Vol. 68 (1978), pp. 17–33; R. A. Cybriwsky and J. T. Meyer, "Geographical Aspects of the Housing Market in a Rejuvenating Neighborhood," *Papers in Geography*, (Pennsylvania State University, No. 16, Dec., 1977); P. R. Levy, *Queen Village: The Eclipse of Community* (Philadelphia: Institute for the Study of Civic Values, 1978); P. O. Muller, K. C. Meyer, and R. A. Cybriwsky, *Metropolitan Philadelphia: A Study of Conflicts and Social Cleavages* (Cambridge, Mass.: Ballinger, 1976), pp. 1–33; and N. Smith, "Gentrification and Capital: Theory, Practice and Ideology in Society Hill," *Antipode*, (in press).

[22] R. Fitcher, *Young Professionals and City Neighborhoods* (Boston: Parkman Center for Urban Affairs, Aug., 1977); R. Fusch, "Historic Preservation and Gentrification: A Search for Order in the Urban Core," paper presented at the annual meeting of the Association of American Geographers, New Orleans, April 9–12, 1978; F. J. James, "Back to the City: An Appraisal of Housing Reinvestment and Population Change in Urban America" (Washington, D.C.: The Urban Institute, June 1977, draft); Research Division, Urban Land Institute, *New Opportunities for Residential Development in Central Cities* (Washington, D.C.: The Urban Land Institute, 1976); and A. Yezer, "Living Patterns: Why People Move into the Inner City," *Washington Post*, June 25, 1977.

[23] D. F. Ley, "Inner City Resurgence in Its Societal Context," paper presented at the annual meeting of the Association of American Geographers, New Orleans, April 12, 1978.

[24] J. B. Quinn, "The Comforts of Homes," *Newsweek*, Jan. 1, 1979, p. 43.

[25] Research Division, Urban Land Institute, op. cit., note 22, p. 9.

[26] Ibid.

[27] Fitcher, op. cit., note 22, p. 2.

[28] Research Division, Urban Land Institute, op. cit., note 22, p. 10.

[29] D. Hodge, "Residential Change in Inner City Seattle Neighborhoods," paper presented at

the annual meeting of the Association of American Geographers, New Orleans, April 12, 1978 and R. Reinhold, "Seattle's Families Are Pulling Out, But the City May Learn to Like It," *New York Times*, March 28, 1977.

[30] Research Division, Urban Land Institute, op. cit., note 22, p. 10.

[31] Ibid.; J. Pastier, "Welcome to Downtown L.A.," *Horizon*, Vol. 20 (1977), pp. 10–19; and Downtown Is Looking Up," op. cit., note 8.

[32] Fitcher, op. cit., note 22; E. Karask, "Suburbs? Foo! Some Are Moving Back to the City," *Philadelphia Inquirer*, Sept. 4, 1977; and J. Sharkey and J. Davidson, "New 'Pioneers' Leaving Suburbs for City," *The Evening Bulletin* (Philadelphia), June 17, 1977.

[33] Fusch, op. cit., note 22, p. 7.

[34] Ibid., p. 5.

[35] R. Thayer and P. Waidhas, "What Do In-Town Investors Want?" *Urban Land*, June, 1977, p. 20.

[36] D. S. Bradley, "Neighborhood Transition: Middle-Class Home Buying in an Inner City, Deteriorating Community," paper presented at the annual meeting of the American Sociological Association, Chicago, Sept. 8, 1977, p. 20.

[37] D. R. Goldfield, "The Limits of Suburban Growth: The Washington, D.C., SMSA," *Urban Affairs Quarterly*, Vol. 12 (1976), pp. 83–102.

[38] For example, Bradley, op. cit., note 36, p. 19.

[39] P. O. Muller, "Suburbia, Geography, and the Prospect of a Nation Without Important Cities," *Geographical Survey*, Vol. 7 (1978), pp. 4–5.

[40] R. E. Datel, "Historic Preservation and Neighborhood Change," paper presented at the annual meeting of the Association of American Geographers, New Orleans, April 9–12, 1978, p. 4.

[41] Clay, op. cit., note 4.

[42] The National Urban Coalition, *Displacement: City Neighborhoods in Transition* (Washington, D.C.: The National Urban Coalition, 1978), p. 6.

[43] D. Wilson, E. Dayton, K. Hudson, and T. Burns, "Queen Village Neighborhood Study," unpublished seminar paper submitted to W. J. Young, Temple University, Dec. 14, 1978.

[44] Bradley, op. cit., note 36, pp. 13–16.

[45] The median family income in New Orleans was approximately $9,000 per year (Thayer and Waidhans, op. cit., note 34, p. 20).

[46] C. Winter, "Rejuvenation with Character: The Coming-Into-Being of Some New Types of Neighborhoods in New York, San Francisco, Boston, and Washington," paper presented at the annual meeting of the Association of American Geographers, New Orleans, April 12, 1978, p. 1.

[47] S. Laska and D. Spain, "Inner City Renovation: What Can We Expect?" *Louisiana Business Survey*, Oct., 1978, p. 5.

[48] J. R. Hudson, "Changing Land-Use Patterns in SoHo: Residential Invasion of Industrial Areas," unpublished paper, Feb. 20, 1978.

[49] This contention is most often found in articles in newspapers and popular magazines. For example, see the references in note 32 and Allman, op. cit., note 8.

[50] Laska and Spain, op. cit., note 47, p. 5.

[51] Ibid.

[52] D. Wilson et al., op. cit., note 43.

[53] A large percentage of Virginia-Highlands residents are newcomers to Atlanta; more than 50% have lived in the city 8 years or less (Bradley, op. cit., note 36, p. 17).

[54] G. Grier and E. S. Grier, *Movers to the City: New Data on the Housing Market for Washington, D.C.* (Washington, D.C.: The Washington Center for Metropolitan Studies, 1977), p. 11.

[55] D. Wilson et al., op. cit., note 43.

[56] C. Weiler, *Reinvestment Displacement: HUD's Role in a New Housing Issue*, report

submitted to the U.S. Department of Housing and Urban Development, Washington, D.C., Jan., 1978, p. 19.

[57]M. Shill, "Dealing with the Costs of Gentrification," paper presented at the Conference on Urban Redevelopment, Woodrow Wilson School of Public and International Affairs, Princeton University, Nov. 29, 1978, p. 2.

[58]However, there is a different, minority viewpoint on this. For example, James Greene has argued that opposition to gentrification is being fueled by sociologists who have "invented a new field of study which permits them to question [the] madness of community improvement (J. Green, "Attack from a New Quarter: Urban 'Gentrification'," *The Brownstoner*, Vol. 9 (1978), pp. 1 and 12).

[59]The National Urban Coalition, op. cit., note 42, and P. Myers, *Neighborhood Conservation and the Elderly* (Washington, D.C.: The Conservation Foundation, 1978).

[60]Clay, op. cit., note 4, p. 7.

[61]Levy, op. cit., note 21, p. 26.

[62]C. Richards and J. Rowe, "Restoring a City: Who Pays the Price?" *Working Papers for a New Society*, Vol. 4 (1977), p. 4, quoted in Schill, op. cit., note 57, p. 4.

[63]The National Urban Coalition, op. cit., note 42, p. 5.

[64]Levy, op. cit., note 21, p. 26.

[65]R. Cybriwsky, "Benefits and Social Costs of Gentrification in Inner City Philadelphia," paper presented at the annual meeting of the Association of American Geographers, New Orleans, April 12, 1978.

[66]Schill, op. cit., note 57, pp. 6–7.

[67]The National Urban Coalition, op. cit., note 42, p. 6.

[68]My research has indicated that some Spring Garden realtors steer Puerto Ricans to Kensington and another nearby neighborhood after evicting them, thereby making profits at both ends from the same people.

[69]S. Franklin, "Where Do Elderly Go as the Young Move in?" *The Bulletin* (Philadelphia), Nov. 12, 1978, pp. 1 and 5.

[70]For a detailed study of the impact of change in Fairmount see Cybriwsky, op. cit., note 21.

[71]Levy, op. cit., note 21, p. 41.

[72]The newcomer had bought the house for $12,000 and spent $67,000 in repairs and renovations (W. Storm, "Remodeled House Firebombed by Vandals Near Art Museum," *The Evening Bulletin* (Philadelphia), June 3, 1977.

[73]P. Lewis, "To Revive Urban Downtown, Show Respect for the Spirit of the Place," *Smithsonian*, Vol. 6 (1975), pp. 32–41 and W. F. Naedele, "Queen Village Fears Invasion of Honky-Tonk Bars," *The Evening Bulletin* (Philadelphia), Feb. 22, 1977, pp. 13 and 15.

[74]For example, the study by Laska and Spain is based on a total of 92 interviews in the 12 neighborhoods surveyed. Thayer and Waidhas had 62 respondents to their questionnaire, and the Queen Village study cited in note 43 had a sample of 117, 69 of whom were classified as newcomers.

[75]Schill, op. cit., note 57, p. 4.

[76]Urban Consortium, op. cit., note 18, p. 2.

[77]The National Urban Coalition, op. cit., note 42, p. 27.

Chapter 3

Suburbanization in the 1970s: Interpreting Population, Socioeconomic, and Employment Trends

Peter O. Muller

While inner city neighborhood revitalization represents a recent process in urban America, a more enduring process is suburbanization. The growth that has occurred since 1950 around cities has often resulted in rings that completely surround the central city. Suburban growth continued in the 1970s with two notable features: a slower rate, especially in the largest SMSAs in the Northeast and North Central states, and a still rapid growth in the Sunbelt. The economic and legal changes that have occurred in suburbia since 1950 have resulted in suburbs becoming more heterogeneous, even though there are fewer minorities and poor compared to central cities. What has transpired with the out-migration of residents from central cities and the decentralization of business and industry is that suburbia has become an "outer city" in its own right. This suburban independence of the central city can be illustrated for a number of cities, including Baltimore, Philadelphia, New York, St. Louis, and San Francisco. Continued decentralization and suburbanization represent additional features of post-industrial urban economies.

As the other chapters have shown, the 1970s are witnessing an accelerated redistribution of population within the U.S. that is transforming the nation's metropolitan and nonmetropolitan settlement patterns.[1] Among these trends, *suburbanization* of population inside the expanding metropolis continues to be the mainstay of national growth: The latest (1977) data reveal that since 1970 suburban rings of SMSAs have grown by more than 9% while nonmetropolitan areas grew by 5% and central cities declined by over 3%. To be sure, these figures reflect a slowing down in the growth rates which characterized suburbia in the 1950s and 1960s. Yet they also show a widening lead over nonsuburban America and more strongly

Table 3. Percentage Share of Total U.S. Population, 1950 to 1975

Years	Suburbs	Central cities	Nonmetropolitan areas
1950	24.4	34.6	41.0
1960	33.2	33.8	33.0
1970	37.6	31.4	31.0
1975	39.1	29.6	31.3

reinforce the major finding of the 1970 Census that the U.S. had become a suburban nation in a decidedly suburban age (Table 3). Although residential suburbanization persists as the leading component of population growth, the decisive development of the 1970s has been the rapid emergence—and fast-approaching dominance—of suburbia as home for highest order, nonresidential metropolitan activity. It is the purpose of this chapter to briefly examine these intrametropolitan deconcentration trends by presenting and interpreting 1970 to 1975 demographic, socioeconomic, and employment data trends with emphasis on their geographical dimensions and consequences.[2]

SUBURBAN POPULATION TRENDS SINCE 1970

As implied above, the definition of suburbia employed here is the one most widely used by urban researchers: all territory lying outside the central city within the SMSA. The 1970 to 1975 change in suburban population for all 257 SMSAs in the conterminous U.S., utilizing suburban percentages of the total SMSA population to facilitate longitudinal and intermetropolitan comparisons, is presented in Table 4.[3] For the nation as a whole, the suburbanization trend continued during the first half of the 1970s as the mean percentage advanced by almost 2% (comparable pre-1970 data were not available, but it is likely that the 1.8% increase also represents a slowdown compared to the preceding intercensal period). A number of major internal variations also occurred, making a regional and metropolitan size-class breakdown of these patterns a worthwhile consideration at this point.

The 1970 and 1975 breakdown by major census region shows the continuing suburbanization of the metropolitan population to be a nationwide trend (Table 5). Highest percentages are observed along both coasts, with only the Pacific region—already exhibiting a high overall suburbanization level—gaining less than the national mean for the period. The recording of no gain for the West Coast, however, is something of a statistical fluke since the figure of zero is derived as an unweighted mean: Large Pacific SMSA suburban rings continue to grow apace (the five biggest advanced an average of 2.9%), while more numerous small- and middle-sized metropolises have experienced faster central city growth, mostly through annexation of former suburbs. The nation's largest gains in New England are probably accentuated in the other direction by that region's underbounded cities, such as Boston, which have long been unable to absorb much additional urban growth. Highest relative levels in the Middle Atlantic region are very likely attributable to the pull of suburbanization in the gigantic New York metropolis, which also contains among its satellite SMSAs the nation's only such statistical unit (Long Island's Nassau-Suffolk) that lacks a central city altogether; a more realistic measure of the Greater New York urban concentration, perhaps, is the Standard Consolidated Area which saw the non-New York City portion of the region advance from 54.9% in 1970 to 55.9% in 1975.

Suburbanization is widespread in the interior of the country as well. Both the Midwest (East North Central) and Inland South (East South Central) now rank above the 50% level and are among the large gainers since 1970 (Table 5). Between the Mississippi River and the Pacific Coast states, however, suburbanization levels are noticeably lower in the heavily rural Great Plains (most of West North Central and West South Central) and Mountain regions where urbanization has traditionally lagged well behind the rest of the nation in an area whose relatively sparse population can support few cities. Yet even here the suburbs are growing faster than the central cities and the prognosis is for continued rapid metropolitan development, particularly if the contemporary migration trends described elsewhere in this book persist and intensify as they are expected to do in the 1980s. It is noteworthy that the fastest growing suburban rings in this part of the U.S. are contained in the most rapidly burgeoning SMSAs, metropolises which also happen to rank among the area's largest: Denver (7.2%), Phoenix (5.7%), New Orleans (5.6%), Minneapolis-St. Paul (5.2%), Dallas-Fort Worth (5.1%), and Houston (4.7%). The significance of this phenomenon is that rapid suburbanization is entering the Plains-Mountain region simultaneously at precisely the places where hierarchical diffusion models developed by geographers tell us to expect future spreading of innovations downward through the regional urban system. Thus, barring intervention by outside forces, such as new government anti-growth controls, suburbanization can be expected to "trickle down" to smaller SMSAs throughout this area for at least as long as the Interior West continues to maintain its current popularity as a destination for interstate migrants. Undoubtedly, these effects are already beginning to be felt in such intermediate-sized SMSAs as Austin (3.3%), Salt Lake City (4.3%), and Spokane (2.3%). Elsewhere, as in western Texas, annexation is still a strong force that operates against suburbanization. However, these traditions may now be losing hold and a significant harbinger of things to come may have occurred at the edge of Houston in the spring of 1978: For the first time, an affluent suburb is resisting annexation to that city (which has doubled in size by that method of growth since the early 1960s) for the same reasons—loss of local control, fear of property value losses, and negatively perceived taxation—that suburbs around the nation have been avoiding political unification with central cities for decades.

The breakdown of suburban percentages by metropolitan size-class is presented in Table 6. Most evident is the symmetrical relationship between SMSA size and degree of suburbanization: Both percentage levels and 1970 to 1975 gains decrease as the size of the metropolis declines. Nonetheless, suburbs are again observed to be growing faster than central cities in every category, and only the smallest SMSA size-class ranks below 50%. This 70,000 to 150,000 category, however, should be

Table 4. Suburban Percentage of the SMSA Population, 1970 and 1975

SMSA	Suburban in 1970 (%)	Suburban in 1975 (%)	SMSA	Suburban in 1970 (%)	Suburban in 1975 (%)
Abilene, TX	26.6	24.9	Fort Lauderdale-Hollywood, FL	60.3	67.9
Akron, OH	59.5	62.3	Fort Myers, FL	74.0	76.7
Albany, GA	24.9	26.8	Fort Smith, AR-OK	60.9	67.9
Albany-Schenectady-Troy, BY	67.0	69.2	Fort Wayne, IN	50.9	50.3
Albuquerque, NM	26.9	27.4	Fresno, CA	59.8	60.4
Alexandria, LA	58.0	59.1	Gadsden, AL	42.7	47.2
Allentown-Bethlehem-Easton, PA-NJ	64.2	66.4	Gainesville, FL	38.4	44.3
Altoona, PA	53.5	55.3	Galveston-Texas City, TX	40.7	44.5
Amarillo, TX	12.0	8.7	Gary-Hammond-East Chicago, IN	47.9	50.8
Anaheim-Santa Ana-Garden Grove, CA	68.6	71.2	Grand Rapids, MI	63.3	66.7
Anderson, IN	48.9	49.7	Great Falls, MT	26.5	28.1
Ann Arbor, MI	57.4	59.6	Greeley, CO	56.4	56.0
Anniston, AL	69.4	71.2	Green Bay, WI	44.5	47.1
Appleton-Oshkosh, WI	60.1	61.7	Greensboro-Winston-Salem-High Point, NC	53.0	53.1
Asheville, NC	64.2	64.5	Greenville-Spartanburg, SC	77.7	79.9
Atlanta, GA	69.0	75.6	Hamilton-Middletown, OH	48.4	48.9
Atlantic City, NJ	72.7	76.8	Harrisburg, PA	83.4	86.3
Augusta, GA-SC	78.3	80.5	Hartford-New Britain-Bristol, CT	71.3	74.0
Austin, TX	20.8	24.1	Houston, TX	37.3	42.0
Bakersfield, CA	78.9	77.5	Huntington-Ashland, WV-KY-OH	63.9	66.8
Baltimore, MD	56.3	60.3	Huntsville, AL	51.2	52.3
Baton Rouge, LA	27.6	28.4	Indianapolis, IN	34.2	37.2
Battle Creek, MI	78.3	76.2	Jackson, MI	68.3	70.1
Bay City, MI	57.9	60.6	Jackson, MS	40.5	42.3
Beaumont-Port Arthur-Orange, TX	42.8	44.8	Jacksonville, FL	18.9	22.8
Billings, MT	29.5	29.2	Jersey City, NJ	57.2	57.8
Biloxi-Gulfport, MS	44.2	48.4	Johnstown, PA	83.5	84.9
Binghamton, NY-PA	78.8	80.0	Johnson City-Kingsport-Bristol, TN-VA	77.0	75.2
Birmingham, AL	60.1	65.1	Kalamazoo-Portage, MI	53.8	55.4
Bloomington, IN	43.1	46.1	Kankakee, IL	68.2	70.8
Bloomington-Normal, IL	36.4	35.8	Kansas City, MO-KS	47.7	50.4
Boise City, ID	33.2	27.3	Kenosha, WI	33.2	34.4
Boston-Lowell-Brockton-Lawrence-			Killeen-Temple, TX	56.9	57.8
Haverhill, MA-NH	75.6	76.1	Knoxville, TN	57.4	57.9
Bridgeport-Stamford-Norwalk, Danbury, CT	50.1	52.2	LaCrosse, WI	36.4	42.3
Brownsville-Harlingen-San Benito, TX	27.9	23.2	Lafayette, LA	37.2	39.8
Bryan-College Station, TX	11.4	11.8	Lafayette-West Lafayette, IN	41.4	38.7
Buffalo, NY	65.7	69.3	Lake Charles, LA	46.4	49.4
Burlington, NC	62.7	62.2	Lakeland-Winter Haven, FL	74.6	75.0
Canton, OH	72.1	74.6	Lancaster, PA	82.0	83.4
Cedar Rapids, IA	32.2	34.5	Lansing-East Lansing, MI	57.8	60.2
Champaign-Urbana-Rantoul, IL	29.6	30.0	Laredo, TX	5.3	5.0
Charleston-North Charleston, SC	80.1	84.5	Las Vegas, NV	54.0	56.1
Charleston, WV	72.2	73.8	Lawton, OK	31.1	25.7
Charlotte-Gastonia, NC	48.3	44.2	Lewiston-Auburn, ME	27.8	32.0
Chattanooga, TN-GA	54.9	58.7	Lexington-Fayette, KY	34.6	36.4
Chicago, IL	51.8	55.8	Lima, OH	74.4	75.7
Cincinnati, OH-KY-IN	67.3	70.1	Lincoln, NE	11.0	12.0
Clarksville-Hopkinsville, TN-KY	43.3	45.6	Little Rock-North Little Rock, AR	40.4	44.8
Cleveland, OH	63.6	67.5	Long Branch-Asbury Park, NJ	89.5	91.0
Colorado Springs, CO	43.6	38.5	Longview, TX	62.3	58.5
Columbia, MO	27.3	28.3	Lorain-Elyria, OH	48.8	48.9
Columbia, SC	64.8	69.6	Los Angeles-Long Beach, CA	55.0	56.2
Columbus, GA-AL	29.8	28.5	Louisville, KY-IN	58.3	62.2
Columbus, OH	47.0	49.9	Lubbock, TX	16.8	16.9
Corpus Christi, TX	28.2	27.7	Lynchburg, VA	59.4	55.7
Dallas-Fort Worth, TX	47.9	53.0	Macon, GA	46.0	48.6
Davenport-Rock Island, Moline, IA-IL	46.3	47.7	Madison, WI	40.3	45.7
Dayton, OH	71.4	75.4	Manchester-Nashua, NH	35.9	40.8
Daytona Beach, FL	73.3	77.1	Mansfield, OH	57.7	56.4
Decatur, IL	27.7	29.6	McAllen-Pharr-Edinburg, TX	61.1	59.8
Denver-Boulder, CO	53.0	60.2	Melbourne-Titusville-Cocoa, FL	62.2	63.5
Des Moines, IA	36.0	41.4	Memphis, TN-AR-MS	21.2	23.7
Detroit, MI	65.9	69.8	Miami, FL	73.6	74.6
Dubuque, IA	31.2	34.4	Midland, TX	9.1	9.1
Duluth-Superior, MN-WI	49.9	52.2	Milwaukee, WI	48.9	52.8
Eau Claire, WI	61.2	60.8	Minneapolis-St. Paul, MN-WI	62.1	67.3
El Paso, TX	10.3	9.1	Mobile, AL	49.6	51.3
Elmira, NY	60.7	62.7	Modesto, CA	68.3	62.7
Erie, PA	51.0	52.9	Monroe, LA	51.2	51.4
Eugene-Springfield, OR	51.5	47.8	Montgomery, AL	40.9	38.6
Evansville, IN-KY	51.3	53.5	Muncie, IN	46.5	39.4
Fargo-Moorhead, ND-MN	30.9	33.8	Muskegon-Norton Shores Muskegon Heights, MI	52.0	54.3
Fayetteville, NC	74.8	71.7	Nashville-Davidson, TN	39.1	43.4
Fayetteville-Springdale, AR	62.8	63.8	Nassau-Suffolk, NY	100.0	100.0
Flint, MI	61.9	66.4	New Bedford-Fall River, MA	55.3	56.8
Florence, AL	71.1	72.2	New Brunswick-Perth Amboy-Sayreville, NJ	86.2	85.9
Fort Collins, CO	51.8	53.7	New Haven-West Haven-Waterbury-Meriden, CT	52.4	54.7

Table 4. (cont'd)

SMSA	Suburban in 1970 (%)	Suburban in 1975 (%)	SMSA	Suburban in 1970 (%)	Suburban in 1975 (%)
New London-Norwich, CT	69.9	70.3	San Francisco-Oakland, CA	65.4	68.3
New Orleans, LA	43.3	48.9	San Jose, CA	56.7	52.7
New York, NY-NJ	20.8	21.7	Santa Barbara-Santa Maria-Lompoc, CA	51.5	53.5
Newark, NJ	81.4	83.0	Santa Cruz, CA	74.1	75.7
Newport News-Hampton, VA	22.3	25.0	Santa Rosa, CA	75.6	73.5
Norfolk-Virginia Beach-Portsmouth, VA-NC	19.3	21.2	Sarasota, FL	66.6	71.0
Northeast Pennsylvania, PA	73.9	73.7	Savannah, GA	43.1	45.7
Odessa, TX	14.6	14.5	Seattle-Everett, WA	58.9	61.9
Oklahoma City, OK	47.2	51.0	Sherman-Denison, TX	35.1	38.7
Omaha, NE-IA	35.7	35.2	Shreveport, LA	45.6	46.3
Orlando, FL	78.2	80.6	Sioux City, IA-NE	26.0	28.7
Owensboro, KY	36.7	37.5	Sioux Falls, SD	23.9	26.1
Oxnard-Simi Valley-Ventura, CA	51.3	49.7	South Bend, IN	55.2	57.9
Parkersburg-Marietta, WV-OH	58.8	63.8	Spokane, WA	40.7	43.0
Pascagoula-Moss Point, MS	47.0	54.0	Springfield, IL	46.3	51.3
Paterson-Clifton-Passaic, NJ	38.7	41.3	Springfield, MO	28.5	29.8
Pensacola, FL	75.5	76.0	Springfield, OH	56.3	58.7
Peoria, IL	62.9	64.1	Springfield-Chicopee-Holyoke, MA	48.2	54.0
Petersburg-Colonial Heights-Hopewell, VA	35.7	31.2	Steubenville-Weirton, OH-WV	65.0	67.2
Philadelphia, PA-NJ	59.5	62.2	Stockton, VA	62.9	60.7
Phoenix, AZ	39.9	45.6	Syracuse, NY	69.0	71.8
Pine Bluff, AR	32.7	34.7	Tacoma, WA	62.4	63.6
Pittsburgh, PA	78.3	80.2	Tallahassee, FL	34.3	39.6
Pittsfield, MA	61.8	63.2	Tampa-St. Petersburg, FL	54.6	61.8
Portland, ME	61.7	73.9	Terre Haute, IN	59.9	62.6
Portland, OR-WA	62.1	67.1	Texarkana-Texarkana, TX-AR	53.6	52.0
Poughkeepsie, NY	85.6	86.5	Toledo, OH-MI	49.7	52.8
Providence-Warwick-Pawtucket, RI	62.5	63.9	Topeka, KS	30.8	33.1
Provo-Orem, UT	42.8	46.1	Trenton, NJ	65.6	68.4
Pueblo, CO	17.6	16.0	Tucson, AZ	25.2	33.2
Racine, WI	44.3	46.1	Tulsa, OK	40.0	43.4
Raleigh-Durham, NC	47.7	49.7	Tuscaloosa, AL	43.4	44.0
Reading, PA	70.4	73.3	Tyler, TX	40.5	42.8
Reno, NV	39.8	46.2	Utica-Rome, NY	58.4	60.7
Richland-Kennewick, WA	55.5	52.5	Vallejo-Fairfield-Napa, CA	41.0	39.7
Richmond, VA	54.0	59.7	Vineland-Millville-Bridgeton, NJ	26.5	25.3
Riverside-San Bernardino-Ontario, CA	73.0	74.2	Waco, TX	35.4	37.7
Roanoke, VA	54.7	53.2	Washington, DC-MD-VA	74.0	76.4
Rochester, MN	36.1	36.5	Waterloo-Cedar Falls, IA	20.9	17.6
Rochester, NY	69.2	72.5	West Palm Beach-Boca Raton, FL	75.4	76.7
Rockford, IL	45.8	46.3	Wheeling, WV-OH	73.6	75.7
Sacramento, CA	68.2	70.4	Wichita, KS	29.0	31.2
Saginaw, MI	58.2	62.0	Wichita Falls, TX	24.9	27.3
St. Cloud, MN	70.5	73.0	Williamsport, PA	66.5	68.7
St. Joseph, MO	26.4	22.1	Wilmington, DE-NJ-MD	83.9	85.3
St. Louis, MO-IL	74.2	77.8	Wilmington, NC	56.9	58.1
Salem, OR	63.4	62.3	Worcester-Fitchburg-Leominster, MA	60.3	62.0
Salinas-Seaside-Monterey, CA	51.6	49.1	Yakima, WA	68.6	67.9
Salt Lake City-Ogden, UT	65.2	69.5	York, PA	84.7	86.0
San Angelo, TX	10.1	11.3	Youngstown-Warren, OH	61.9	64.9
San Antonio, TX	26.3	21.2			
San Diego, CA	48.7	51.2	**Mean percentage 257 SMSAs**	51.6	53.4

Table 5. Suburban Percentage of the SMSA Population, by Region 1970 and 1975

Region	1970	1975	Change
New England	56.4	59.5	+3.1
Middle Atlantic	68.1	69.9	+1.8
South Atlantic	58.4	60.4	+2.0
East South Atlantic	49.1	51.4	+2.3
West South Atlantic	35.4	36.4	+1.0
East North Atlantic	53.6	55.6	+2.0
West North Atlantic	36.9	38.7	+1.8
Mountain	40.4	42.2	+1.8
Pacific	60.5	60.5	−
Conterminous U.S.	51.6	53.4	+1.8

Table 6. Suburban Percentage of the SMSA Population, by
Metropolitan Size-class, 1970 and 1975

SMSA Size-class	1970	1975	Change
More than 1,000,000	59.8	63.0	+3.2
500,000–1,000,000	56.1	58.5	+2.4
250,000–500,000	53.7	55.2	+1.5
150,000–250,000	51.2	52.6	+1.4
70,000–150,000	42.7	43.5	+0.8
Mean for all SMSAs	51.6	53.4	+1.8

viewed critically: Most of its moderate-sized urban concentrations are not really worthy of the appellation "metropolitan," and elimination of this size category from Table 6 results in a 4% increase in the national mean percentage for both 1970 and 1975. Among these small-central city SMSAs are such dubious "metropolises" as Bloomington, Ind.; Billings, Mont.; LaCrosse, Wis.; Elmira, N.Y.; Pine Bluff, Ark.; and Altoona, Pa. Moreover, the list of smallest SMSAs keeps growing vigorously and includes the following, added in mid-1977 after the latest SMSA listing at this writing had gone to press: Grand Forks, N.D.; Kokomo, Ind.; Lawrence, Kan.; and both Panama City and Bradenton in Florida.

SOCIOECONOMIC CHANGE IN SUBURBIA SINCE 1970

Economic class and racial divisions of long standing persist between the residential population of central cities and suburban rings. Whereas post-1970 trends do not signal a dramatic break with the past, they have been somewhat mixed with certain city-suburb differences heightening while others narrowed. In order to better discern the current situation, income, race, and overall social heterogeneity are examined.

An income disparity has always existed between central cities and suburbs. Post-1970 data, presented in Table 7, reveal that the gap is now widening as central city percentage of suburban median family income recedes further. In 1970, the difference between an average suburban and central city family's income was 17.8%; by 1975, that suburban family's income had climbed another 4.6% while its central city counterpart's income fell by 0.3%. A study by Berry and Dahmann reported that poverty is becoming more heavily concentrated in central cities, where the share of national poverty increased by 3.2% in the first half of the 1970s to 37.4%, and more than 10% of central city families now receive public assistance payments as opposed to less than 4% in suburbia.[4]

A pronounced racial dichotomy continues to characterize the population of the central city and suburban outer ring. By the mid-1970s, three-fifths of all U.S. blacks resided in the central cities compared to only one-quarter of the nation's white, whose metropolitan population living in suburbia grew from 59 to 62% in

Table 7. Median Family Income, Central Cities and
Suburban Rings, 1969 and 1974

Metropolitan Categories	1969	1974
Central cities	$9,157	$11,343
Suburban rings	$11,003	$14,007
Central cities percent of suburban rings	83.2	81.0

Source: U.S. Bureau of the Census, 1975.

the 1970 to 1975 period. On the other hand, only 17% of all blacks reside in the outer ring vs. 42% of the total white population. Although this racial imbalance shows no real sign of dissipating, blacks have found suburbia more accessible in the 1970s. These gains continue the minuscule increase that occurred during the 1960s when the black proportion of the suburban population rose from 4.78% in 1960 to 4.82% in 1970. The 1970 to 1975 gain has been slightly larger, and increased the black suburban presence to 5.0%. Some reports claim that post-1970 black suburbanization rates—based, of course, on very much lower base figures—have out-distanced those of whites. While this may technically be true, there is no evidence, however, that blacks are entering white residential areas in meaningful numbers. In other words, ongoing black suburban migration is overwhelmingly directed toward already black enclaves or advancing inner suburb ghettos that simply involve the spillover of central city ghettos across the city line. Thus, desegregation is not occurring and the dual housing market—through whose operation whites express their universal unwillingness to share residential space with blacks—continues to dominate the social geography of suburbia. Within the black community, however, there are signs of a deepening division between the increasingly middle-income, new suburbanites and the inner city underclass, a trend highlighted by Berry and Dahmann's finding that in 1975 suburban black income levels were 20% higher than those for central city residents vs. only a 15% differential for whites.[5]

Measures of suburban social heterogeneity for 1970 and 1975 show an increasing trend in that direction (Table 8). Quite clearly, the long-accepted image of a suburbia dominated by middle class nuclear family lifestyles—which several sociologists insist was always an inaccurate stereotype—is in need of revision in the late 1970s. Childless couples in every adult age group, single-parent families, the elderly, and particularly single persons have all increased their presence in suburban society in the first half of the 1970s. Undoubtedly, the enormous increase of multiple-dwelling units in the suburbs since the late 1960s has abetted this diversification of lifestyles. However, all evidence indicates that this lifestyle heterogeneity has occurred with minimal change in the social status quo of suburban communities. In other words, the newcomers are overwhelmingly alike in their income and status levels to those prevailing in the preexisting local population. Thus, the new

Table 8. Selected Measures of Suburban Social Heterogeneity,
1970 and 1974

Variable	1970	1974
% families without children under 18	39.5	42.1
% families headed by women	8.4	9.5
% family heads under 25	6.2	7.0
% family heads over 65	11.1	11.5
Median age	27.4	28.1
Single persons over 21 (in millions)	12.7	15.4

Source: U.S. Bureau of the Census, 1975.

suburban social heterogeneity of the 1970s is limited to those who can pay the price of admission, and excludes, through zoning and other quasi-legal mechanisms, those of lower income as well as nearly all ethnics of color.

POST-1970 EMPLOYMENT SUBURBANIZATION AND ITS CONSEQUENCES

As was pointed out at the beginning of this chapter, it is the deconcentration of high-order economic activity that has been the most dynamic suburban trend of the 1970s. In almost every major metropolis today, suburbia is emerging as an *outer city* in its own right that increasingly captures the leading urban functions of the central city which spawned it. Unfortunately, comprehensive data are not available to fully document this most significant new metropolitan trend, and detailed analysis must therefore await publication of the 1980 Census. Nevertheless, usable data of limited geographical coverage are available for the 1970 to 1975 period, and relate to the suburbanization of employment at the county level. These data series are published annually in *County Business Patterns*, and permit a fairly detailed look at employment deconcentration in those large SMSAs whose central cities coincide with county boundaries. There are eight such metropolises and they fortunately span the major regions of the U.S.: New York, Philadelphia, Baltimore, Washington, D.C., New Orleans, St. Louis, Denver, and San Francisco.

Employment breakdowns by economic sector for these eight metropolises in 1970 and 1975 are presented in Table 9. The four northeastern Megalopolis metropolitan areas all reveal rapid suburbanization of economic activities in the 1970s. Baltimore lags somewhat behind the others, but suburbanization in every sector except manufacturing has leaped ahead by at least 10 percentage points during the half-decade. Much of this suburban activity growth has occurred in the circumferential expressway (Beltway) corridor that rings the central city and is rapidly turning the Baltimore metropolis inside out. The idential phenomenon is repeated in the neighboring Washington metropolis to the south, where the Capital Beltway is already known as the urban region's "Main Street." By 1975, *every single category*

Table 9. Suburban Percentage of SMSA Employment, by Economic Sector, 1970 to 1975

	1970	1975		1970	1975
Baltimore:			*New Orleans:*		
Total employment	39.3	*49.6*[a]	Total employment	27.0	38.6
Manufacturing	47.4	*53.4*	Manufacturing	40.9	*49.6*
Wholesale trade	24.6	40.7	Wholesale trade	20.7	40.4
Retail trade	46.9	*61.0*	Retail trade	34.1	47.8
F.I.R.S.	10.5	25.6	F.I.R.S.[b]	21.3	31.9
Services	17.8	27.2	Services	29.2	44.7
Business services	20.2	*49.9*	Business services	19.6	29.6
Health services	21.3	38.9	Health services	22.1	30.3
Denver:			*New York:*[c]		
Total employment	33.3	45.3	Total employment	45.1	*50.3*
Manufacturing	45.8	*49.6*	Manufacturing	*55.5*	*61.2*
Wholesale trade	13.1	30.0	Wholesale trade	40.5	*51.6*
Retail trade	42.6	*56.0*	Retail trade	*53.4*	*59.9*
F.I.R.S.	17.0	30.8	F.I.R.S.	25.2	30.1
Services	30.3	40.7	Services	38.0	43.2
Business services	24.7	36.1	Business services	32.0	40.2
Health services	35.3	41.3	Health services	47.0	*51.5*
Philadelphia:			*San Francisco:*[d]		
Total employment	48.8	*56.7*	Total employment	*58.9*	*59.0*
Manufacturing	*54.5*	*63.2*	Manufacturing	*71.9*	*77.0*
Wholesale trade	39.7	*54.1*	Wholesale trade	*51.5*	*64.3*
Retail trade	*55.9*	*64.7*	Retail trade	*68.3*	*71.9*
F.I.R.S.	31.0	43.0	F.I.R.S.	33.7	37.8
Services	29.2	44.7	Services	*54.0*	*54.8*
Business services	38.2	42.7	Business services	46.8	*49.6*
Health services	46.1	*52.3*	Health services	*66.3*	*62.1*
St. Louis:			*Washington, D.C.:*		
Total employment	*51.6*	*61.5*	Total employment	*54.1*	*63.2*
Manufacturing	*53.9*	*60.3*	Manufacturing	*57.6*	*69.1*
Wholesale trade	34.7	*54.7*	Wholesale trade	*53.6*	*68.5*
Retail trade	*63.4*	*72.7*	Retail trade	*65.7*	*74.8*
F.I.R.S.	42.7	*51.1*	F.I.R.S.	47.7	*54.4*
Services	45.4	*58.9*	Services	43.4	*51.9*
Business services	29.5	*51.0*	Business services	*51.9*	*67.6*
Health services	*52.0*	*58.1*	Health services	*54.6*	*60.9*

Notes: [a]Greater than 49.5% suburban proportion underlined. [b]Finance, insurance, and real estate. [c]Metropolis defined as Standard Consolidated Area. [d]City of Oakland included in suburban ring.

Source: U.S. Bureau of the Census, *County Business Patterns*, 1970, 1975.

of metropolitan employment activity was present to a greater degree in the suburbs than in the District of Columbia. The national capital area's largest employer, the federal government, has also suburbanized many of its major facilities. Although nobody apparently keeps track of the intraurban decentralization of federal jobs, the best guess of a knowledgeable U.S. Department of Labor economist is that at least 50% of these jobs in the Washington SMSAs were located outside the central city by the mid-1970s. Metropolitan New York (defined as the Standard Consolidated Area, as discussed earlier) exhibits many of the same trends, with the central city finally relinquishing its share of more than half the area's jobs in 1975. Despite its recent financial difficulties, Manhattan's national business community still hangs together. However, a large number of leading corporate headquarters have recently left the city for suburbia, and the danger of further unraveling of the city's economy, as expressed in the 8% suburban gain of the region's business service jobs between 1970 and 1975, is ever-present.[6]

The fourth northeastern metropolis, Philadelphia, exhibits identical employment trends with each suburban sector gaining 5% or more. Philadelphia is also one of the very few SMSAs that has kept track of annual changes in central city/suburban ring employment, and because this metropolitan economy has usually performed close to the national norm in the past it may be that the trends observed in Figure 10 are typical of older, large urban regions. Suburban gain concomitant with central city erosion since 1960 is the dominant spatial employment trend on this graph, a widening gap interrupted only by the effects of the mid-1970s recession which appeared to have ended by early 1978 (Table 10).

Elsewhere in the nation, both St. Louis and San Francisco exhibit current suburban employment trends similar to those of the Northeast. The structure of the St. Louis economy is very much like Philadelphia's: an overindustrialized employment base that is undergoing rapid deterioration as the national economy becomes increasingly a post-industrial one emphasizing the production of services and decision-making based on highly specialized information. It is also interesting that even though St. Louis is a century "younger" than Philadelphia, the midwestern metropolis is now experiencing a more broad-based economic decline, with the suburbs taking over in every employment sector by 1975. With the exception of financial and real estate activities, San Francisco's employment pattern is also dominated by its suburbs, although the inclusion of a major satellite city (Oakland) does inflate the percentages of that outer ring. The Bay Area metropolis also includes the only central city job-sector gain observed anywhere in Table 9: San Francisco's 5% rise in health services employment that is at least partially attributable to the recent expansion of the University of California's leading medical-facility complex in that city. Denver and New Orleans both exhibit the nascent employment deconcentration pattern that we would expect to be associated with the beginnings of mass suburbanization in the largest SMSAs of the Interior West. Both metropolises show sizable suburban gains in all economic sectors, and if current deconcentration trends persist both will soon attain the dispersed intra-metropolitan employment distribution that dominates large SMSAs in other parts of the country.

Although it is hazardous to generalize from only eight metropolises, an

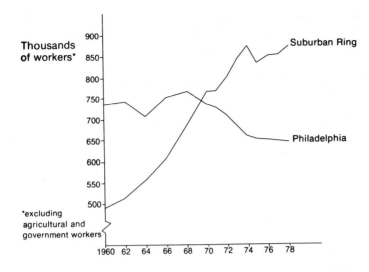

Fig. 10. Employment trends in Philadelphia SMSA.

intermetropolitan comparison of job-sector suburbanization in the 1970s can at least be broadly sketched from the data in Table 9. It does appear that manufacturing and retail trade pave the way for activity suburbanization, a finding consistent with the literature on the economic geography of the postwar metropolis. It is also evident that the specialized services of the metropolitan office industry are among the last to deconcentrate from the central city, another finding compatible with recent research. Yet apart from these interesting but limited observations, we really understand very little about the dimensions, let alone the causes, of the

Table 10. Suburban Percentage of Metropolitan Employment, Philadelphia SMSA, 1960 to 1978[a]

Year	Suburban percentage of SMSA employment	Year	Suburban percentage of SMSA employment
1960	40.1	1972	53.0
1962	41.0	1973	55.2
1964	43.9	1974	57.0
1966	44.7	1975	56.1
1968	47.3	1976	56.6
1970	51.2	1977	56.7
1971	51.4	1978	57.5

[a]Agricultural and governmental workers excluded.
Source: Various publications of Mideast region, U.S. Bureau of Labor Statistics.

sudden rapid post-1970 suburbanization of economic activities. Most unfortunate too is the lack of available data beyond the information presented in this chapter. The U.S. Department of Labor through its Bureau of Labor Statistics does report monthly figures on total metropolitan employment, but unfortunately defines workers by residence rather than workplace—as if commuting and particularly reverse commuting across the central city line did not even exist—so that it will be impossible to discern city/suburb job trends for all the remaining SMSAs until the detailed findings of the 1980 Census are published in 1981 or 1982.

CONCLUSIONS

Within the limitations imposed by the availability of pertinent information, this chapter has examined macrogeographical aspects of post-1970 suburban demographic, socioeconomic, and employment data trends. A few conclusions may be drawn from these observations. *First*, suburban population growth—though now increasing at a slower rate than in the quarter-century following World War II—remains strong throughout the nation despite the recent energy crisis, economic recession, and astounding inflation in the price of new and used housing. *Second*, income disparities between the central city and suburban ring are widening and, while suburbia is becoming more heterogeneous in its lifestyles, there is no evidence of meaningful change in long-standing patterns of suburban racial and economic segregation. And *third*, high rates of employment suburbanization in eight large northeastern, mid-western, southern, and western SMSAs reinforce much other less formal evidence that suburbia has approached economic independence from the central city in the late 1970s.

As we enter the 1980s, it is clear that a new intrametropolitan reality has been forged with the suburban ring now comprising the essence of the contemporary American city. Geographers and other students of the evolving American metropolitan system must now begin to weigh the enormous consequences of this truly historic development, and participate in the shaping of policies and plans designed to improve urban life in the transformed metropolis.

NOTES

*The author gratefully acknowledges the support of a Temple University Summer Research Fellowship in gathering and analyzing the data on which this chapter is based.

[1] For a geographical overview of these trends, see Brian J. L. Berry and Donald C. Dahmann, *Population Redistribution in the United States in the 1970s* (Washington, D.C.: National Academy of Sciences, 1977) and Curtis C. Roseman, *Changing Migration Patterns Within the United States* (Washington, D.C.: Association of American Geographers, Resource Papers for College Geography No. 77-2, 1977).

[2] For an extended exposition, see Peter O. Muller, *The Outer City* (Englewood Cliffs, N.J.: Prentice-Hall, 1980).

[3] This listing, with the elimination of Anchorage, Alaska and Honolulu, Hawaii, follows the latest SMSA list of the Bureau of the Census in its publication, Series P-25, No. 709, Sept. 1977

("Estimates of the Population of Counties and Metropolitan Areas: July 1, 1974 and 1975"). The main differences with respect to past listings are the elimination of Puerto Rican SMSAs and the grouping together of New England SMSAs into multiples of counties rather than individual aggregations of townships.

[4] Berry and Dahmann, op. cit., note 1, pp. 32–33.

[5] Ibid.

[6] Peter O. Muller, "The Suburbanization of Corporate Headquarters: What Are the Trends and Consequences?" *Vital Issues* (Washington, Conn.: Center for Information on America, Vol. 27, No. 8, April, 1978).

Chapter 4

Exurban Areas and Exurban Migration

Curtis C. Roseman

A major reason for exurban problems is attributed to the post-1970 population growth in nonmetropolitan areas. This "rural renaissance" represents a dramatic turnaround from the migration pattern of previous decades. Many of the "rural" areas are nonmetropolitan by definition but are functionally a part of a metropolitan system. The migration patterns characteristic of exurban areas are the focus of the discussion in this chapter. A technique known as the Automatic Interaction Detector (AID) is used to identify the most important variables associated with net migration in exurban areas from 1970 to 1975. Different types of exurban growth occurred, some dependent on the attraction of amenity environments, some on government employment, and others on commuting to nearby metropolitan areas. In a pilot study of migration streams to and from 10 selected exurban areas, the variety of patterns in migration evident from 1955 to 1960 continues to be evident in the 1965 to 1970 period. The nature and extent of exurban nonmetropolitan growth represent an important element in studying metropolitan systems in the future.

INTRODUCTION

The recent resurgence of nonmetropolitan population in the U.S. sometimes referred to as "rural renaissance" is today an issue of considerable importance.[1] Closely linked with this nonmetropolitan trend has been the gradual decline in growth rates in metropolitan areas leading to the absolute loss of population in many large U.S. SMSAs during the last few years. This gradual redistribution of population from metropolitan to nonmetropolitan areas is not unique to the U.S. nor is it something which suddenly occurred in 1970.[2] It has been the product of several long-term trends. For instance, during the 1960s many SMSAs were experiencing net out-migration, which went largely unnoticed because these areas were still growing in population.[3] It was not until after 1970, when birth rates went down and out-migration increased further, that these components of population change were translated into absolute losses of population.[4]

The most important component of the "turnaround" has been a steady increase in out-migration from metropolitan areas. Whereas migration streams to metropolitan areas have been declining, the more important migration component was the rise in migration from metropolitan to nonmetropolitan areas.[5] Further, the most important proportion of that stream has been directed toward nonmetropolitan places near metropolitan areas. It has been estimated, for instance, that about 63% of the nonmetropolitan net in-migration between 1970 and 1974 was in counties adjacent to SMSAs.[6] Such an estimate is consistent with the findings of residential location preference studies which show that (1) among metropolitan residents there is a majority preference for nonmetropolitan places and (2) among that majority the most common preference is for nonmetropolitan places near metropolitan areas.[7] Most persons who are able to act on a preference for nonmetropolitan places apparently locate near metropolitan areas. This movement has been termed "exurban" migration and a rapidly growing set of "exurban" places is emerging in this country—a set of places which are officially "nonmetropolitan" but which clearly and functionally are a part of the metropolitan system.

This chapter is concerned with exurban places and exurban migration. It focuses first on all nonmetropolitan U.S. counties which are adjacent to metropolitan areas and classifies them according to factors which are associated with their post-1970 net migration—an effort to uncover the characteristics of exurban places growing through migration. Second, the chapter reports the results of a small pilot study of migration streams affecting some exurban places prior to 1970—partially to document the longer term nature of the population turnaround and partially to gain insight into the specific types of migration streams which are most affecting population change in exurban areas. The chapter concludes by commenting on the nature of exurban places and exurban migration, with an eye toward the kinds of issues needed to be addressed in future research.

EXURBAN PLACES

The first analysis focuses upon 762 U.S. nonmetropolitan counties which are adjacent to, but not part of, SMSAs (using the 1970 definition of SMSA). The question is posed: To what extent do various characteristics of these exurban counties relate to recent (post-1970) population change attributable to migration? A dependent variable is defined for each county as the estimate of net migration from 1970 to 1975 as a percent of the 1970 population.[8] A set of independent variables is chosen as representative of various factors which are believed to influence contemporary nonmetropolitan migration. Full discussions of these factors are presented by McCarthy and Morrison and by Morrill.[9]

The first independent variable represents both the dependence of exurban counties upon, and their access to, adjacent metropolitan areas, potentially key factors in the recent growth of exurban counties (Table 11). The next four variables are resident population characteristics. Population density and rural non-farm population characterize the settlement character of exurban areas, the latter being particularly important to nonmetropolitan growth in general. Median age and median income are population characteristics which may indirectly relate to the attraction of places and/or describe the migrants who are selecting growing exurban environments.

Percentages employed in government and living in group quarters measure the presence of governmental and other institutional activities which have contributed to overall nonmetropolitan growth for some time (e.g., universities, military communities, and state capitals). The remaining two independent variables represent private industrial developments. The mining industry has recently been influential in population growth in parts of Appalachia and the Interior West. Percent of farms owned by a corporation does not itself represent a characteristic directly related to in- or out-migration, but is a surrogate for other processes which are so related. Areas with relatively few corporate farms, such as the Middle West and parts of the South, are much more dependent upon agriculture as a mainstay of their economy and hence are less likely to grow due to migration. Conversely, many specialized farming areas, such as the fruit and vegetable areas of Florida and the Southwest, extensive cattle areas of the interior West, and truck farming areas near many large cities, possess attractive environments for nonmetropolitan-bound migrants.

The technique chosen for this analysis is AID.[10] AID is ideally suited to this analysis because it will: (1) determine the relative importance of the independent variables in discriminating between counties with different rates of net migration, (2) specify complex interactions among the independent variables which best predict net migration, and (3) classify counties on the basis of their migration response to different combinations of the predictor variables. AID starts by selecting

Table 11. Independent Variables for Aid Analysis

1. % working in another county
2. Population per square mile
3. Rural nonfarm population
4. Median age
5. Median family income
6. % employed in government
7. % living in group quarters
8. % of mining establishments
9. % of farms with sales $2500 and over operated by a corporation

Source: U.S. Bureau of the Census (1973).

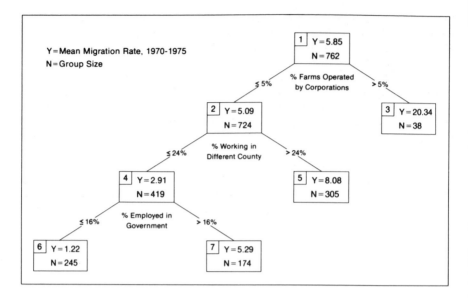

Fig. 11. AID analysis: Nonmetropolitan adjacent counties.

the one independent variable which accounts for the greatest difference in the dependent variable between two subsets of counties using variance analysis techniques.[11] At this point, the universe of counties is split into two groups whose net migration means account for more of the total sum of squares than do the means of any other two groups that could be defined by the independent variables. The analysis continues by repeating this procedure for each of the two subgroups, entering the variable which best discriminates among net migration within each. The program proceeds until it is no longer possible to split subgroups at greater than a specified level of significance or until a specified minimum group size cannot be met. The analysis results in a "tree graph" that describes all the interrelationships.

Figure 11 shows the independent variables and a tree graph for the analysis of exurban counties. The overall unweighted mean percent net migration for all 762 counties is +5.85 (box number 1).[12]

In the classification of the 762 exurban counties, a rather clear pattern emerged (Fig. 11). The initial split separates out a group of 38 counties which have high percentages of corporation operated farms and are growing at rapid rates due to migration (group 3). Most of these counties are located in Florida, the Southwest, and scattered locations in the Eastern Seaboard area, principally in areas which have citrus or vegetable farms. The growth of these counties is probably not due to that type of agriculture per se, but to the general attractiveness of those areas for exurban migration or amenity-related migration. A critical variable divided the remainder: Group 5 emerged as a set of counties with a high level of commuting dependence upon other counties. These counties are perhaps the truly "exurban" areas—counties which are adjacent to and dependent upon metropolitan areas. These counties are the recipients of recent exurban migrants who seek nonmetropolitan living environments and yet may be tied through their job to at least the fringes of the metropolitan area. These counties, formally classified as nonmetropolitan in 1970, were functionally a part of the metropolitan system.

Of the remaining counties, a subgroup with relatively large employment in government (group 7, n = 174) has a mean net migration rate near the overall mean, while the remainder (group 6), those counties not benefiting from commuting ties, corporation farm environments, or high government employment, have a mean rate less than that for most nonadjacent counties.

It is clear that adjacency by itself is not a determinant of population growth through migration but probably is a facilitator of growth. Adjacency to metropolitan area, when coupled with commuting, government employment, or an advantageous regional environment, characterized growth through migration in the early 1970s.

EXURBAN MIGRATION

The second analysis is a pilot study of changing migration streams affecting 10 selected nonmetropolitan State Economic Areas (SEAs). Partly in the belief that significant aspects of the recent "rural renaissance" had begun before 1970 and partly because detailed flow data are not available after 1970, migration flows to and from these areas for 1955 to 1960 and 1965 to 1970 are compared.[13] The 10 areas were selected because they are located near metropolitan areas and are within commuting ranges of the SMSA fringes, but they are clearly outside of the contiguous built-up urbanized area and the mass tract housing developments so characteristic of suburban environments. To have been selected, each area must also have been growing due to migration in the 1965 to 1970 period. The 10 are near metropolitan areas in a variety of regions and with a variety of population sizes (Table 12).[14]

The positive net migration of all 10 sample SEAs from 1965 to 1970 represented a reversal from the previous decade for 4 of them (Table 12). Particularly striking reversals were experienced in Georgia 3 and Texas 14. In only two cases (Ohio 3 and Indiana 5) was the 1965 to 1970 net migration less than that for 1955 to 1960.

Some understanding of these trends is revealed in two types of migration stream breakdowns. First, when net migration with respect only to the neighboring metropolitan SEA is isolated, in every case a substantial increase in net migration toward the exurban SEA is found. The result is a positive net migration from 1965 to 1970 for the exurban SEAs, except in the case of Kentucky 7 which essentially broke even. In general, a variety of patterns of net migration changes with respect to the neighboring metropolitan SEAs is seen, but the trend consistently indicates increasing decentralization of population toward these exurban areas.

Any net migration figure is the result of two opposing migration streams. Thus, the second breakdown shows changes in individual migration streams for each

Table 12. Migration Patterns, Selected "Exurban" SEAs

SEA		Nearby metropolitan areas	Net migration		Net migration with respect to adjacent metropolitan area(s)	
			1955-60	1965-70	1955-60	1965-70
NY	1	Rochester	778	991	1,403	8,978
NY	9	New York City	26,289	29,926	28,078	44,897
MD	2	Baltimore	331	15,727	2,171	9,785
OH	3	Dayton/Columbus	4,553	1,884	2,756	4,504
MI	8	Detroit	-1,344	4,149	4,856	8,978
IN	5	Indianapolis	14,975	12,571	-10,404	12,546
GA	3	Atlanta	-2,641	11,741	-1,320	6,102
KY	7	Lexington	-1,626	2,430	-1,666	-34
TX	14	Houston	-8,560	5,754	-3,673	1,199
CA	2	San Francisco	17,915	22,705	11,177	18,020

Percent change in migration streams between 1955-60 and 1965-70

SEA		Nearby metropolitan areas	From adjacent metropolitan area(s)	From elsewhere	To adjacent metropolitan area(s)	To elsewhere
NY	1	Rochester	21.4	35.8	18.4	33.8
NY	9	New York City	46.1	18.9	13.7	44.0
MD	2	Baltimore	113.0	39.5	23.6	8.9
OH	3	Dayton/Columbus	15.7	13.2	9.9	29.0
MI	8	Detroit	30.0	21.4	- .1	6.3
IN	5	Indianapolis	146.8	-8.3	-36.6	85.3
GA	3	Atlanta	83.3	45.5	-5.5	6.3
KY	7	Lexington	68.2	24.8	4.2	3.8
TX	14	Houston	95.1	26.9	32.3	.3
CA	2	San Francisco	38.3	18.4	10.0	31.0

Source: U.S. Bureau of the Census (1967 and 1972).

exurban SEA to and from both neighboring metropolitan SEAs and elsewhere. In-migration streams from adjacent metropolitan areas all increased more than 15%, some more than doubling (Maryland 2 and Indiana 5). In all except two cases, percentage changes in this stream were the greatest of any in- or out-migration stream. Therefore, the change in migration which most influenced the growth due to migration in the sample exurban SEAs were those streams associated with metropolitan decentralization through outward residential movements (exurban migration).

Nonetheless, rather consistent increases in in-migration streams originating elsewhere can be seen, suggesting an attraction for migrants which has a broader base than simply from contiguous metropolitan areas. Out-migration patterns are somewhat more mixed and either decreased or increased at generally lower levels. But it is important to note that there are many cases of increased out-migration from exurban areas, some of which is directed toward the adjacent metropolitan SEAs. In general, these exurban SEAs are becoming migrationally "active" in the sense that they are experiencing increasing out-migration which comes with rapid growth and the influx of migrants who, in turn, are highly prone to migrate again.

This pilot study points toward the conclusion that, in spite of a variety of migratory movements affecting these exurban places, the increase in exurban streams from adjacent metropolitan areas is rather consistent. In this sample, exurban growth is largely an extension of outwardly-directed movements of outwardly-directed movements of migrants and not generally due to the lessening of migration back toward the metropolitan areas. Yet there is also a rather persistent increase in the attraction of migrants from other places. Thus, these exurban areas are growing on the basis of migration from a variety of places, but most importantly from the nearby suppliers of exurban migrants.

DISCUSSION

From these two analyses it appears that (1) metropolitan adjacency by itself does not guarantee growth of nonmetropolitan places and (2) growing exurban areas are consistently drawing increasing numbers of exurban migrants originating nearby, are also drawing increasing numbers of migrants from elsewhere, and are typically not ceasing to supply out-migrants.

In one sense, exurban migration and the growth of exurban places can be viewed as the simple continuation of the dispersal of metropolitan populations. This view suggests that we adhere to a broader spatial definition of "metropolitan" to include exurban places. The annexation to official SMSAs of many adjacent counties since 1970 is consistent with this perspective.

While in this view it may be logical to include more and more of the landscape into "metropolitan" areas, the recent exurban migration trends could represent much more than a simple extension of previous decentralization trends. There could be an important qualitative difference. The idea that bucolic residential settings are desirable has been embraced by part of our population for a long time, but it is now diffusing widely into the middle class. More and more people now apparently desire a "rural" character in their residential environment. The traditional "pull" exerted by tract-housing suburban environments (especially in the 1950s) may be waning, giving way to the "pull" of places with a "rural" or "small-town" image. The large metropolitan fringe, now spatially much more extensive than 20 years ago, may be developing as a region characterized by essentially nonmetropolitan places, populated by urban and suburban refugees, within a metropolitan system.

The explosion of interest in metropolitan to nonmetropolitan migration among social scientists has been disproportionately aimed at movements to more distant nonmetropolitan places, while migrants themselves have been going in greater numbers to exurban locations. Research is needed on the origins (e.g., central city vs. suburban), socioeconomic characteristics, motivations, and choice processes of exurban migrants. Similarly, more research is needed upon community impacts of exurban growth, such as social conflicts and the provision of municipal services, and on the extent to which such places are linked to the metropolitan system through commuting and metropolitan loyalties or through cultural ties retained by exurban migrants.

NOTES

[1] Peter A. Morrison and Judith P. Wheeler, "Rural Renaissance in America? The Revival of Population Growth in Remote Areas," *Population Bulletin*, Vol. 31 (1976), (Washington, D.C.: Population Reference Bureau).

[2] Daniel R. Vining, Jr. and Thomas Kontuly, *Population Dispersal from Major Metropolitan Regions: An International Comparison* (Philadelphia: Regional Science Research Institute, Discussion Paper No. 100, 1977).

[3] William Alonso, *The System of Inter-Metropolitan Population Flows* (Berkeley: University of California, Institute of Urban and Regional Development, Working Paper No. 155, 1971).

[4] Peter A. Morrison, *Emerging Concerns over U.S. Population Movements in an Era of Slowing Growth* (Santa Monica, Calif.: and Paper No. P-5873, 1977).

[5] Curtis C. Roseman, *Changing Migration Patterns within the United States* (Washington, D.C.: Association of American Geographers, Resource Paper No. 77-2, 1977), p. 19.

[6] Calvin L. Beale, *The Revival of Population Growth in Nonmetropolitan America* (Washington, D.C.: U.S. Department of Agriculture, Economic Research Service, ERS-605, 1975).

[7] Glenn V. Fuguitt and James J. Zuiches, "Residential Preferences and Population Distribution," *Demography*, Vol. 12 (1975), pp. 491–504.

[8] U.S. Bureau of the Census, *Current Population Reports, Population Estimates* (Washington, D.C.: U.S. Government Printing Office, Series P-25 and P-26, various numbers, 1976).

[9] Kevin F. McCarthy and Peter A. Morrison, "The Changing Demographic and Economic Structure of Nonmetropolitan Areas in the United States," *International Regional Science Review*, Vol. 2 (1977), pp. 123–42 and Richard L. Morrill, "Population Redistribution, 1965–75," *Growth and Change*, Vol. 9 (1978), pp. 35–43.

[10] For a discussion of the AID technique, see J. A. Sonquist and J. N. Morgan, *The Determination of Interaction Effects* (Ann Arbor: University of Michigan, Survey Research Center, 1964). AID has been applied in other migration analyses by Julian Wolpert, "The Basis for Stability of Interregional Transactions," *Geographical Analysis*, Vol. 1 (1969), pp. 152–80; George F. Rengert, *Migration Probabilities: A Study of Migration from the Agricultural Villages around Ojuelos, Mexico*, unpublished Ph.D. Dissertation, University of North Carolina, 1971; and Dennis Seniffel and Seymour Goldstone, "Employment, Induced In-Migration, and Labor Market Equilibrium," *Growth and Change*, Vol. 7 (1976), pp. 33–40.

[11] In order to be received by the AID routine, each independent variable had to be coded into ordinal categories; hence five categories were defined for each independent variable.

[12] This compares to +3.91 for all U.S. counties and +3.32 for nonmetropolitan, non-adjacent counties.

[13] Migrants are defined as persons 5 years of age and older who were living in a different SEA 5 years before the census date, 1960 or 1970.

[14] For this pilot study no attempt was made to obtain a random sample. The analysis, instead, is intended to be descriptive of the variety of changing migration patterns which are affecting exurban areas.

Chapter 5

Spatial and Behavioral Aspects of the Counterstream Migration of Blacks to the South

James H. Johnson, Jr. and Stanley D. Brunn

The nonmetropolitan migration streams described by Roseman in Chapter 4 represent one of the many migration streams occurring throughout the metropolitan system. A relatively insignificant stream in numbers but one of growing importance is the movement of blacks to the South. The volume, direction, and reasons for that migration are treated in this chapter. Before examining the origins, destinations, and motives of that counterstream migration, this chapter traces the patterns of massive black migration from the rural South to the urban North earlier in this century. Blacks moving South today seem to follow similar South-North streams. Two distinct groups are moving South, each for different reasons. The return migrants include older, blue-collar, widowed, and divorced people who are returning home because the social climate has improved since the 1960s. The new or primary migrants are young, highly educated, and white collar; they perceive the race relations and quality of life to have improved sufficiently to merit a move. The destinations of those in the counterstream movement are mainly metropolitan areas from Virginia to Texas; their origins are from industrial areas in the Northeast, Middle West, and California. Nonmetropolitan areas near Dallas, Houston, and Atlanta are also attracting migrants from the North. The extent of this migration will become more apparent in the 1980 Census. Insights into the extent of future black migration are offered by a survey of students in predominantly black colleges. The preference patterns for Pennsylvania students were the South and California, the Northeast states by North Carolina students, and Sunbelt states by Texas students.

The purpose of this chapter is to examine recent trends in black migration within the U.S. Specifically, the objectives are threefold: (1) to determine and map the volume and direction of these recent movements as well as the specific origins and destinations of the movers; (2) to identify the major motivational factors associated with recent population shifts; and (3) to present empirical evidence of possible future trends in black migration. Since an understanding of present trends is predicated upon an appreciation of past population shifts, this analysis begins with a brief discussion of early 20th century black migration.[1]

20th CENTURY BLACK MIGRATION

Traditionally, black population shifts at the national scale in the U.S. have been total displacement moves from the South to the North and the West. This pattern originated during the decade ending in 1920 when between 300,000 and 1,000,000 blacks left the South in what has been referred to as the Great Migration. The motives for the mass movement are summarized in the popular folklore piece:[2]

> Boll-weevil in de cotton
> Cutworm in de cotton
> Debil in de white man
> Wah's going on.

Indeed, the devastation of cotton, the South's major cash crop, by the boll weevil and the cutworm, and especially the harsh treatment—floggings, lynchings, and burnings—blacks received in the South were major "push" factors. And the curtailment of foreign immigration and the concomitant demand for unskilled labor as a result of World War I were major "pull" factors.[3] But perhaps most important were interpersonal communication links whereby blacks discovered that life in the North was far better than the racially oppressive environment south of the Mason-Dixon line. Indeed, many Afro-Americans trekked North in search of a psycho-socially less stressful environment.[4]

Blacks followed well-defined migratory streams or channels in their exodus from the South to the North. For instance, the majority of those moving from the South Atlantic states migrated north along the Atlantic seaboard to the large industrial centers in the Middle Atlantic states. Cities in the East North Central region were the primary destinations for those moving out of the East South Central states, and the urban centers in the West North Central region were terminus for blacks in the West South Central region.[5] Specifically, such cities as New York, Philadelphia, Pittsburgh, Detroit, and Chicago received the majority of the southern Blacks.

The movement along these well-defined streams, although fluctuating markedly from one decade to the next, has persisted to the present. Between 1935 and 1940, the first time the census included a question pertaining specifically to migration, nearly 120,000 blacks migrated to the North, in spite of the Great Depression.[6] The volume increased to just over 300,000 during the 1955 to 1960 period, but declined to approximately 285,000 between 1965 and 1970.[7] This decrease, however, was paralleled by an increased flow of blacks to the South.

E. G. Ravenstein's fourth law of migration states that for every dominant stream or channel there is a smaller "counterstream" or flow in the opposite direction.[8] While the dominant flow was from the South to the North during the early decades of this century, the number of Afro-Americans moving in the opposite direction has grown to noticeable proportions since 1955. For instance, only 33,000 migrated from the North to the South between 1935 and 1940, less than one-third the volume from the South to the North during this period.[9] But approximately 98,000 blacks left the northern "promised land" for Dixie during the 5-year period ending in 1960, and between 1965 and 1970 another 161,000 migrated South.[10] While almost half as many were moving to the South as were leaving the region during the 1965-70 period, recent census reports reveal that between 1970 and 1977 the number of black migrants to the South exceeded by 52,000 the flow to the North and the West.[11] These figures suggest that a radical shift is occurring in the patterns of 20th century black migration, with the South actually experiencing net black in-migration since 1970.

COUNTERSTREAM BLACK MIGRATION

The recent counterstream movement of blacks to the South has been studied primarily by demographers and sociologists. Some of these writers have scrutinized aggregated census data to discern the volume of movement, the socio-economic and demographic characteristics of the migrants, and the major determinants of the population shift.[12] Others have identified and queried individual migrants as to their motives for moving to the South.[13] And from these and other studies Campbell and Johnson suggested propositions for the counterstream black migration.[14] But as Roseman observed:[15]

> Much of our knowledge of the spatial aspects of the [counterstream] migration lacks specification of exact location, specification that is useful for understanding the site and situation attributes at the origins and destinations which are important in the locational decisions of the migrants.

Thus, the geographer's task is to fill this void.

ORIGINS AND DESTINATIONS OF COUNTERSTREAM MIGRANTS

Regional Patterns

Approximately 175,000 Afro-Americans left the North and the West for destinations in the South between 1965 and 1970.[16] While the bulk of these migrants (81%) left the Middle Atlantic (67,000), East North Central (46,000), and Pacific (30,000) regions, the West North Central and the Mountain regions contributed

Table 13. Regional Origins and Destinations of Counterstream Black Migrants

Origins region, 1965	Destination region, 1970						
	Total in-migrants	South Atlantic		East South Central		West South Central	
		n	(%)	n	(%)	n	(%)
New England	9,664	7,742	80	632	7	1,290	13
Middle Atlantic	66,772	55,570	83	5,924	9	5,278	8
East North Central	45,860	17,272	37	18,230	40	10,358	23
West North Central	14,537	4,702	32	3,884	27	5,951	41
Mountain	9,927	3,903	39	1,158	12	4,866	49
Pacific	30,494	13,045	43	3,709	12	13,740	45

Source: U.S. Bureau of the Census, *Mobility For State and Nation*, 1973.

almost 15,000 and 10,000 respectively. The counterstream migrants also followed well-defined streams. Over 80% of those leaving the Middle Atlantic and New England states, for example, moved south along the Atlantic seaboard into the South Atlantic states (Table 13). Blacks migrating from the East North Central region followed one of two distinct channels: the East South Central region was the destination for 40%, and another 38% moved into the South Atlantic states. Although states in the West South Central region were the primary destinations for those leaving the West North Central region, secondary streams flowed into the South Atlantic (32%) and East South Central states (27%). Migrants from the Mountain and Pacific regions also followed two distinct streams: 46% were destined for states in the nearby West South Central region, and the more distant South Atlantic region was the terminus for 40%.

State Origins and Destinations

Nearly 8 out of every 10 blacks moving to the South between 1965 and 1970 originated in 1 of 8 states: New York, California, Illinois, New Jersey, Pennsylvania, Ohio, Michigan, or Missouri (Table 14). A much smaller but also significant number moved from Indiana, Massachusetts, Connecticut, Washington, and Kansas; the remaining non-South states contributed 20,000. Although a few of the migrants left rural areas, the majority were former residents of metropolitan areas in the North (Table 14).

Texas experienced the greatest influx of blacks from the non-South states, and North Carolina and Virginia were second and third, respectively. While Maryland, South Carolina, Georgia, and Florida received between 12,000 and 15,000 each, between 8,000 and 10,000 moved into each of the following states: Tennessee, Alabama, Mississippi, and Louisiana. Each of the remaining six southern states experienced an influx between 1,000 and 5,000, with West Virginia receiving the smallest number.

Table 14. State Origins of Counterstream Migrants, 1965 to 1970
(Total migrated: 177,254)

Rank	Total	% of total	% Non-metro
1 New York	38,173	21.5	5.6
2 California	23,635	13.8	8.3
3 Illinois	18,629	10.5	5.2
4 New Jersey	14,366	8.1	12.8
5 Pennsylvania	14,233	8.0	5.3
6 Ohio	10,690	6.0	6.5
7 Michigan	9,941	5.6	15.6
8 Missouri	7,155	4.0	25.8
	136,822	77.0	
9 Indiana	4,841	2.7	14.8
10 Massachusetts	3,982	2.2	4.1
11 Kansas	3,806	2.1	54.1
12 Connecticut	3,658	2.1	15.1
13 Washington	3,617	2.0	13.2
	19,904	10.1	
14 Other non-south states	20,528	12.0	

Source: U.S. Bureau of the Census, *Mobility for States and Nation*, 1973.

To identify more specifically the destinations of blacks within each of the southern states, data gathered by the U.S. Bureau of the Census for population shifts between SEAs were scrutinized. These data are based on a 15% sample of the population 5 years or older, generalized to the entire population. SEAs are census defined areal units whose boundaries correspond with those of SMSAs (metropolitan SEAs) or with those of rural counties with similar social and economic functions (nonmetropolitan SEAs).[17]

SEA Destinations

Metropolitan SEAs were the destinations for 6 out of every 10 blacks migrating to the South between 1965 and 1970. Metropolitan areas of special importance were Washington, D.C., Baltimore, Atlanta, Houston, and Memphis, which along with the much smaller Norfolk-Hampton SEA was each the destination of more than 3,000 black migrants (Fig. 12). Cities and hinterlands receiving 2,000 to 2,999 included New Orleans, La.; Newport News, Va.; Jacksonville and Miami, Fla.; and San Antonio, Texas. Each of the following received between 1,500 and 1,999: Birmingham, Ala.; St. Petersburg, Fla.; Nashville, Tenn.; Columbus, Ga.; Columbia and Charleston, S.C.; and Richmond and Alexandria, Va. Between 1,000 and 1,499 Afro-Americans established residences in the cities and hinterlands of Austin, Tex.; Louisville, Ky.; Augusta, Ga.; Shreveport, La.; Oklahoma City and Tulsa, Okla.;

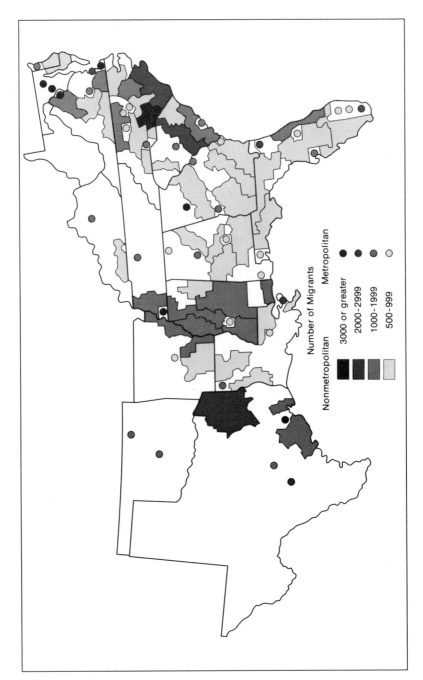

Fig. 12. Inmigration fields of black migrants from North and West, 1965–1970.

Number of Migrants

Nonmetropolitan   Metropolitan

3000 or greater
2000 - 2999
1000 - 1999
500 - 999

Charlotte, N.C.; and Wilmington, Del. And 500 to 999 blacks settled in each of the following metropolitan SEAs: Raleigh, Durham, and Greensboro, N.C.; West Palm Beach, Fla.; Mobile, Huntsville, and Montgomery, Ala.; Jackson, Miss.; Savannah, Ga.; and Baton Rouge, La.

Northern blacks also moved to nonmetropolitan areas in the South (58,000). Rural SEA 9 in North Carolina, for instance, was the destination for more than 3,000, and SEA 12 in Texas, SEA 11 in North Carolina, and SEA 6 in South Carolina all experienced an influx of between 2,000 and 2,999. But these SEAs, with the exception of SEA 12 in Texas, are atypical of most southern nonmetropolitan SEAs; they are areas within which the U.S. Army (SEA 7 in North Carolina and SEA 6 in South Carolina) and Marine Corp (SEA 11 in North Carolina) training installations are located, and more than likely these institutions are responsible for the seemingly large number of black in-migrants. Otherwise, the majority of those destined for the nonmetropolitan South (more than two-thirds) distributed themselves either in 1 of 14 SEAs, each of which received from 1,000 to 1,999, or in 1 of 26 others, each of which was terminus for between 500 to 999.

Some of the SEAs actually experienced net in-migration during the 5-year period ending in 1970, especially the metropolitan SEAs. While Prince Georges and Montgomery Counties in Maryland registered the greatest net influx, three of the recently designated "super" and "most liveable" cities for Afro-Americans also made considerable gains: Atlanta (10,800), Houston (10,000), and Dallas (7,300).[18] Among the numerous other southern metropolitan SEAs experiencing net black in-migration are those including such cities as Tulsa, Okla.; San Antonio and Fort Worth, Tex.; St. Petersburg, Fla.; Columbia, S.C.; Charlotte, N.C.; and Richmond and Alexandria, Va. (Fig. 13).

But the in-migration from the North and the West has contributed little to the growth of the black population in southern metropolitan areas. The majority of the in-migrants moved from nonmetropolitan and to a lesser extent other metropolitan areas within the South. For example, of the 23,000 black in-migrants to the Atlanta SEA, almost 85% changed residences within the South, and more than two-thirds originated in southern nonmetropolitan SEAs (Fig. 14). In fact, the rural counties of Georgia alone contributed nearly 10,000, almost three times the number moving from the North and the West. Similarly, 87% of the nearly 26,000 in-migrants to the Houston SEA were already residents of the South, moving primarily from rural areas within Texas (9,100) and nearby Louisiana (4,100) (Fig. 15). In neither case did the counterstream migrants comprise as much as 20% of the total in-migration.

These data indicate clearly that the counterstream movement between 1975 and 1970, as Stangler observed, was "no runaway train," that recent population shifts have been mainly intraregional, from rural to metropolitan areas, whereas traditionally blacks migrated out of the South.[19] That all but two nonmetropolitan SEAs experienced net out-migration between 1965 and 1970, in spite of the influx of blacks from outside the South, is also evidence that the counterstream was relatively insignificant.

Although the movement from the North and the West between 1965 and 1970 was relatively small (compared to black population shifts within the South), it is

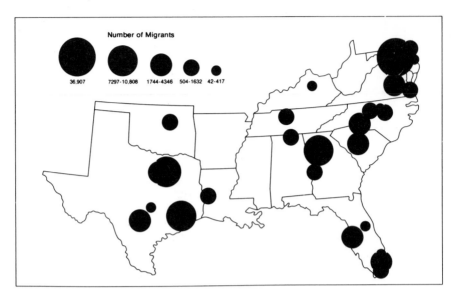

Fig. 13. Net inmigration fields of counterstream black migrants, 1965–1970.

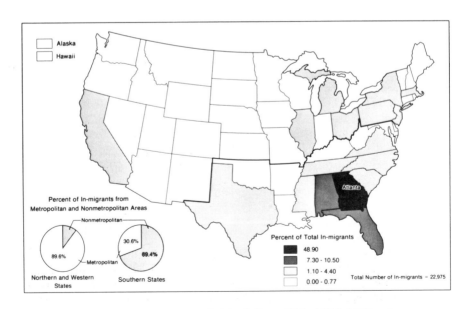

Fig. 14. Inmigration fields, Atlanta SEA, 1965–1970.

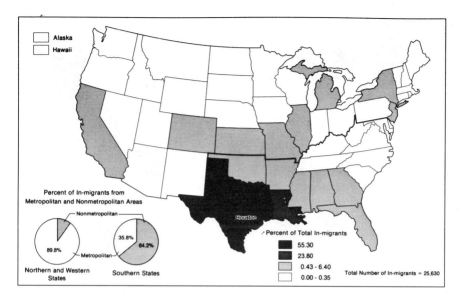

Fig. 15. Inmigration fields, Houston SEA, 1965-1970.

nevertheless worthwhile to identify the reasons for the counterstream migration. It is also important to determine whether the movement is an anomaly or perhaps an emerging trend. The motivational factors are discussed below, and a subsequent section focuses on possible future trends.

MOTIVES FOR COUNTERSTREAM BLACK MIGRATION

Two distinct groups of blacks are migrating to the South: those moving to an area of previous residence (return migrants) and those establishing households in the South for the first time (primary migrants). The primary migrants are characterized as young, highly educated singles and couples, who are employed primarily in white-collar jobs, and the returnees as older, mainly blue-collar workers, many of whom are widowed, separated, or divorced females.[20] Because little research has been done on the primary migrant, the motivational factors discussed here are largely based on Johnson's study of 101 return migrants to Birmingham, Ala., and on news and magazine accounts of return migrants to the South.[21]

To identify the specific motivational factors operating at the origins and the destinations, the migrant's decision *to move* and the decision of *where to move* were considered separately, although the two decisions are usually made simultaneously in actual moving situations.[22]

A majority of the return migrants indicated that their decision to move was based on the steadily deteriorating quality of Afro-American life in northern cities. The most frequently mentioned motive was fear resulting from increasing crime and violence.[23] Exorbitant rents for deteriorated, overcrowded housing, extensive drug traffic, and the rapid pace of inner city life were just a few of the many other motivational factors. In short, as Coombs succinctly articulated:[24]

> Many of the [return migrants] began to look around them, and they could find no sweetness in the ravaged litter-strewn streets of the neighborhood they called home. They began to look homeward—really homeward—and they began to like what they saw.

For the most part, the return migrants attributed their decision of where to move to the changing race relations in the South. According to one return migrant to Jackson, Miss.:[25]

> Before I left years ago . . . there were places you [blacks] couldn't go, places you couldn't even eat, and you couldn't make a decent living. But [now] I can live in peace here. I can walk anywhere in town without fear.

And Claire Jupiter, who grew up in a black middle class family in New Orleans, went North to be educated at Yale, and recently returned home, states that:[26]

> It is a new day down here [South] because blatant racism is ending. There is a measure of security and a black person can even begin to call the South "home."

In addition to changing race relations, some of the migrants gave family related reasons for returning home.[27] For example, Ellistine Perkins Lewis, now an assistant professor of music at Jackson State, gave the following reason for leaving Ann Arbor, Mich., and returning home:[28]

> I wanted to enjoy my mom, be closer to her. I left home early and missed that whole stage during which we could relate as adults. I had no relatives in Michigan, and I found as time went on, I missed being able to participate in family groups. Even though I spent my maturing years in the North—that's where I got my sense of who I am—my roots are here [the South].

More than half of the 101 return migrants to Birmingham, Ala., interviewed by Johnson also gave similar reasons for coming back "home."[29]

Of note is the almost insignificant role of economic factors in the return migrant's locational decision. Only 20% of those interviewed by Johnson, for example, gave reasons that could be classified as economic, and, in most cases, these reasons were secondary to improved race relations and family ties in the South.[30] In fact, Viola Bullock, a former resident of Albany, N.Y., suggested that an improved social environment was more important.[31]

> I don't regret at all the hard work I put in during those 11 years in the North, but there's always (sic) time to know when to come home [Raleigh, N.C.]. We don't

Table 15. Cost of Living Indexes for
Selected U.S. Cities, 1976[a]
(U.S. average = 100)

City	Index
Northern cities	
Chicago	116.9
Detroit	109.2
Newark	104.5
New York	124.9
Southern cities	
Atlanta	99.7
Birmingham	101.7
New Orleans	101.6
Little Rock	97.2
Jackson	101.5
Houston	101.3

[a]Index based on a "middle management
family of four with an annual income of $18,000
to $20,000."
Source: Cost of Living Indicators, 1976.

make nearly as much money as we once did. But we have a nice home, pleasant
neighbors, healthy children, and we no longer have to take any nonsense from
white people.

Other factors mentioned by the returnees include a more hospitable climate
and a more reasonable cost of living. As Table 15 indicates, the cost of living in
southern cities is indeed less than that for comparable cities in the North.

Very little data have been gathered on the primary migrant's reasons for moving
to the South. Several writers have speculated that rapidly expanding employment
opportunities, improved race relations, and the images of major southern cities
(e.g., Atlanta) as contemporary centers of black socio-cultural life are the major
factors luring new migrants to the South.[32] While these motives seem plausible,
much research remains to be done, as the relative weight of each factor in the
primary migrant's locational decision is obscure.[33] Even though there is a lack of
sufficient information on the primary migrant, it is generally agreed that the
counterstream movement of blacks to the South is a "quality of life migration."[34]

Despite recent census estimates indicating that blacks in the North and the West
continue to move to the South in steadily increasing numbers, the extent to which
this reverse migration is an established and, most importantly, meaningful movement (in terms of numbers arriving at specific destinations in the South) will not
be specifically known until the 1980 Census, not likely to appear before 1982.[35]
The next section speculates on future migration trends via an analysis of black
residential preferences.

BLACK RESIDENTIAL PREFERENCES

Although the correlation between peoples' preferences for specific geographic environments and their actual migratory behavior is usually extremely weak, residential preferences have nevertheless been used as crude indicators of future population shifts.[36] To determine possible future trends in black migration, students enrolled in introductory geography classes at three predominately black colleges in Pennsylvania, North Carolina, and Texas were asked to rank the 48 contiguous states of the U.S. according to their residential preference upon graduation.[37] College students were selected because, as Gould and White indicated, "They are the most educated and mobile members of an incredibly mobile society."[38]

The student rankings were factor analyzed, and the resulting factor scores grouped into five classes using an iterative classification that minimized within group and maximized between group variance. This classification was done for mapping purposes so that the scores assigned to each of the 48 states could be categorized into one of five nominal classes ranging from highly desirable to highly undesirable.

Pennsylvania Viewpoint

The students at Cheyney State College are clearly biased in favor of the south-eastern states. With the notable exception of Alabama, the entire belt of states extending from West Virginia to Louisiana is viewed as a highly desirable place to live (Fig. 16). Although California must be added to this group, it is interesting that the factor scores for the southeastern states were higher than the scores assigned to California. Pennsylvanians, surprisingly, did not display a particular affinity for their home state. Rather, a second tier of states (Alabama, Ohio, Tennessee, and Kentucky) immediately adjacent to the highly preferred southeastern seaboard states were more favored than Pennsylvania, Texas, Oklahoma, and Washington. Maryland, Rhode Island, and Massachusetts were also more favored than Pennsylvania. States in New England, the Upper Great Lakes, and the Great Plains were viewed with indifference or as undesirable areas; Arkansas, Iowa, Utah, and New Mexico were considered very undesirable.

North Carolina Viewpoint

The most desirable areas of the country for this group consists of a band of states along the northeastern seaboard extending from Virginia to New York and including Maryland, New Jersey, and Pennsylvania; Florida and California also belong in this group (Fig. 16). North Carolina is not among the most preferred; it received only a moderate rating similar to that of Washington, Texas, South Carolina, Ohio, Connecticut, and Vermont. In general, the Great Plains, Upper Middle West, and New England states are viewed as moderately undesirable. The Deep South states, plus Kentucky, Iowa, Idaho, and Arizona, are least desired.

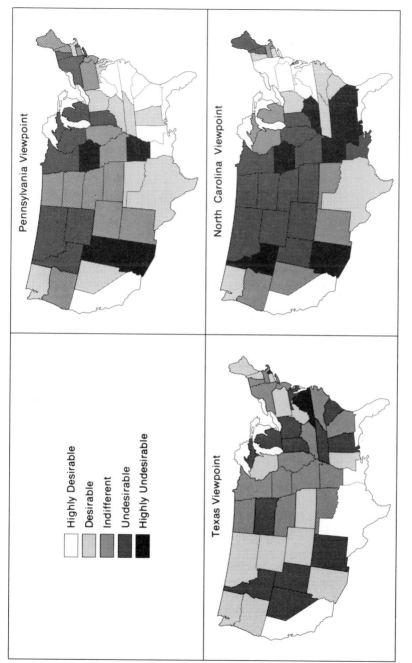

Fig. 16. Afro-American residential preference patterns.

Pennsylvania Viewpoint

North Carolina Viewpoint

Texas Viewpoint

Highly Desirable
Desirable
Indifferent
Undesirable
Highly Undesirable

Texas Viewpoint

Texans ranked California, Louisiana, Florida, and especially their home state as the most desirable states (Fig. 16). Areas viewed as only moderately desirable include a variety of locations, several in the Northeast (Pennsylvania, Connecticut, Vermont, and Maine), Wisconsin, Mississippi, several Rocky Mountain states, plus Washington, Oregon, and Arizona. Virginia is the least preferred. States in the eastern Middle West and Alabama, South Carolina, and Tennessee are considered undesirable.

From these three surveys of Afro-Americans it is concluded that California and Florida are consistently viewed as desirable. Beyond this generalization, however, the residential preferences vary with the college student sample in question. Pennsylvania blacks are biased toward the South, while those in North Carolina favor the northeast. And blacks in Texas primarily view Sunbelt states as highly desirable.

These preference patterns suggest that future population shifts may reflect existing trends in black migration. Although the movement from the South to the North has declined since the 1950s, the preferences of the North Carolina student sample suggest that some blacks will continue to follow the traditional southeast to northeast stream. On the other hand, the preferences of the Pennsylvania sample reveal that blacks in the Northeast will continue to migrate to the Sunbelt, and the Texas group's preference for the Sunbelt states suggests that recent population shifts within the South may continue.

SUMMARY AND CONCLUSIONS

This chapter has (1) examined the spatial aspects of the reverse migration of Afro-Americans to the South, (2) discussed the reasons for the population shift, and (3) speculated on future black migratory trends. This analysis revealed that (a) the reverse migration is primarily a movement from metropolitan areas in the North to such areas in the South; (b) while the gross numbers migrating to the South appear large, the number moving to specific destinations within the region is extremely small, especially compared to the massive intraregional population shifts; (c) the counterstream movement is a "quality of life migration"; and (d) blacks will continue their exodus from the northern "Promised Land" to the Sunbelt.

NOTES

[1] John Fraser Hart, "The Changing Distribution of the Negro," *Annals*, Association of American Geographers, Vol. 50 (1960), p. 242.

[2] Seth M. Scheiner, *Negro Mecca: A History of the Negro in New York 1865-1920*, (N.Y.: New York University Press, 1965), p. 71.

[3] For geographic treatments of these factors, see Richard L. Morrill and O. Fred Donaldson, "Geographical Perspectives on the History of Black America," *Economic Geography*, Vol. 48

(1972), pp. 1-23 and George A. Davis and O. Fred Donaldson, *Blacks in the United States: A Geographic Perspective* (Boston: Houghton-Mifflin, 1975), pp. 53-91.

[4]This notion is discussed in Walter C. Farrell, Jr. and James H. Johnson, Jr., "Black Migration as a Response to Social-Psychological Stress: A Note on Migrant Letters, 1916-1918," *Geographical Survey*, Vol. 7 (1978), pp. 22-27 and Walter C. Farrell, Phillip E. Kitchart, and Kenneth A. Jordan, "Psychosocial and Other Factors in Black Migration," *Negro History Bulletin*, Vol. 41 (1978), pp. 812-13.

[5]The spatial patterns are displayed cartographically in Morrill and Donaldson, op. cit., note 3, pp. 12-13.

[6]U.S. Bureau of Census, *Census of Population*, "Internal Migration 1935-1940" (Washington, D.C.: U.S. Government Printing Office, 1943).

[7]U.S. Bureau of Census, *Census of Population: 1960*. Subject Reports. "Lifetime and Recent Migration," Final Report PC (2)-2D. (Washington, D.C.: U.S. Government Printing Office, 1963); U.S. Bureau of Census, *Census of Population: 1970*, Report PC (1)-C1. U.S. Summary. "General Social and Economic Characteristics," (Washington, D.C.: U.S. Government Printing Office, 1972).

[8]E. G. Ravenstein, "The Laws of Migration," *Journal of the Royal Statistical Society*, Vol. 52 (1889), pp. 241-301.

[9]U.S. Bureau of Census, op. cit., note 6.

[10]U.S. Bureau of Census, op. cit., note 7.

[11]U.S. Bureau of Census, *Current Population Reports*, Series P-20, No. 273, "Mobility of the Population of the United States: March 1970 to March 1974" (Washington, D.C.: U.S. Government Printing Office, 1974); U.S. Bureau of Census, *Current Population Reports*, Series P-20, No. 320 "Geographical Mobility: March 1975 to March 1977" (Washington, D.C.: U.S. Government Printing Office, 1978).

[12]Rex R. Campbell, Daniel M. Johnson, and Gary J. Stangler, "Return Migration of Black People to the South," *Rural Sociology*, Vol. 39 (1974), pp. 514-28; idem, "Counterstream Migration of Black People to the South: Data from 1970 Public Use Sample," *Review of Public Data Use*, Vol. 3 (1975), pp. 13-21; Daniel M. Johnson, Gary J. Stangler, and Rex R. Campbell, "Black Migration to the South: Primary and Return Migrants," paper presented at the Rural Sociological Society Annual Meeting, Montreal, Canada, 1974; Larry H. Long and Kristen A. Hansen, "Trends in Return Migration to the South," *Demography*, Vol. 12 (1975), pp. 601-13; idem, "Selectivity of Black Return Migration to the South," *Rural Sociology*, Vol. 42 (1977), pp. 317-31; Anne S. Lee, "Return Migration in the United States," *International Migration Review*, Vol. 8 (1974), pp. 283-308; Richard J. Cebula, Robert M. Kohn, and Richard K. Vedder, "Some Determinants of Interstate Migration of Blacks, 1965-1970," *Western Economic Journal*, Vol. 2 (1973), pp. 500-505; and James B. Kau and C. F. Sirmans, "New Repeat, and Return Migrants: A Study of Migrant Types," *Southern Economic Journal*, Vol. 43 (1976), pp. 1114-48.

[13]Daniel M. Johnson, *Black Return Migration to a Southern Metropolitan Community: Birmingham, Alabama*, unpublished doctoral dissertation (University of Missouri, Columbia, 1973).

[14]Rex R. Campbell and Daniel M. Johnson, "Propositions on Counterstream Migration," *Rural Sociology*, Vol. 41 (1976), pp. 127-44.

[15]Curtis C. Roseman, "Migration as a Spatial and Temporal Process," *Annals*, Association of American Geographers, Vol. 61 (1971), p. 589.

[16]U.S. Bureau of Census, *Census of Population: 1970*, Subject Reports, Final Report PC (2)-2B. "Mobility For States and the Nation." (Washington, D.C.: U.S. Government Printing Office, 1973).

[17]U.S. Bureau of Census, *Census of Population: 1970*. Subject Reports, Final Report PC (2)-2E. "Migration Between State Economic Areas." (Washington, D.C.: U.S. Government Printing Office, 1972).

[18]"The Ten Best Cities For Blacks," *Ebony*, Vol. 33 (1978), pp. 95–102.

[19]Jerome Mondesire, "Reverse Migration: A Complex Pattern," *Today, The [Philadelphia] Inquirer Magazine*, March 13, 1977, p. 31.

[20]Johnson, Stangler, and Campbell, op. cit., note 12.

[21]Johnson, op. cit., note 13; "The South Today," *Ebony*, Vol. 26 (1971), entire issue; Orde Coombs, "The Black Woman Finds Her Roots," *Redbook*, Vol. 49 (1977), pp. 56, 60, 62, 67; Harriet Jackson Scarapa, "Reverse Migration," *Essence*, Vol. 8 (1977), pp. 66–7; 116–18; Bernard E. Garnett, "Going Home, More Black Americans Return to the South From Exile in the North," *The Wall Street Journal*, Nov. 10, 1972, p. 1; Jermoe Mondesire, "A Black Family's Return to the Changing South," *Today, The [Philadelphia] Inquirer Magazine*, Mar. 13, 1977, pp. 18–20, 26–29, 32; and Walter C. Farrell, Jr., "Black Migration," *Today, The [Philadelphia] Inquirer Magazine*, Apr. 10, 1977.

[22]The locational decisions of the migrants are discussed in Ira Lowry, *Migration and Metropolitan Growth: Two Analytical Models* (San Francisco, Calif.: Chandler Publishing Co., 1966); John A. Jakle, Stanley D. Brunn, and Curtis C. Roseman, *Human Spatial Behavior: A Social Geography* (North Scituate, Mass.: Duxbury Press, 1976), pp. 148–51; and Curtis C. Roseman, *Changing Migration Patterns Within the United States*, Resource Papers for College Geography No. 7–72. (Washington, D.C.: Association of American Geographers, 1977), pp. 4–6.

[23]"The South Today," op. cit., note 21, p. 66.

[24]Coombs, op. cit., note 21, p. 56.

[25]"The South Today," op. cit., note 21.

[26]Coombs, op. cit., note 21, p. 67.

[27]The vastly improved race relations in the South can be attributed to the Civil Rights Movement and the Voting Rights Act of 1965. Since the mid-'60s, for example, more than 2 million southern Afro-Americans have registered to vote, and black elected officials increased from 100 to 2,200 in 1975. This increased political power, Ayers suggests, is the primary social change agent. It is the reason South Carolina Senator Strom Thurmond, for long a diehard segregationist, now has blacks on his staff and his child enrolled in an integrated school; for George Wallace's more moderate political philosophy, and his recent trip to the University of Alabama, where he once blocked the schoolhouse door to keep blacks out, to crown a black homecoming queen; and for school desegregation being much more advanced in the South than in the North. For a complete discussion, see: *The Voting Rights Act: Ten Years After: A Report of the United States Commission on Civil Rights*, (Washington, D.C.: U.S. Commission on Civil Rights, 1975); Howell Raines, "Revolution in South: Blacks at Polls and In Office," *New York Times*, Apr. 3, 1978, pp. 1, 16; "Increase in Black Elected Officials," *The Crises*, Vol. 85 (1978), p. 70; "The Growing Black Role in Democratic Politics of the South," *New York Times*, Apr. 4, 1978, p. 33C; B. Drummond Ayers, Jr., "Decade of Black Struggles: Gains and Unmet Goals," *New York Times*, Apr. 2, 1978, pp. 1, 18; and John Herbers, "Montgomery Relaxes as Racism Recedes," *New York Times*, April 14, 1978.

[28]Scarapa, op. cit., note 21, pp. 66–67.

[29]Johnson, op. cit., note 13, p. 84.

[30]Johnson, op. cit., note 13, p. 84.

[31]Coombs, op. cit., note 21, p. 67.

[32]"Minorities, The Poor and the Sunbelt Boom: Five Opinions," *Network*, Vol. 5 (1976), p. 4.

[33]Campbell, Johnson, and Stangler, op. cit., note 14 and Louis A. Ploch, "Notes on Counterstream Migration," *Newsline*, Vol. 6 (1978), pp. 20–22.

[34]Farrell, op. cit., note 21.

[35]Bureau of Census, op. cit., note 11.

[36]Peter R. Gould and Rodney White, *Mental Maps* (Baltimore, Md.: Penguin Books, 1974); Gary Fuller and Murray Chapman, "On the Role of Mental Maps in Migration Research," *International Migration Review*, Vol. 8 (1974), pp. 491–506; and Roseman, op. cit., note 22, pp. 6–7.

[37]The students participating in the survey attended Cheyney State College, Cheyney, Pa.; North Carolina Central University, Durham, N.C.; and Prairie View A & M University, Prairie View, Tex.

[38]Gould and White, op. cit., note 36, p. 93.

Chapter 6

Geopolitical Fragmentation and the Pattern of Growth and Need: Defining the Cleavage Between Sunbelt and Frostbelt Metropolises

Donald J. Zeigler and Stanley D. Brunn

Both metropolitan growth and decline involve the reorganization of political space, i.e., administrative problems that transcend a variety of governmental and administrative units separated by boundaries. The scope and scale of geopolitical fragmentation is the topic addressed in this chapter. Variations in the degree of fragmentation are examined vis-a-vis changes in metropolitan growth in the Sunbelt and Frostbelt in light of a Per Capita Needs Index (PCNI) devised by the Department of Housing and Urban Development. The most politically fragmented metropolitan areas are in the Northeast quarter of the U.S., a mosaic of overlapping, tightly fitted jurisdictions with underbounded central cities containing only a fraction of their metropolitan area's population. An Index of Geopolitical Fragmentation (IGF) is devised based on the number of local governments per 100,000 population and percent of the population in the central city. According to this index the least fragmented metropolitan areas are in the Sunbelt and New England. Two methods introduced to remodel the political shell and eliminate outmoded and overlapping political boundaries are territorial annexation and consolidation. Central city annexation and city-county consolidation are most frequently in the South and East, with little in the Northeast and North Central regions. Special districts are also used to achieve a better political organization; however, they often fragment governmental responsibilities. The PCNI is related most closely to the slowest growing and oldest industrial cities in the Northeast and North Central regions. What often occurs are needy and declining central cities that are surrounded by affluent suburbs, a picture that illustrates the acuteness of boundaries in the solution to metropolitan area wide problems.

Metropolitan growth and change take place within the confines of an administrative framework assembled from the building blocks of counties, townships, and municipalities. Antiquated but inviolate political boundaries often pose dilemmas for both declining and growing metropolitan areas in the U.S. These boundaries condition the pattern of community need which emerges from official statistics and, at the same time, limit options for coping with that need. This cellular framework of administrative units may be envisioned as a political shell analogous to the physical shells of Ekistics theory. One constitutes the political structures, whereas the other constitutes the physical structures, within which "man lives and carries out his different functions."[1]

Just as the pattern of metropolitan growth and decline is not a random one, neither are the patterns of geopolitical fragmentation and community need. Ample note has been afforded the growth of Sunbelt metropolises allegedly at the expense of declining areas in the Frostbelt. *Fortune, Saturday Review, Harper's, Nation's Cities, Money*, and other popular magazines have all carried cover stories or major articles on the disparities in state and metropolitan growth rates along North-South lines. All of them note the geographic regularities which emerge from an analysis of current growth trends.

Geopolitical fragmentation, the division of metropolitan areas into a multitude of separate or overlapping jurisdictions, exhibits a pattern of regional variation which parallels the regional cleavages in population growth and the manifestations of urban need as expressed in a PCNI devised for the Department of Housing and Urban Development. Metropolitan population change often triggers the emergence of new problems or accentuates the severity of old ones. Since many of these problems demand solutions, formulated or at least implemented at the local level, the structure of the political shell may facilitate or hinder the problem-solving process. Patterns of geopolitical fragmentation and community need, and their interrelationships with the pattern of population change, will be examined in this chapter in light of the Sunbelt-Frostbelt debate in an effort to advance a more comprehensive geography of growth and decline.

THE PATTERN OF METROPOLITAN GROWTH AND DECLINE

Between 1970 and 1976, 37 SMSAs experienced an absolute decline in population (Fig. 17).[2] Twenty-eight of these negative growth SMSAs were located in the Northeast or North Central census regions. A similar pattern emerges when the regional distribution of slowly-growing SMSAs is examined. Of the 37 metropolitan areas which experienced a positive annual growth rate of .35% or less, 28 were located in the same two regions.

Almost all of the declining and slowly growing metropolitan areas fall into at least one of the following categories: (1) the older industrial areas of the American manufacturing belt; (2) the smaller and more isolated metropolitan areas of the South, many of which are in the growth shadows of rapidly growing urban agglomerations; and (3) the nation's largest metropolitan areas. Of the 15 largest SMSAs

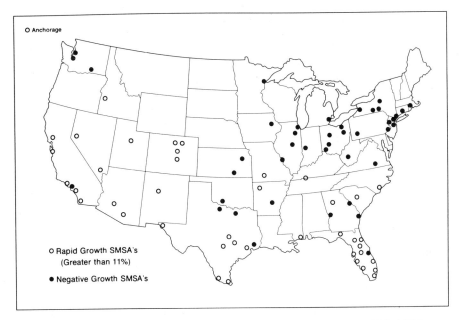

Fig. 17. Population growth and decline in metropolitan areas, 1970–1976.

in 1970, in fact, 8 experienced a net population loss, and 4 more were among the most slowly growing in the United States.

In contrast, all of the 37 metropolitan areas which experienced the most rapid growth between 1970 and 1976 were located in the Sunbelt and Rocky Mountains amenity regions of the South and West. Florida, Texas, and California alone accounted for over three-fifths of the SMSAs which grew more than 19% during the 6-year period.

The National Planning Association (NPA) has projected what the fastest growing SMSAs will be between 1970 and 1990 and what the largest metropolitan areas will be in 1990 (Table 16 and 17).[3] All except 1 of the 38 fastest growing SMSAs are projected to be in the South and West census regions. Florida, Texas, Arizona, California, Nevada, Utah, and Colorado are each projected to have 2 or more metropolitan areas among the 38 most rapidly growing between 1970 and 1990.

According to the NPA, the largest SMSAs in 1990 are supposed to reveal a pattern of distribution very similar to that of the 1970s. Only Fort Lauderdale, Salt Lake City, and Sacramento are forecast to move into the top 40 from lower ranks, ousting Hartford-New Britain-Bristol, Louisville, and Dayton. What is even more significant from the standpoint of metropolitan growth and decline is the relative position of SMSAs within the top 40. Of the 19 largest in the Northeast and North Central census regions, 14 are projected to lose rank, whereas 15 of the 21 largest SMSAs in the South and West are projected to move up in rank. The three largest metropolitan areas, plus Atlanta, are expected to remain unchallenged.

Table 16. Metropolitan Areas Projected to have the Most Rapid Growth Rates by the National Planning Association, 1975 to 1990

Rank	SMSA	Projected annual growth rate (%)	Rank	SMSA	Projected annual growth rate (%)
1	Sarasota, FL	4.56	20	Salt Lake City, UT	2.79
2	Fort Myers, FL	3.86	21	Fort Lauderdale, FL	2.73
3	Anchorage, AK	3.62	22	Sioux Falls, SD	2.69
4	Pascagoola, MS	3.58	23	Lakeland, FL	2.67
5	Phoenix, AZ	3.35	24	Miami, FL	2.66
6	Fort Collins, CO	3.34	25	Las Vegas, NV	2.62
7	Gainesville, FL	3.28	26	Houston, TX	2.62
8	Austin, TX	3.24	27	Richland, WA	2.61
9	Albuquerque, NM	3.22	28	El Paso, TX	2.59
10	Kileen, TX	3.15	29	Anaheim, CA	2.58
11	Tucson, AZ	3.13	30	Provo, UT	2.56
12	Lafayette, LA	3.13	31	Denver, CO	2.56
13	Daytona Beach, FL	3.12	32	Colorado Spring, CO	2.56
14	Tallahassee, FL	3.06	33	Ann Arbor, MI	2.55
15	Greeley, CO	3.00	34	San Diego, CA	2.51
16	Boise City, ID	2.95	35	Columbia, SC	2.50
17	Orlando, FL	2.89	36	Bryan, TX	2.46
18	San Jose, CA	2.87	37	Santa Cruz, CA	2.36
19	Reno, NV	2.82	38	Lincoln, NE	2.35

Source: National Planning Association, *Regional Economic Projection Series*, Vol. 1 (1977), Table IV, p. 39.

THE PATTERN OF GEOPOLITICAL FRAGMENTATION IN METROPOLITAN AREAS

Almost all of the metropolitan areas in the U.S., regardless of location or growth rate, are politically fragmented into a puzzling jigsaw of civil jurisdictions. Of the 281 SMSAs defined by the Department of Commerce, 38 include territory in more than one state, and 5 overlap three states. Of the 281 SMSAs, 175 are comprised to two ore more counties; 1 SMSA, Atlanta, encompasses a total of 15 counties. Compounding the fragmented political complextion of metropolitan space are the virtually thousands of municipalities, townships, and special districts.

The pattern of political fragmentation has been most often measured by comparing the number of units of local government to the total population served. At the state scale, the most politically fragmented SMSAs are found in that group of states stretching from New Jersey to North Dakota and Oklahoma. States in which metropolitan areas are the least fragmented are (1) the Southwestern states and

Table 17. The Largest Metropolitan Areas in 1990: Projected by the National
Planning Association

Projected rank in 1990	SMSA	Rank in 1970	Projected rank in 1990	SMSA	Rank in 1970
1	New York, NY	1	21	Miami, FL	26
2	Los Angeles, CA	2	22	Denver, CO	27
3	Chicago, IL	3	23	Phoenix, AZ	36
4	Detroit, MI	5	24	Tampa, FL	30
5	Philadelphia, PA	4	25	San Jose, CA	31
6	Washington, DC	8	26	Milwaukee, WI	21
7	Dallas, TX	12	27	Cincinnati, OH	22
8	Houston, TX	16	28	Seattle, WA	19
9	San Francisco, CA	7	29	Riverside, CA	28
10	Boston, MA	6	30	Kansas City, MO	25
11	Nassau County, NY	9	31	Portland, OR	34
12	Minneapolis, MN	17	32	Columbus, OH	33
13	Anaheim, CA	20	33	Indianapolis, IN	29
14	St. Louis, MO	10	34	New Orleans, LA	32
15	Baltimore, MD	13	35	Buffalo, NY	24
16	Pittsburgh, PA	11	36	San Antonio, TX	38
17	San Diego, CA	23	37	Fort Lauderdale, FL	61
18	Atlanta, GA	18	38	Salt Lake City, UT	51
19	Cleveland, OH	14	39	Rochester, NY	37
20	Newark, NJ	40	40	Sacramento, CA	42

Source: National Planning Association, *Regional Economic Projection Series*, Vol. 1 (1977), Table IV, p. 39.

Colorado, (2) selected states of the Southeast, and (3) the states of southern New England. At the metropolitan scale, the number of local governments (excluding special districts) varies from 94 per 100,000 population in Fargo-Moorhead to one unit of local government serving the more than 630,000 inhabitants of the city-county consolidation of Honolulu.[4]

Another equally important aspect of political fragmentation is the divisive impact of the boundary which separates the central city from its companion jurisdictions. Often the central city or cities of an SMSAs contain only a minority of the metropolitan area's total population, giving rise to many of the problems which beset the modern metropolis. As Nathan Glazer has noted, "Mayors do not preside over metropolitan areas in which they can balance off growth in the suburbs against decline in the center. They preside over cities. And this is a dilemma of policy which we have never been able to get around."[5]

Glazer's comment is especially true of so many, often declining metropolises in the Northeast and North Central regions, exemplified in the extreme by Long Branch-Asbury Park, N.J., an SMSA in which only 10.5% of the total population resides in the two central cities.[6] The Advisory Commission on Intergovernmental Relations surveyed the nation's 85 largest SMSAs and found that central cities in the Northeast contained an average of only 34% of their metropolitan area populations, whereas the central cities of SMSAs in the South contained an average of 61%.[7]

An Index of Geopolitical Fragmentation

Combining two aspects of jurisdictional fragmentation into a single index facilitates regional comparisons and correlations with other variables. Since the magnitude of political fragmentation is directly proportional to the number of local governments per 100,000 population and inversely proportional to the percentage of the metropolitan population residing in the central cities of an SMSA, an IGF can be computed by dividing the first quantity by the second. Low scores on the index reflect few governmental units per 100,000 population and a high proportion of the metropolitan population living in the central city or cities.

IGFs were computed for all of the 264 SMSAs listed in the 1972 *Census of Governments*. The indexes ranged from 0.3 for Honolulu to 274 for Johnstown, Pa., a single-county SMSA with 116 units of local government serving 266,000 inhabitants, of whom only 16.1% lived in the central city (Table 18). The geographic distribution of metropolitan areas in the top and bottom quintiles (the least and most fragmented SMSAs, respectively) reveals some important regional dimensions of geopolitical fragmentation (Fig. 18).

The least politically fragmented SMSAs are strongly concentrated in the Sunbelt and in New England, with a few outlyers such as Toldeo, Baltimore, and Pueblo. The most politically fragmented, on the other hand, are almost all located in the Frostbelt, except for four residuals in the South. The political organization of metropolitan space in the northeastern quadrant of the country is basically a pattern of overlapping or tightly fitted jurisdictions with central cities containing only a small proportion of the metropolitan area's population. In the South and West, by contrast, metropolitan areas are typically less crowded by governmental units. Here, as well, central cities are more likely to take advantage of state statutes permitting annexations when warranted by a changing settlement pattern.

With the notable exception of New England, the geographical configuration of metropolitan fragmentation in the U.S. reveals a decided Sunbelt-Frostbelt cleavage. In the New England states, administrative problems result not so much from multitudinous and overlapping local governments as from boundaries which are administrative antiques established during the agrarian past. Because of the regional cleavage in the remainder of the U.S., many of the SMSAs experiencing the most rapid growth are also those which are the least politically fragmented. By contrast, one-quarter of the SMSAs which are losing population are among the most jurisdictionally fragmented. Of the 53 SMSAs in the most fragmented quintile on the GFI, 29 experienced either an absolute decline in population or grew at a rate of .5% or less per year between 1970 and 1976. Just as the metropolitan areas of the nation's industrial heartland are disadvantaged by a technologically outmoded physical shell, they are equally disadvantaged by an antiquated political shell which has not kept up with the pace of change in urban areas.

Table 18. Geopolitical Fragmentation: Top and Bottom Quintiles on the
Geopolitical Fragmentation Index (GFI)

Least politically fragmented SMSAs (GFI ≤ 5.8)		Most politically fragmented SMSAs (GFI ≥ 35.3)	
Rank	SMSA	Rank	SMSA
1	Honolulu, HI	212	Dubuque, IA
3	El Paso, TX	213	Cincinnati, OH-KY-IN
3	Jacksonville, FL	214	St. Louis, MO-IL
3	Norfolk-VA Beach-Ports, VA	215	La Cross, WI
5	Tucson, AZ	216	Bay City, MI
5	Tuscaloosa, AL	217	Saginaw, MI
7	Albuquerque, NM	218	Scranton, PA
8	Newport News-Hampton, VA	219	Altoona, PA
9	Meriden, CT	220	Pine Bluff, AR
10	Baton Rouge, LA	220	Florence, AL
11	Lexington, KY	222	Richland-Kennewick, WA
13	Baltimore, MD	223	Allentown-Beth.-East., PA
13	Richmond, VA	224	Dayton, OH
13	San Diego, CA	225	Anderson, IN
15	New London, CT	226	Elmira, NY
16	New York, NY	227	Muskegon-Musk. Heights, MI
17	Los Angeles-Long Beach, CA	228	Wilmington, DE-NJ-MD
18	Memphis, TN	229	Rochester, MN
19	Albany, GA	230	Sioux Falls, SD
19	Tallahassee, FL	231	Davenport-RI-Moline, IA-IL
21	Laredo, TX	232	Syracuse, NY
22	San Angelo, TX	233	Atlantic City, NJ
23	Austin, TX	234	Mansfield, OH
24	Phoenix, TX	235	Texarkana, TX-AR
25	Midland, TX	236	Parkersburg-Marietta, WV-OH
27	Bristol, CT	237	Utica-Rome, NY
27	Nashua, NH	238	Springfield, IL
27	San Jose, CA	239	Lansing-East Lansing, MI
29	Stamford, CT	240	Champaign-Urbana-Rantoul, IL
31	Nashville, TN	241	Jackson, MI
31	Norwalk, CT	242	Pittsburgh, PA
31	Odessa, TX	243	Appleton-Oshkosh, WI
33	Las Vegas, NV	244	West Palm Beach-Boca Raton, FL
33	Toledo, OH	245	Fort Smith, AR-OK
35	Amarillo, TX	246	Battle Creek, MI
35	San Antonio, TX	247	Steubenville-Weirton, OH-WV
37	Pueblo, CO	248	Bloomington-Normal, IL
37	Reno, NV	249	Peoria, IL
39	Roanoke, VA	250	Wilkes-Barre-Hazleton, PA
41	Columbus, GA-AL	251	Reading, PA
41	Lewiston-Auburn, ME	252	Wheeling, WV
41	Montgomery, AL	253	Duluth-Superior, MN-WI
43	Manchester, NH	254	Terre Haute, IN
44	Lubbock, TX	255	Poughkeepsie, NY
45	New Britain, CT	256	Lancaster, PA
46	Jersey City, NJ	257	Long Branch-Asbury Park, NJ
47	Bridgeport, CT	258	Binghamton, NY
48	Fall River, MA	259	Fargo-Moorhead, ND-MN
49	Biloxi-Gulfport, MS	260	Williamsport, PA
50	Macon, GA	261	Lima, OH
52	Bryan-College Station, TX	262	Harrisburg, PA
52	Charlotte, NC	263	York, PA
52	San Francisco-Oakland, CA	264	Johnstown, PA

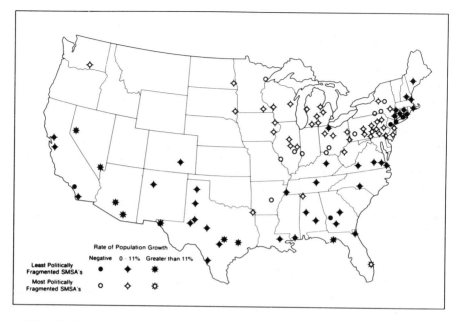

Fig. 18. Geopolitical fragmentation in metropolitan areas: top and bottom quintiles on the GFI.

Remodeling the Political Shell

To cope with the geographic expansion of urbanized areas and the growing complexity of urban management, the political shell of metropolitan areas must either be remodeled or devices found to eliminate the divisive nature of outmoded political boundaries. "The expanding urban tissue of metropolitan areas has gone too far without the proper reorganization of administration on a metropolitan level."[8] Two methods of coping with a changing urban settlement pattern are (1) the elimination of outmoded boundaries through annexation or city-county consolidation and (2) the creation of special districts in which political boundaries remain even though their functions are diminished. Both annexation and consolidation move the metropolitan area toward a single, unified leadership, whereas the creation of special districts often further fragments the responsibility for administering a metropolitan area and coming to grips with the problem of slow growth.

The most popular method of keeping pace with the changing settlement geography of urban areas has been territorial annexation. The use of annexation to increase the area of incorporated places at the expense of unincorporated territory is, however, as rare in the Northeast and many parts of the North Central region as it is common in the West and South.

Patterns of boundary alteration activity reveal strong regional differences engendered by variations in state statutes regulating annexations and detachments. Of the 19 states in which over 80% of the municipalities changed boundaries between 1970 and 1975, 13 are in the West and none are in the Northeast.[9] Changing settlement patterns in the West and South, whether characterized by growth or decline, are likely to be reflected in the adaptable political boundaries of cities, towns, and villages. Municipal boundaries in the Northeast and, to a lesser extent, in the North Central region, on the other hand, rarely reflect changing urban patterns. Factors which account for this inflexibility in many states include (1) rigid state statutes governing annexations, (2) the abundance of municipalities and incorporated townships which tend to hem each other in, (3) the lack of unincorporated territory to annex, forcing any boundary alteration activity to take the form of consolidations or mergers, and (4) the historical inertia of some of the oldest boundaries in the country.

The record of the most extensive central city annexations also reveals a Sunbelt orientation. Of the 41 central cities which annexed 10 square miles or more of territory between 1970 and 1975, none is in the Northeast and only 3 are in the North Central region (Table 19).[10] Curiously, 10 are state capitals. This group of

Table 19. Central Cities Reporting Net Increases in Land Area of 10 Square Miles or More, 1970 to 1975

City	Net increase in square miles	City	Net increase in square miles
Columbus, GA	132.9	Vallejo, CA	16.7
Anchorage, AK	127.3	Roanoke, VA	16.0
San Antonio, TX	79.5	Tuscaloosa, AL	14.9
Corpus Christi, TX	75.1	Fresno, CA	14.1
Memphis, TN	62.7	Jackson, MS	14.1
Chattanooga, TN	62.1	Petersburg, VA	14.1
Houston, TX	55.3	San Jose, CA	13.1
Kansas City, KS	53.7	Waco, TX	13.1
Dallas, TX	43.7	Albany, GA	12.3
El Paso, TX	42.8	Tucson, AZ	11.7
Columbus, OH	38.0	Baton Rouge, LA	10.8
Wichita Falls, TX	34.2	Pueblo, CO	10.8
Charlotte, NC	32.4	Shreveport, LA	10.8
Austin, TX	28.9	Springfield, IL	10.6
Colorado Spring, CO	25.5	Topeka, KS	10.6
Phoenix, AZ	25.5	Birmingham, AL	10.3
Fort Worth, TX	25.1	Clarksville, TN	10.3
Lynchburg, VA	25.1	Orlando, FL	10.3
Muncie, IN	18.8	Salt Lake City, UT	10.3
Denver, CO	18.4	Amarillo, TX	10.0
North Charleston, SC	17.4		

Source: U.S. Bureau of the Census. *Boundary and Annexation Survey 1970-1975* (1978), Table 4, p. 15.

cities represents SMSAs along the entire growth continuum, though, predictably, rapidly growing SMSAs outnumber declining SMSAs by more than two to one. As a more politically feasible method of keeping up with the pace of change than the city-county consolidation, many Southern and Western SMSAs such as Charlotte, Phoenix, and Houston have maintained active annexation programs.

An alternative and less popular method of remodeling the political shells of urban areas is the city-county consolidation. There are currently 25 city-county consolidations in existence, 7 of which represent 19th and early 20th century attempts of major American cities and Honolulu to keep up with urban growth (Table 20). Given the expansion of such metropolitan areas as Boston and San Francisco since that time, however, the city-county boundaries no longer define the limits of a metropolitan system.

The remaining consolidations are post-World War II creations brought into existence, with one exception, by referenda at the local level. Considering both the number of metropolitan areas that could benefit from a simplified political structure and the favorable publicity which has emanated from both academic and non-academic circles, the consolidated city-county government remains a political anomaly.

Of the 59 separate attempts which have been made to create consolidated governments since World War II, only 18 have been approved by referenda and 5 of those 18 are found in Tidewater Virginia.[11] The pattern of consolidation attempts and successes shows a dediced orientation toward the South and, more recently, the West. Only one consolidated government, Indianapolis, has come into existence outside the South and West and that was created by legislative action rather than by referendum.

Bringing a metropolitan area under a single governmental administration has been repeatedly cited as one way to reduce costs, improve services, and equalize the tax base, all of which are problems brought into sharp focus by population decline compounded by a fragmented political shell. Both annexations and city-county consolidations are most common in that part of the country where metropolitan areas are least fragmented and more rapidly growing rather than in the Northeast where innovative geographic and administrative solutions to the problems of slow and negative growth are sorely needed.

While special districts may superimpose even more boundaries on an already fragmented political shell, their creation is perceived to represent comparatively little threat to established administrations. Their popularity has consequently grown considerably as the range of cross-jurisdictional problems in metropolitan areas has increased. Between 1942 and 1972, the total number of special districts (excluding school districts which have been declining in number) almost tripled. Of the four census regions, the North Central and West have made the most extensive use of special districts. The Northeast and South have had fewer in number but the rate of increase in the South led all other regions in the period from 1962 to 1972, while the rate of increase in the Northeast was the lowest in the nation. Though popular, it should be noted that too many special districts prevent the citizens from keeping abreast of what is going on in a community. As a result, the Advisory Commission on Intergovernmental Relations recommended that no

Table 20. City-County Consolidations

City	County	State	Year
City-County Consolidations Prior to World War II			
New Orleans	Orleans Co.	LA	1805
Boston	Suffolk Co.	MA	1821
Philadelphia	Philadelphia Co.	PA	1854
San Francisco	San Francisco Co.	CA	1856
New York	New York Co.	NY	1874
	Queens Co.		1898
	Richmond Co.		1898
Denver	Denver Co.	CO	1904
Honolulu	Honolulu Co.	HI	1907
City-County Consolidations Since World War II			
Baton Rouge	E. Baton Rouge Pa.	LA	1947
Hamptom	Elizabeth City Co.	VA	1952
Newport News	Newport News Co.	VA	1958
Nashville	Davidson Co.	TN	1962
South Norfolk	Norfolk Co.	VA	1962
Virginia Beach	Princess Anne Co.	VA	1962
Jacksonville	Duval Co.	FL	1967
Carson City	Ormsby Co.	NV	1969
Indianapolis	Marion Co.	IN	1969
Juneau	Greater Juneau Bo.	AL	1969
Columbus	Muscogee Co.	GA	1970
Sitka	Greater Sitka Bo.	AL	1971
Suffolk	Nansemond Co.	VA	1972
Lexington	Fayette Co.	KY	1974
Anchorage	Greater Anchorage Bo.	AL	1975
Anaconda	Deer Lodge Co.	MT	1977
Butte	Silver Bow Co.	MT	1977
Chesapeake	Chesapeake Co.	VA	1977

Sources: Glendening and Atkins, and Marando (see note 11).

new special districts be permitted where there are already existing governments which can provide the needed service.[12]

THE PATTERN OF URBAN NEED

East St. Louis, Ill., and Laredo, Tex., are the "neediest" cities in the U.S. according to a factor analytic study of city need carried out by Harold Bunce as one method for evaluating the disbursement of Community Development Block Grant funds.[13] Four hundred and thirty-five "entitlement" cities (central cities and other

88   Zeigler and Brunn

Table 21. Components of the Per Capita Needs Index

Variables subjected to factor analysis	Factors defined and weighted
Persons aged 65 and over Crime rate Nonwhite population Persons over 25 with less than a high school education Female headed families below the poverty level Poor persons under 18 Persons below the poverty level Housing units lacking one or more plumbing facilities Occupied housing units with more than 1.01 persons per room Unemployed persons Housing units built before 1939 Persons per square mile Owner-occupied houses	Poverty (.35) Age of housing stock (.25) Density (.20) Crime and unemployment (.10) Lack of economic opportunity (.10)

Source: U.S. Department of Housing and Urban Development, *An Evaluation of the Community Development Block Grant Formula* by Harold Bunce (1976), pp. 49–51.

cities over 50,000 population) were rank ordered on the basis of a PCNI computed for each. Variables reflected in the PCNI include many related to poverty, urban blight, and neighborhood instability. Five factors were derived from the 13 variables and these 5 factors were weighted and consolidated into the final, standardized index value (Table 21). The PCNI was designed to serve as a yardstick for evaluating the formula used to allocate Block Grant funds, and to compare it with alternative formulas that would stress poverty less and other dimensions of community need more. Beyond its utilitarian value, however, the PCNI reveals a significant pattern of relationships with metropolitan growth and geopolitical fragmentation.

Not surprisingly, the most needy cities are to be found in the eastern half of the nation, with the Northeast itself accounting for almost half of the entries in the top quintile. Here and in older industrialized areas of the North Central region, cities load heavily on the age and density dimensions of need. The South, where cities load heavily on the poverty factor, also accounts for a large number of the most needy cities. The West, on the other hand, is generally unrepresented in the top quintile, except for a pocket of severe urban need accounted for by Berkeley, San Francisco, and Oakland (Fig. 19). Unlike the formula for allocating Block Grant funds during the first several years of the program, the PCNI seems to be responsive to geographic variations in the dimensions of community need. Of the 20 neediest cities, for instance, 10 are in the Northwest and North Central regions and 10 are in the South.

Of the pattern of least needy entitlement cities, it can be said that most are large suburban entities often in the orbit of needy central city cores. Of the 16 least needy cities, for example, 7 are suburbs of Detroit and 1 is a suburb of St.

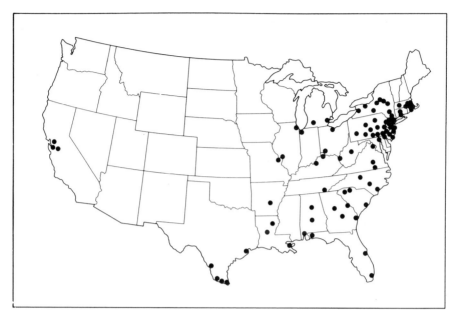

Fig. 19. The neediest entitlement cities: top quintile on the per capita needs index.

Louis. This pattern of opulence and decay encapsulated in independent municipalities within a single metropolitan area is characteristic of the Northeast and North Central regions where the neediest and least needy cities are frequently located side by side. Nathan and Adams have examined the needs of SMSAs over 500,000 population and computed a city-to-suburb or intrametropolitan hardship ratio for each. One of their findings is that disadvantaged central cities are in the Northeast and Midwest where there are the most serious cases of city boundaries which encase only the "poverty impacted cores" of metropolitan areas.[14]

In contrast to the proximity of needy and affluent cities in metropolitan areas of the North is the general absence of southern cities in the lowest need quintile. Only 15 of the 87 least needy cities are in the South, and all but 2 of these are in the growth states of Florida and Texas. That large affluent municipalities are not typical of metropolitan areas in the Deep South is a reflection of both the general lack of local resources to combat need and the geopolitical configuration of metropolitan areas which reduces the number of suburban political entities in many states.

A city's need as measured on the PCNI and its population growth rate are closely related. Bunce noted that 38 of the 50 neediest cities lost population between 1960 and 1973; of the 12 which gained population, 10 were in the South. Likewise, the 50 cities which experienced the most severe population loss all scored above average on the PCNI, whereas only 3 of the 50 fastest growing cities scored above average. This relationship is attributed to the older housing stock, higher concentration of low income persons, and higher levels of per capita expenditures and taxes which characterize declining cities.[15] The fiscal needs of growing and declining cities are further contrasted by Muller who concluded that whether the population is growing or declining has a major influence on the level of per capita outlays in cities.[16]

Central cities often precede the fall of their metropolitan areas into the abyss of negative growth. Between 1960 and 1970, for instance, 121 central cities, but only 21 metropolitan areas, experienced a net loss in population. By 1976, however, the number of declining metropolises had increased to 37 and the number of declining central cities continued to grow. Of the 87 neediest cities (those in the top quintile), almost a third were located in the heart of metropolitan areas which declined in population between 1970 and 1976. Of greater significance, however, is the reciprocal statistic: Over two-thirds of the neediest cities are in growing metropolitan areas, though only 4 (all southern) are among the 42 fastest growing. There consequently emerges a group of metropolitan areas in which central cities with declining populations and high per capita needs are found in the midst of overall metropolitan growth. Yet, because of the geopolitical fragmentation of these metropolitan areas, the central cities cannot take advantage of the potential benefits of growth. Of the 42 declining cities in the top PCNI quintile which are located in growing metropolitan areas, almost two-thirds rank above the median on the GFI. Those which do not are most often southern and New England cities. The point might even be made that a declining central city in the heart of a growing metropolitan area reflects only the location of constricting political boundaries. Certainly such a case could be made for the exceptional example of Atlantic City, N.J., which declined in population by 22% between 1960 and 1973 while the single-county SMSA grew by 16%. Atlantic City is the nation's fourth most needy city and the SMSA is one of the most politically fragmented, ranking 233 out of 264 metropolitan areas.

Geopolitical fragmentation makes possible the division of metropolitan areas into poor central cities, victims of their political geography, and often affluent suburbs, a fact so well illustrated by the aforementioned example of Detroit surrounded by such well-to-do jurisdictions as Livonia, Sterling Heights, St. Clair Shores, and Dearborn Heights. Unfortunately, "the current balkanization of metropolitan areas into dozens and often hundreds of local governments encourages 'beggar-thy-neighbor' strategies"[17] and discourages the intrametropolitan equalization of financial resources resulting in the pattern of municipal need as seen especially in such cities as East St. Louis, Atlantic City, Newark, Wilmington, Camden, and Harrisburg. Of the 20 most politically fragmented SMSAs, 15 have at their cores cities which rank in the top two quintiles on the PCNI. It should be noted, however, that an examination of the least politically fragmented SMSAs reveals a more diverse pattern of need. Of the city-county consolidations, none ranks in either the highest or lowest quintiles of need; and, of the 25 least politically fragmented SMSAs, only 3 rank in the extreme quintiles. In cases like these, intrametropolitan differences in need are averaged out. Almost certainly, if a northeastern-like political shell were imposed on consolidations like Jacksonville or on such actively annexing cities as Charlotte, Memphis, or Houston, a much different picture of need would arise, particularly with respect to the city cores.

CONCLUSIONS

When the patterns of metropolitan growth, geopolitical fragmentation, and urban need are examined, a clearer picture of both Frostbelt and Sunbelt metropolitan areas emerges. Profile characteristics of a Frostbelt SMSA are slow or negative rates of population growth and severely fragmented political shells, but diverse patterns of city need, ranging from some of the neediest central cities to some of the most affluent suburban jurisdictions. Typical Sunbelt metropolises, on the other hand, exhibit more unified political shells but more diverse patterns of growth, ranging from the most rapidly growing metropolitan areas to the most rapidly declining. In terms of need, cities in the Southeast appear to be among the neediest in the country, while cities in the growth areas of the Southwest, parts of Texas, and Florida are typically less needy.

Of significance to the Sunbelt-Frostbelt debate is the fairly well-defined North-South cleavage which results from mapping metropolitan growth rates and geopolitical fragmentation, and the similarly well-defined East-West cleavage which results from mapping the PCNI. City need apparently does not follow Sunbelt-Frostbelt lines; it does, however, manifest different characteristics in the Northeast than in the South. Formulas for allocating federal Block Grant funds must therefore avoid favoring cities in either region.

Both population growth and geopolitical fragmentation have an impact on the pattern of community need which emerges in a metropolitan area and on the availability of specific options for coping with that need. Slow and negative growth rates have been studied and closely correlated with severe hardship, fiscal pressure, and urban need; but, assuming that the relationship is not necessarily causative, it would now seem wise to explore the possibilities of Nathan Glazer's asseration that "there is no reason why declining metropolitan areas cannot offer as many opportunities, as high a quality of life as growing areas."[18] Remodeling the political shell of metropolitan areas may make this more possible since intrametropolitan boundaries often pose barriers to the evolution of the qualitative organic growth which must occur if metropolises are to resolve internal conflicts and replace competitive modes of operation with cooperative ones.

NOTES

[1] Constantinos A. Doxiadis, *Ekistics* (N.Y.: Oxford University Press, 1968), p. 21.

[2] U.S. Bureau of the Census, *Estimates of the Population of Counties and Metropolitan Areas: July 1, 1975 and 1976,* Current Population Reports, Series P-25, No. 739 (Washington, D.C.: U.S. Government Printing Office, 1978), pp. 5–24.

[3] T. B. Sivia, D. W. Fay, and J. W. Lee, *Regional Economic Projection Series; State and Metropolitan Growth Patterns 1960–1990* (Washington, D.C.: National Planning Association, 1977), p. 39.

[4] U.S. Bureau of the Census, *Census of Governments 1972,* Vol. 1, *Governmental Organization* (Washington, D.C.: U.S. Government Printing Office, 1974).

[5] Nathan Glazer, "Social and Political Ramifications of Metropolitan Decline," in George Sternleib and James W. Hughes, eds., *Post-Industrial America* (New Brunswick, N.J.: Center for Urban Policy Research, Rutgers University, 1975), p. 243.

[6] U.S. Bureau of the Census, *Census of Population: 1970*, Vol. 1, *Characteristics of the Population*, Part 1, *United States Summary* (Washington, D.C.: U.S. Government Printing Office, 1973), Table 34.

[7] Advisory Commission on Intergovernmental Relations, *Trends in Metropolitan America* (Washington, D.C.: Advisory Commission on Intergovernmental Relations, 1977), p. 3.

[8] Doxiadis, op. cit., note 1, p. 421.

[9] U.S. Bureau of the Census, *Boundary and Annexation Survey 1970-1975*, Report GE 30-2 (Washington, D.C.: U.S. Government Printing Office, 1978), p. 4.

[10] Ibid., p. 15.

[11] Parris N. Glendening and Patricia S. Atkins, "The Politics of City-County Consolidation," in *The County Yearbook 1977* (Washington, D.C.: National Association of Counties/International City Management Association, 1978), p. 64; Vincent L. Marando, "Voting in City-County Consolidation Referenda," *Western Political Quarterly*, Vol. 26 (1973), p. 91.

[12] Bernard J. Frieden, *Metropolitan America: Challenge to Federalism* (Washington, D.C.: U.S. Government Printing Office, 1966), p. 125.

[13] U.S. Department of Housing and Urban Development, *An Evaluation of the Community Development Block Grant Formula* by Harold Bunce (Washington, D.C.: Department of Housing and Urban Development, 1976).

[14] Richard P. Nathan and Charles Adams, "Understanding Central City Hardship," *Political Science Quarterly*, Vol. 91 (1976), p. 50.

[15] U.S. Department of Housing and Urban Development, op. cit., note 13, pp. 124, 139.

[16] Thomas Muller, "The Declining and Growing Metropolis—A Fiscal Comparison," in George Sternlieb and James W. Hughes, eds., op. cit., note 5; *Growing and Declining Urban Areas: A Fiscal Comparison* (Washington, D.C.: The Urban Institute, 1975).

[17] William Alonso, "Urban Zero Population Growth," *Daedalus*, Vol. 102 (1977), p. 194.

[18] Nathan Glazer, op. cit., note 5, p. 237.

Chapter 7

Lending Practices and Policies Affecting the American Metropolitan System

Joe T. Darden

The inter- and intra-governmental problems of administration and financing that Zeigler and Brunn discuss at a national and regional level also exist in another form within specific metropolitan areas. This chapter treats the geographic and social variations in various lending practices. Redlining techniques and mortgage lending practices, whether used by banks, savings and loans, or by government agencies, are examples of policies that result in distinct spatial patterns. Variations in lending patterns are primarily a function of location, race, and class within cities and metropolitan areas. Because variations exist, some areas and groups experience differential neighborhood quality, growth, decline, and homeownership. An analysis of published data on various lending practices reveals the primary beneficiaries of loans and assistance from the federal government and private sector are white and middle class suburban residents in the South and West. This chapter concludes by offering specific recommendations to existing legislation that would insure a more even distribution of mortgage lending.

The pattern of lending within and between metropolitan areas has a great impact on the quality, growth, and decline of areas in general and residential areas in particular, since housing construction and rehabilitation and homeownership are very much dependent on the practices and policies of lending institutions. In any society, housing is costly to construct. Because of the tremendous production cost, builders and developers generally borrow most of the money they need to put up new housing. About 75% of all the money used to finance new housing production in the U.S. is borrowed.[1] Thus, the housing industry and the housing market in this country are very much dependent on borrowed money, i.e., credit.

The major sources of mortgage credit for financing both existing and new housing are banks and other large financial institutions. These financial institutions have tremendous amount of control over the supply of housing, i.e., how much, if any, gets built *where* for whom, and over the cost of housing, i.e., who can afford to live in it, *where*. Therefore, if the pattern of lending is not evenly distributed within American metropolitan areas and among all groups, some areas and groups will experience differential neighborhood quality, growth, decline, and homeownership.

To the extent that the U.S. government provides assistance or subsidies to both financial institutions (by lowering their operating cost through tax concessions) and home buyers (by lowering the cost of housing through tax deductions), the *national* interest should be served, i.e., all areas and groups should have equal access to mortgage financing.[2] Because of government assistance in the form of tax concessions, part of the operating costs of lending institutions is paid by the institutions and part by the American population. Also, part of the cost of the house is paid by the buyer and part by the American population through taxes. While it may seem unjust to require others to bear part of the cost of an individual family's house as a matter of public policy, as long as equal assistance and equal opportunity in financing exist for every family, no one bears an unjust burden. However, in reality, equal governmental assistance and equal opportunity lending practices and policies have not and do not exist in the American metropolitan system.

The major thesis of this chapter is that the pattern of lending within the American metropolitan system is primarily a function of location, race, and class. Mortgage loans are most available in the newer suburbs within metropolitan areas of the South and West and least available within older central cities of the Northeast. They are most accessible to white middle and upper class families and least accessible to non-white lower class families.

THE PATTERN OF MORTGAGE LENDING WITHIN METROPOLITAN AREAS

Mortgage lending does not occur uniformly across neighborhoods within metropolitan areas. Instead, it varies spatially. Mortgage loans are difficult to obtain in some neighborhoods and easy to obtain in other. Thus, mortgage lending is, in part, a function of geography. Geography is so important in mortgage lending that, in assessing the value of property, the appraiser emphasizes the geographical location even to the point that a poorly built, aging structure in a growing, highly desirable neighborhood may have lending priority over a newly built structure in an economically declining neighborhood. When a potential borrower is denied a loan by a local lender because of the *location* of the property, the practice is referred to as "redlining."[3]

The Concept of Redlining

Redlining is a multifaceted concept with the behavior of mortgage lenders and geographic location as unifying factors. There are minor and major forms of redlining. Redlining in its major form involves the practice by mortgage lenders of denying loans on properties located in a specific geographic area. Among the minor forms of redlining are the following: (1) the requirement of higher down payments than those usually necessary for comparable properties in other areas, (2) the requirement of loan maturities below the number of years to maturity set for comparable mortgages in other areas, and (3) the requirement of higher interest rates than those usually charged for financing comparable properties in other areas. In both minor and major forms of redlining, such behavior by mortgage lenders occurs without regard to the credit rating of the borrower or the quality of the specific property. Some authors have extended the concept to include not only geographic location but the arbitrary denials of financing based on racial and ethnic considerations or any consideration which is not justified on the basis of legitimate, demonstrable economic criteria.[4]

Some neighborhood groups in search of a more operational definition have stated that a lending institution is practicing redlining if during a specified time period, perhaps one year, it made a lower percentage of total loans to a certain neighborhood than the percentage of the institution's total deposits which originate from that neighborhood. In other words, when a neighborhood's loans do not equal its deposits, it is being redlined.

The practice of denying loans for certain properties in a specific geographic area has been coined "redlining" because it is believed that lending officials draw a red line on a map around the borders of an area to indicate to the staff the location of properties on which real-estate loans are not to be made or else made at terms substantially less favorable than those available in other areas of the city.[5] For example, loans may be made in the "redlined" areas only with larger down payments or at higher interest rates or for shorter terms than in other areas, or no loans may be made to the area on any terms. Some lending institutions may refuse to make loans in an area if most of the properties are above a certain age, say, 30 years. For example, if houses built before 1940 predominate in a certain area, the area could be considered ineligible for loans just as though it were redlined on a map.[6] Thus, customers for more recently built homes in the area suffer the same consequences of loan denial as buyers of older homes. The lender usually justifies his refusal to make a loan by citing the location of the collateral, not necessarily the collateral itself. Location is translated to mean demand, and demand is interpreted to mean the safety of the remaining loan balance in the event the borrower defaults. The lenders lump the good housing with the bad, the old with the more modern, and deny them both new mortgage credit. As a result, those neighborhoods that are typically redlined tend to have the following characteristics: (1) older housing, though structurally well built; (2) middle class or blue-collar income groups; (3) racially integrated, white ethnic, or black populations; and (4) location adjacent to poorer neighborhoods.[7]

Redlining Techniques

Redlining is very difficult to identify. The issue is one of access to mortgage financing, and the process of discouraging a potential borrower can be a very subtle one. Probably a large amount of redlining occurs without any record to indicate that there was a loan request. In other words, many potential borrowers are discouraged prior to submitting a written loan application.

There are several techniques used to discourage a potential borrower:

(1) *High interest rate technique*, whereby the lending officer simply tells the potential borrower that the firm cannot compete with the interest rates of other lending institutions and suggests that the loan request be made elsewhere in the neighborhood. Or a very high interest rate may be quoted in order to discourage the submission of an application and at the same time leave the impression that the borrower is receiving a favor by being directed toward institutions with lower interest rates.

(2) *Age of housing technique.* The lending officer simply indicates that his institution will not finance housing older than, say, 20 years. This procedure is very effective in discouraging many potential borrowers who wish to buy property in central cities, particularly inner city areas, because it is highly probable that the property they wish to buy is at least that old.

(3) *Low maximum loan technique.* The potential borrower is told that the lending institution has a low maximum loan amount policy, which means that it cannot make mortgages above, for example, $35,000 when the potential borrower has requested a $45,000 loan. Thus, a higher down payment would be necessary.

(4) *Short-term mortgage technique.* The potential borrower is told that the lending institution is only making mortgages of, say, 25 years. The potential borrower, however, has requested a 30-year loan.

(5) *Low-value technique.* The loan officer, for example, tells the potential borrower that the lending institution will not make a loan above 75% of value. This would require the potential borrower to provide at least 25% as a down payment.

These techniques effectively discourage many potential borrowers. By convincing the potential borrowers that the loan conditions are matters of policy and beyond the loan officer's authority, the officer is effectively removed from any responsibility, with the implication that the actual decisions are made elsewhere. The truth is that the "policy" may have been created in order to discourage a potential borrower from formally applying for a loan on property interpreted to be located in a "high risk" or "hazardous" area.

The Origins of Redlining in American Cities

Although organized neighborhood resistance to redlining is of recent origin, the practice itself is not. Redlining is probably as old as cities, capitalism, and the rent theory of value. An early capitalist lender may have perceived risk to lending money on property located near a slaughterhouse, for example. Thus, loans may have been refused to those who wanted to buy property near that or any other slaughterhouse. Therefore, properties located near slaughterhouses were redlined because of the perception that, should the borrower default on the mortgage, the lender would incur a high risk of finding another buyer for the property since few people are willing to live near slaughterhouses.[8] The practice of redlining in American cities can be traced back at least to the 1930s following the establishment of the Federal Home Bank Board and similar organizations such as the Home Owners

Loan Corporation. In 1940 the former organization provided statistics to mortgage lending institutions on various neighborhoods in American cities. It classified neighborhoods into "high risk" and "low risk" areas. The areas classified as "high risk" or ranked low were predominantly black.[9] These were the areas in which loans were not to be made. The latter organization prepared a detailed survey and classification of mortgage credit risk areas in Oakland and Berkeley, Calif. Four classes were established, and each neighborhood was color coded on an accompanying map. Areas labeled "hazardous" were colored red. The purpose of the government-administered survey was to guide mortgage lenders in making loans in the cities. The primary criterion used to classify an area as "hazardous" for home loans was the proportion of "undesirable population," a synonym for "minority population."[10]

As early as 1944, Swan warned of the consequences of redlining in New York City. He wrote that, if the policies of lenders refusing to provide credit to certain areas were allowed to continue, an entire city could gradually be effectively prevented from receiving new loans.[11] More recent evidence indicates that several urban areas are experiencing serious difficulties obtaining new mortgage money.[12] It appears, then, that the old practice of denying loans to certain areas within the city has become policy with some lending institutions.[13] The consequences are that the entire city eventually suffers as the stages in the redlining process lead to greater and greater deterioration.

Stages in the Redlining Process

The redlining process consists of nine stages. The early stages (one to three) are subtle and go largely undetected. However, the impact of the succeeding stages is much more severe. The following are characteristic of the redlining process:

Stage (1). Higher down payments on mortgages are required.

Stage (2). Higher interest rates on loans are required.

Stage (3). Shorter loan maturities are given.

Stage (4). Older houses are denied mortgage loans altogether. Homeowners are forced to borrow from mortgage banking firms who obtain their funds from out-of-town insurance companies or pension funds. As housing deteriorates in one area, the remainder of the neighborhood soon follows in a self-perpetuation cycle of decay.[14]

Stage (5). Home improvement loans are denied in the area. This often leads to poor maintenance and eventually to the occurrence of slum conditions and housing abandonment.

Stage (6). Conditions worsen and property insurance is denied or is provided only at exorbitant rates. Neighborhood businesses, already suffering from a lack of credit, begin to leave, taking essential services and important sources of cash flow out of the neighborhood. People are forced to shop out of the neighbrohood, leaving less and less of a market for the remaining businesses.[15]

Stage (7). Property values in the redlined neighborhood continue to decrease but at an accelerated rate. Loans or insurance of any kind is difficult to obtain. The few remaining young middle class families migrate from the area, leaving behind the poor and the aged.

Stage (8). The declining property values in the redlined neighborhood are financially felt by the entire city as revenue declines while the demand for social services increases. Redlining spreads to other neighborhoods.[16]

Stage (9). In this final stage the entire city is drained of so much revenue because of redlining that the quality and quantity of essential services are reduced as the tax rate of the city is substantially increased. Loans within the entire city are either denied or difficult to obtain.

Thus, the practice of redlining guarantees that property values will decline and generally leads to neighborhood deterioration, destruction, and abandonment. This process makes more credit available for the resale and refinancing of homes in other neighborhoods, thus perpetuating differential neighborhood quality, growth, decline, and homeownership. Financial institutions justify this lending behavior on the basis of risk. However, community groups have argued that lenders refuse to make mortgage or home improvement loans to certain areas solely on "perceived risk" which is unfounded in reality. Where spatial variation in lending activity has been documented, lenders state that to make loans in certain areas would be so risky as to constitute an unsound economic practice. The present emphasis by financial institutions on safety and soundness is a historical vestige of the Great Depression days when many financial institutions failed. So ingrained is the fear of institutional failure that in spite of the development since the 1930s of deposit insurance and periodic examinations designed to insure sound management, some lenders continue to equate risk in lending with a variety of neighborhood factors that bear little or no relationship to safety. Proving actual risk is difficult or impossible since inadequate data exist on default and foreclosure rates by location.

The difficulty of measuring risk is also encountered in establishing loan-to-value ratios. Raising or lowering the ratio is a matter of lender's discretion. Community groups argue that in their efforts to protect themselves from "perceived risk" lenders erect unreasonable and discriminatory barriers to potential borrowers in certain areas. For example, a low loan-to-value ratio requires a higher down payment. When spatial variation in loan-to-value ratio has been documented, the lenders defend it on the grounds that a low loan-to-value ratio gives them a greater assurance that the borrower will not default. The lender can also draw upon empirical research to defend his or her position. At least one study specifically indicated that the loan-to-value ratio is the single most significant variable in predicting default.[17]

Lenders issue or deny property and mortgage insurance coverage on the basis of the same underwriting criteria they use for extending or denying a mortgage.[18] Property insurance rates do in fact vary by the geographic location of the structure. In certain areas regarded as "high risk," insurance agents may refuse to extend coverage to any property regardless of its individual quality. Certain community groups have labeled such a consideration of neighborhood factors as discriminatory.

Lending Discrimination on the Basis of Race

Just as discrimination in mortgage lending exists on the basis of geographic location, it also exists on the basis of race. This is true despite the passage of the

Federal Fair Housing Law of 1968 which prohibited discrimination against non-whites in obtaining mortgage financing.[19] Mortgage lenders still treat non-white home buyers differently from white home buyers.[20] White, male dominated lending institutions use imprecise, subjective criteria in granting mortgages; these criteria are applied differently. Such subjective criteria include the borrower's relationship to his/her family and friends, the borrower's reputation for living a harmonious or troubled home life, the reputation of the borrower's associates, and whether the borrower participates in civic affairs.[21]

The evaluation of the credit worthiness of the applicant is also partly subjective and has an adverse effect on non-whites. For example, a survey of savings and loan associations by the Federal Home Loan Bank Board revealed that 26% of the associations sought information on arrest records, and 12% automatically disqualified applicants who had been arrested and 14% disqualified applicants if they had been convicted.[22] Because non-whites are arrested in disproportionate percentages, the disqualification on the basis of arrest records alone has a discriminatory effect.

Typically, most American families must successfully pass a three stage screening process before obtaining a mortgage loan. They are screened initially by a real estate broker, next by a loan officer, and finally by the institution's loan committee. Non-white families, however, are much more closely scrutinized than white families, and each stage is fraught with the possibility of discriminatory rejection because of race. Usually, the rejection is informal and the non-white families rarely know the precise reasons why they are rejected. Indeed, lending institution officials themselves frequently cannot explain these reasons by reference to *objective* credit factors. Although most families may have some difficulty in obtaining the financing necessary to purchase a home, non-white families often encounter insurmountable obstacles when they approach the mortgage lending institutions.

Measuring the extent to which the mortgage finance system results in discriminatory treatment on the basis of race is a difficult task because data are often unavailable, inadequate, or difficult to obtain. This is because data on individual cases which are used by the lenders are usually not accessible for use in research at the present time, even with the passage of the Home Mortgage Disclosure Act of 1975. Where data have been obtained, the results are consistent with allegations that at least some banks discriminate against non-white applicants. One of the most comprehensive studies of urban mortgage lending revealed that in four of the five largest metropolitan areas in New York State, black applicants have a much greater chance of being turned down for a loan than do white applicants, even though the socioeconomic, property, and neighborhood conditions are otherwise equal.[23] In the Buffalo metropolitan area, black applicants have a 24% chance of denial compared to 12% for similarly situated whites; in the New York and Nassau-Suffolk metropolitan area, the chance of denial for blacks is 21% compared to 11% for similarly situated whites; in the Rochester metropolitan area, it is 14% compared to 4%; and in the Syracuse metropolitan area, it is 15% compared to 7. Only in the Albany-Schenectady-Troy metropolitan area are applicants of different races treated equally.[24]

In New York and Nassau-Suffolk metropolitan area, other non-white applicants (mostly Hispanic and Asian families) have a 15% chance of denial compared to the

11% for similarly situated whites. Other non-white applicants are treated equally with regard to the decision to deny an application in the other four metropolitan areas.

To determine if a similar pattern of discrimination exists for other metropolitan areas in the U.S. will require similar data. The responsibility for requiring data collection of the nation's lenders rests with the federal financial regulatory agencies which have continued to resist promulgating such a regulation. Although present practices of mortgage lenders are more often covert than overt, they nevertheless have the effect of denying many non-white families the opportunity of homeownership. Partly due to racial discrimination in lending, 65% of all white families owned their homes in 1970 compared to only 42% of all black families and 44% of all Spanish speaking families.[25]

Mortgage Lending and Class

In addition to location and race, mortgage lending is also strongly related to the class of the borrower. The likelihood that an application will be denied decreases as income increases. Based on a study of lending decisions in the five largest metropolitan areas of New York State, applicants with incomes in the $15,000 to $25,000 are even less likely to have their applications denied.[26]

The effect of income on mortgage lending, however, varies by racial group. The importance of having income in the highest category is 23% greater for blacks than for similarly situated whites, i.e., whereas blacks in the highest income category are 12.3 percentage points less likely to have their applications denied than are blacks in the lowest category, whites in the highest income category are only 9.9 percentage points less likely to have their applications denied than are whites in the lowest category. Conversely, low-income black applicants are more likely to have their applications denied than are similarly situated low-income white applicants. Income, therefore, is more important in evaluating applications from blacks than those from whites, other aspects of the situation being equal. A similar but smaller effect also holds true for other non-whites when compared to whites.

Furthermore, even when black applicants have higher incomes (over $25,000) than whites ($15,000–$25,000) and otherwise identical applications, the black applications are 20% more likely to be denied.

GOVERNMENT INVOLVEMENT IN MORTGAGE LENDING

The preceding section focused on the pattern of lending by lending institutions within the private sector. This section will analyze the pattern of lending and/or financial assistance of the government. It is shown that the pattern of lending and/or assistance of the government follows that of the private lending institutions. The primary beneficiaries of governmental mortgage loan and/or assistance are suburban residents who live in the South and West and who are white and middle class.

Government participation in mortgage lending has taken several forms. One is through the secondary mortgage market, which at the present time is carried out through the activities of three agencies, viz., (1) the Government National Mortgage Association (GNMA), (2) The Federal National Mortgage Association (FNMA), and (3) The Federal Home Loan Mortgage Corporation (FHLMC).

GNMA's major purposes include retarding or stopping declines in homebuilding and mortgage lending; encouraging mortgage originators to expand their allocations of funds for mortgage investments; and attracting nontraditional sources of long-term investment capital to the mortgage market.[27] GNMA attempts to accomplish its mission through the issuance of commitments to purchase and the actual purchase of mortgages from mortgage originators; sale of such mortgages, and guarantee of securities issued by approved mortgage originators and backed by pools of mortgages. A commitment is an agreement by GNMA to purchase a specific type of mortgage bearing a specified interest rate at a specified price from a mortgage originator. The interest rate stipulated in the commitment is usually lower than the market rate. For example, under GNMA's so called "Tandem plan," it provides an interest subsidy that permits lenders to offer mortgages at a rate of 7.5%, i.e., well below the market rate. GNMA purchases these low-interest mortgages from lenders at the market interest rate, absorbing as a subsidy the difference between 7.5% and the market rate.[28]

Commitments are intended to stimulate home buying and construction by encouraging mortgage originators to make loan committments to home builders. Such commitments aid the builder in obtaining construction financing and enable him or her to advertise the availability of *below* market interest rates mortgages to home buyers. The number and *location* of housing starts and mortgage interest rates are key indicators of the condition of the housing industry. The number of housing starts has not been evenly distributed within metropolitan areas and among regions in the U.S. The central cities have been receiving less and less while the suburbs have been receiving more and more. For example, between 1975 and 1976, 80% of the GNMA homes were located in the suburbs, 16% were in the central cities, and 4% in rural areas (Table 22).

Furthermore, GNMA mortgages purchased for new homes are not distributed uniformly throughout the U.S. In general, the Sunbelt regions get the bulk of the mortgages. For example, between 1975 and 1976 the single largest state where GNMA mortgages were purchased was Texas, followed by California, Georgia, Florida, and Virginia (Table 23). These 5 states accounted for more than 40% of all the GNMA assisted mortgages. At the other extreme, the 6 New England states got less than 2%.

It is the middle class who benefits most under the GNMA program. The median income of most home buyers assisted with GNMA mortgages was about $20,000 in 1975; 9% made $30,000 or more. On the other hand, the median income for all families in 1975 was between $13,000 and $14,000.[29] Only about 13% of the GNMA purchases had incomes between $10,000 and $15,000, figures close to the moderate or median income range. Thus, few moderate and very low income families participate in the GNMA program because the subsidy is insufficient to permit lower income households to take advantage of the somewhat easy terms (Table 24).

The FNMA was chartered in 1934, but was converted to a partly private, partly

Table 22. Distribution of FNMA Mortgages by Type of Location
(in %)

Location	FNMA GNMA		FNMA market	
	N	Amount	N	Amount
Urban	16	16	29	27
Suburban	80	81	67	68
Rural	4	3	4	5
TOTAL	100	100	100	100

Source: U.S. Senate, *Hearings Before the Committee on Banking, Housing and Urban Affairs*; 94th Congress, 2nd session (Washington, D.C.: GOP, 1976), p. 36.

governmental corporation in 1968 by the U.S. Congress. It is private in the sense that its stock is privately owned and traded, it pays full corporate taxes, and its obligations are not backed by the U.S. Treasury. It is not at all, however, a private corporation in the conventional sense. It is chartered by Congress for specific public purposes.

In section 301 of the FNMA Charter Act, Congress intended that four basic purposes be achieved in carrying out the secondary market activity of FNMA. These purposes are as follows: (1) to provide liquidity for mortgage lenders; (2) to perform a stabilization function (i.e., by bringing new sources of mortgage funds into mortgage investments, buying mortgages in periods of credit stringency, and selling them in times of credit ease); (3) to provide *geographical distribution* of mortgages by bringing money from areas of capital surplus to areas of capital shortage; and (4) to provide support for sound market rate government insured mortgages for low and moderate income housing.

FNMA has failed to adequately carry out functions (3) (bringing more capital to capital short areas such as the inner cities) and (4) (allocating a sufficient portion of its purchasing authority to mortgages on low income housing that is inherently sound). Central city areas in general and non-white areas in particular have been traditionally capital short because of the unavailability of mortgage funds even though the income of several individuals in such areas is perfectly adequate to support sound mortgage investments.

In its conventional mortgage program, FNMA has tended to purchase only the most desirable mortgages, typically those on homes in the suburbs (Table 22). In purchasing conventional home mortgages, FNMA has attempted to avoid the inner city. Thus, FNMA's policy has made the Federal Housing Administration (FHA) insured mortgage, which is often the only financing vehicle available in the inner city, less salable and therefore less desirable.

Like GNMA purchases, FNMA market purchased mortgages are concentrated primarily in the South and West. These two regions had more than 75% of the FNMA market purchased mortgages in 1975 (Table 23). Furthermore, FNMA

Table 23. Distribution of Mortgages by Subregion and State, by Program

Subregion and state	FNMA GNMA		FNMA Market		FHLMC GNMA		FHLMC Market	
	N	(%)	N	(%)	N	(%)	N	(%)
New England	231	1	15	*	1,255	2	1,393	2
Maine	–	–	–	–	86	*	19	*
Vermont	–	–	–	–	7	*	4	*
New Hampshire	3	*	–	–	27	*	93	*
Massachusetts	121	*	7	*	582	1	586	1
Connecticut	107	*	8	*	528	1	558	1
Rhode Island	–	–	–	–	25	*	133	*
Mid-Atlantic	2,254	6	512	3	3,657	7	3,451	6
New York	517	1	–	*	909	2	490	1
New Jersey	896	2	176	1	1,024	2	816	1
Pennsylvania	841	2	336	2	1,724	3	2,145	–
South-Atlantic	7,658	20	2,597	17	10,236	20	10,919	19
West Virginia	13	*	–	–	64	*	72	*
Maryland	805	2	651	4	696	1	2,999	5
Delaware	109	*	39	*	210	*	271	*
District of Columbia	–	–	231	2	–	–	330	1
Virginia	1,299	3	1,035	7	3,124	6	3,740	7
North Carolina	873	2	107	1	1,593	3	2,082	4
South Carolina	575	1	7	*	859	2	321	1
Georgia	1,888	5	202	1	1,656	3	650	1
Florida	2,096	5	325	2	2,034	4	454	1
East South Central	3,157	8	452	3	2,708	5	1,602	3
Kentucky	391	1	23	*	255	*	286	1
Tennessee	1,145	3	159	1	846	2	–	–
Mississippi	677	2	127	1	655	1	166	*
Alabama	946	2	143	1	952	2	172	*
East North Central	3,699	9	2,745	18	2,471	15	5,484	10
Wisconsin	388	1	16	*	1,005	2	568	1
Michigan	1,114	3	1,710	11	2,009	4	1,931	3
Illinois	826	2	291	2	1,721	3	1,389	3
Indiana	851	2	716	5	960	2	509	1
Ohio	570	1	12	*	1,776	3	1,087	2
West North Central	1,689	4	139	1	2,986	6	1,940	3
North Dakota	–	–	–	–	–	–	1	*
South Dakota	–	–	–	–	54	*	22	*
Nebraska	183	*	13	*	210	*	56	*
Kansas	191	*	32	*	626	1	1,518	3
Minnesota	357	1	40	*	609	1	51	*
Iowa	262	1	9	*	445	1	77	*
Missouri	696	2	45	*	1,042	2	215	*
West South Central	9,790	25	2,743	18	9,018	18	3,916	7
Texas	6,456	17	2,006	13	6,315	12	2,976	5
Oklahoma	1,145	3	202	1	1,476	3	524	1

Table 23. (cont'd)

Subregion and state	FNMA				FHLMC			
	GNMA		Market		GNMA		Market	
	N	(%)	N	(%)	N	(%)	N	(%)
West South Central								
Arkansas	342	1	50	*	447	1	139	*
Louisiana	1,847	5	458	3	780	2	277	1
Mountain	3,449	9	1,424	10	4,889	10	4,336	8
Idaho	175	*	49	*	277	*	112	*
Nevada	206	1	78	1	180	*	147	*
Arizona	848	2	108	1	868	2	480	1
Montana	27	*	4	*	108	*	199	*
Wyoming	54	*	177	1	242	*	308	1
Colorado	1,000	3	603	4	4,735	3	1,976	4
New Mexico	520	1	209	1	336	1	66	*
Utah	619	2	201	1	1,143	2	1,048	2
Pacific	6,339	17	4,579	30	9,054	18	22,914	41
Washington	1,299	3	811	5	1,865	4	1,948	4
Oregon	245	1	19	*	624	1	393	1
California	4,283	11	3,289	22	6,384	12	18,272	33
Alaska	23	*	289	2	95	*	1,413	3
Hawaii	167	*	171	1	86	*	888	2
Puerto Rico and Virgin Islands	367	1	19	*	114	*	420	1
TOTAL	38,266	100	15,225	100	51,388	100	56,375	100

*Less than 0.5%.

Source: U.S. Senate, *Hearings Before the Committee on Banking and Housing and Urban Affairs*, 94th Congress, 2nd Session (Washington, D.C.: GOP, 1976), p. 73.

benefits primarily the middle and upper classes. Of all the market purchased by FNMA in 1975, 58% went to families in the $15,000 to $25,000 category (Table 24). Whereas 11% went to families earning $30,000 or more, only 1% went to families earning $7,500 to $10,000, and less than one-half of 1% went to families earning less than $7,500.[30]

The FHLMC was chartered in 1970. Like the FNMA and GNMA, its mortgage activity has been concentrated primarily in the suburbs, in the South and West and among the middle and upper classes. In market purchases, for example, 60% of FHLMC mortgages were located in the Pacific and South Atlantic regions with 41% in the Pacific region alone (Table 23). Furthermore, a majority or 51% of FHLMC market purchased mortgages went to families earning $20,000 or more with 13% of the mortgages issued to families earning $30,000 or more. At the other extreme, only 1% of FHLMC's mortgages went to families earning $7,500 to $10,000 and less than one-half 1% went to families earning less than $7,500 (Table 24).

The Revenue Act of 1978 allows taxpayers 55 years of age and over to exclude from their income, on a one time basis, up to $100,000 of the capital gain they receive on the sale of their principal residence. The Act repealed a former provision that allowed people over the age of 65 to exclude a smaller amount of the gain on home sales. In addition to the one time exclusion for those over 55, all taxpayers are allowed to defer payment of taxes on capital gains from their home sales if they purchase new homes of equal or greater value within 18 months of the sale of their former residence.

In sum, the federal government's involvement in mortgage lending has taken several forms, ranging from the secondary mortgage market to special capital gains. Thus, governmental involvement has consisted of both direct and indirect subsidies. In general, however, the benefits of governmental mortgage lending programs have not been evenly distributed. Most of the benefits have gone to one or all of the following: (1) the suburbs (especially those in the South and West), (2) the white population, and (3) the middle and upper classes. Therefore, lending practices and policies of the federal government tend to reflect those of private lending institutions, i.e., the pattern of lending of private institutions and of the government tend to be a function of location, race, and class.

CONCLUSIONS AND POLICY RECOMMENDATIONS

The basic thesis of this chapter was that the lending practices and policies within the metropolitan system tend to be differentially applied on the basis of location, race, and class, thereby affecting the quality, growth, and decline of neighborhoods and the quantity of homeownership among groups. Mortgage loans tend to be most accessible to suburban residents (particularly residents of the South and West), white residents, and middle and upper class families. On the other hand, mortgage loans tend to be most inaccessible to central city residents (especially residents in the inner cities), the non-white population, and low income residents.

The policy recommendations which follow are designed to bring about a more even distribution of the pattern of lending within the American metropolitan system. There is a need for public policy makers to distinguish between two goals: (1) the elimination of discrimination against those actively seeking mortgages on the one hand and (2) the stimulation of affirmative action to meet latent demand for single family housing in older, low and moderate income, racially changing, and non-white neighborhoods on the other. Latent demand exists anywhere that there is a potential need for resources that cannot be met with funds at hand.[36]

In spite of the present laws designed to eliminate discrimination in mortgage lending on the basis of location, race, and source of income, discrimination still exists. It is apparent, therefore, that the present laws are not totally effective and should be amended. The Home Mortgage Disclosure Act, i.e., the Anti-Redlining Act, should be amended to require lending institutions (1) to disclose all loan originations; (2) to include information concerning the number, race, and income of applicants who were and were not approved for credit; (3) to send all disclosure data to a central collection agency which is accessible to the public; (4) to disclose data regardless of the assets of the institutions; (5) to issue harsh civil or criminal penalties against financial institutions that fail to comply with the laws; (6) to disclose data on both oral and written applications; and (7) to include *all* the secondary market institutions, e.g., FNMA, FHLMC, and GNMA so that there would be accessibility to the records of the kinds of loans handled such as where they originate by census tract, where the loans are being bought, and how the secondary market is also affecting the decline of older central city neighborhoods within metropolitan areas.

Congress should require all federal agencies that regulate the lending industry to change certain obsolete appraisal and underwriting standards. One example is the standard of overimprovement whereby the owner or prospective purchaser who wants to pioneer in rehabilitating a home in an older neighborhood is penalized because traditional appraisal standards warn against lending on homes whose improvements exceed those of other homes in the neighborhood. Another example is the standard of conformity which assigns higher lending risks to neighborhoods where mixed land uses exist or are anticipated, or which discourage lending on new homes in older neighborhoods because they are considered nonconforming properties and, therefore, higher risks. Congress should require lending institutions and secondary market institutions to comply with affirmative action employment regulations and employ a proportionate number of non-white loan officers. Finally, Congress should modify FHA statutes to permit the option of 35-year, no downpayment mortgage for single family home purchases. Once the changes above are implemented, there is a high probability that a more even distribution in mortgage lending will occur within the American metropolitan system.

NOTES

[1] Michael Stone and Emily Achtenberg, *Hostage: Housing and the Massachusetts Fiscal Crisis* (Boston: Boston Community School, 1977), p. 2.

[2] Carroll R. Melton, *Housing Finance and Homeownership: Public Policy Initiatives in Selected Countries* (Chicago: International Union of Building Societies and Savings Associations, 1978), p. 5.

[3] Joe T. Darden, "Redlining: A Concept for Study by Urban-Social Geographers," in Harold Winters and Marjorie Winters, eds., *Applications of Geographic Research* (East Lansing: Michigan State University, Department of Geography, 1977), p. 33.

[4] Richard Francis et al., *Interim Report of the Governor's Task Force on Redlining* (Michigan Department of Commerce, Financial Institutions Bureau Report, 1976), p. 2, and Michael Agelasto and David Listokin, *The Urban Financing Dilemma: Disinvestment Redlining*, Council on Planning Librarians Exchange Bibliography No. 890 (Monticello, Ill.: Council of Planning Librarians, 1975), p. 1.

[5] Hilbert Fefferman, *The Redlining of Neighborhoods by Mortgage Lending Institutions and What Can Be Done About It* (Washington, D.C.: Federal National Mortgage Association Special Report, 1976), p. 26.

[6] Gordon Nelson, *Some Perspectives on Redlining.* (Washington, D.C.: Federal National Mortgage Association Special Report, 1976), p. 6, and University of California, Berkeley, Center for Real Estate and Urban Economics, "Redlining," *Current Urban Land Topics 1* (Oct., 1975), p. 1.

[7]U.S. Senate Committee on Banking, Housing, and Urban Affairs, *Home Mortgage Disclosure Act of 1975*, Hearings, 94th Congress, 1st. Session (Washington, D.C.: U.S. Government Printing Office, 1975).

[8]George Sternlieb, *The Tenement Landlord* (New Brunswick, N.J.: Rutgers University Press, 1966), p. 112.

[9]U.S. Commission on Civil Rights, *Understanding Fair Housing* (Washington, D.C.: U.S. Government Printing Office, 1973).

[10]Home Owners Loan Corporation, *Mortgage Risk Areas in Oakland and Berkeley* (Washington, D.C.: Home Owners Loan Corporation, 1936).

[11]Herbert Swan, *The Housing Market in New York City* (N.Y.: Reinhold Press, 1944).

[12]George Sternlieb, *The Urban Housing Dilemma* (N.Y.: Housing and Development Administration, 1972).

[13]Edwin Daniel, "Redlining," *Journal of Housing*, Vol. 32 (1975), pp. 441-44.

[14]Institute for Policy Studies, *Redlining: Mortgage Disinvestment in the District of Columbia* (Washington, D.C.: Public Interest Group, 1975), p. 1.

[15]National Urban League, *The National Survey of Housing Abandonment* (N.Y.: National Urban League, 1971).

[16]George Sternleib and Robert Burchell, *Residential Abandonment: The Tenement Landlord Revisited* (New Brunswick: Center for Urban Policy Research, 1973).

[17]George V. Furstenberg, "The Investment Quality of Home Mortgages," *Journal of Risk and Insurance*, Vol. 37 (1970), p. 443.

[18]Francis et al., op. cit., note 4, p. 14.

[19]Federal Fair Housing Law of 1968 42 U.S.C. Sec. 3601.

[20]U.S. Commission on Civil Rights, *Mortgage Money: Who Gets It* (Washington, D.C.: U.S. Government Printing Office, 1974), p. 3.

[21]U.S. Department of Housing and Urban Development, *Mortgage Credit Risk Analysis and Servicing of Delinquent Mortgages* (Washington, D.C.: U.S. Government Printing Office, 1972), p. 14, and Robert Pease, ed., *Mortgage Banking* (N.Y.: McGraw-Hill, 1965), p. 216.

[22]U.S. Commisstion on Civil Rights, op. cit., note 20, p. 9.

[23]Robert Schafer, *Mortgage Lending Decisions: Criteria and Constraints* (Cambridge: Joint Center for Urban Studies of the Massachusetts Institute of Technology and Harvard University, 1978), Vol. 1.

[24]Ibid., p. xxii.

[25]U.S. Department of Commerce, Bureau of the Census, *1970 Census of Housing: Metropolitan Housing Characteristics*, Final Report No. HC (2)-1 (Washington, D.C.: U.S. Government Printing Office, 1972).

[26]Schafer, op. cit., note 23, p. 51.

[27]U.S. Senate, *Hearings Before the Committee on Banking, Housing and Urban Affairs*, 94th Congress, 2nd Session (Washington, D.C.: U.S. Government Printing Office, 1976), p. 4.

[28]U.S. House of Representatives, *Tax Exempt Boards for Single Family Housing*, Subcommittee on the City of the Committee on Banking, Finance, and Urban Affairs, 96th Congress, 1st. Session (Washington, D.C.: U.S. Government Printing Office, April, 1979), p. 68.

[29]U.S. Senate, op. cit., note 27, p. 47.

[30]U.S. Senate, op. cit., note 27, p. 63.

[31]U.S. Senate, op. cit., note 27, p. 44.

[32]Congressional Budget Office, *The Budget of the United States, Fiscal Year 1980* (Washington, D.C.: U.S. Government Printing Office, Jan., 1979), pp. 3-4.

[33]U.S. Department of Housing and Urban Development, *Summary of the HUD Budget, Fiscal Year 1980* (Washington, D.C.: U.S. Government Printing Office, Jan., 1979), p. 17.

[34]U.S. House of Representatives, op. cit., note 28, p. 70.

[35]Congressional Budget Office, op. cit., note 32, p. 72.

[36]Calvin Bradford, Dennis R. Marino, and Lawrence B. Rosser, *Demand, Supply and Marketing of Single Family Mortgage Credit in Mature Communities* (Chicago: Woodstock Institute, 1977), p. 15.

Chapter 8

Regional and Structural Shifts in the American Economy since 1960

Thomas A. Clark

Since the turn of the century the American economy has undergone several simultaneous and interconnected transformations. As population and gross national product have increased, large metropolitan centers have arisen, forging a new urban order. The rich industrial states of the Northeast have witnessed the development of rival places elsewhere within the nation. Outlying regions which once harnessed limited supplies of labor and capital to produce a few items for national markets now possess highly diversified economies. Interregional and foreign trade relations have consequently been reshaped as the structure of dependency has shifted. Likewise, the mechanism which determines the place, process, and purpose of production has been rebuilt. Government and large corporate structures now seem to propel this mechanism, organizing productive energies, directing economic change, and steadying the motion of societal forces admist a capricious environment.

One of the most striking features of the economic transformation of the U.S. since 1960 has been the emergence of a substantial service-performing sector.[1] This sector, which includes all economic activities other than those devoted to agriculture, mining, construction and manufacturing, is extremely diverse. Today, 7 of every 10 nonagricultural payroll employees are engaged in the service-performing sector. The shift to services represents a long-run secular trend which is both cause and consequence of the other dimensions of national economic change. Growth in the "connecting" services (transportation, communication, and utilities) and the commercial services (wholesale and retail trade) has been closely linked to the twin processes of economic expansion and geographic dispersal. Still others, such as finance, insurance, and real estate services, have concentrated and directed

111

capital into the various forms of production, both to sustain existing functions and to generate new functions by diminishing the individual risk usually inherent in new ventures. Finally, there are services performed by both government and private firms which more directly satisfy human needs. These include a growing plethora of activities in the fields of education, health, welfare, and safety. Expansion in these areas may reflect not only growth in individual purchasing power, but also heightened awareness of their importance in attaining an acceptable living standard. Because human services are often costly to provide and have other characteristics associated with "public goods," government has become a major participant in their division.

The emergence of a strong service-performing sector in the U.S., consequently, has been neither inevitable nor unilineal.[2] Rather, each service category has responded to a different set of pressures and opportunities. Certain classes have emerged in the normal play of market forces.[3] Others, however, were confronted by severe conditions for market entry and consequently required the intervention of extra-market forces set in motion by the communal expedient of political decisions.

Whatever the process of expansion within the service sector, certain general characteristics are shared by many member industries. Most are labor intensive. Their workers are disproportionately oriented to white-collar pursuits, and many relate directly to service consumers. Many of the firms are small, producing an intangible product without the benefit of the kinds of advanced technologies which account for the continuing growth of output in the more capital-intensive, goods-producing industries.[4] Many of the jobs within the sector are low-skill and low-paying. Despite the disproportionate gain in service-performing vs. goods-producing industries since 1900, the service sector's share of total national output value has remained almost constant since the 1930s.[5] This may, of course, understate the real value of service products.[6]

Some find within the emergent service economy a new sociopolitical configuration. Bell, for example, forecasts the rise of a technocratic "post-industrial" society emphasizing "the centrality of theoretical knowledge as the axis around which new technology, economic growth, and the stratification of society will be organized."[7] Gartner and Riessman foresee the development of a new social ethos founded on new values and institutions embodying a new relationship between service producers and consumers.[8] Neither these nor other similar social extrapolations, however, seem to acknowledge the continuing momentum of the current social and political arrangement. It is clear that the service sector is an increasingly important, if not dominant, force in generating wealth, distributing resources, and fashioning the quality of life. The sector is a major source of new employment opportunities. It is an essential ingredient in the economy of regions. It is a conduit for both public and private resources, transcending regional boundaries.

The intent of this chapter is to document the role of service industries within the context of national economic transformation and regional shifts since 1960. In particular, it will examine the differential role which various service industries have played in reshaping the employment structures of the major subnational regions, states, and metropolitan areas of the U.S. Employment trends and patterns will be examined according to the major sub-national regions (Northeast, North

Central, South, and West) and divisions within them identified in the U.S. census and other national tabulations.[9]

NATIONAL EMPLOYMENT TRENDS

Since 1960, total nonagricultural employment in the U.S., excluding Alaska and Hawaii, has increased by almost 29 million jobs. This represents a gain of nearly 55%, while population rose by almost 20%. In 1960, there were 3.4 persons per nonagricultural job, while in 1977 there were 2.7 persons per job. This substantial increase in primarily urban employment opportunities has more than kept pace with population growth, and the reduction in the persons per job ratio has likely more than offset the decline in agricultural employment which these figures do not reflect.

Employment expansion since 1960 is coupled with several structural trans-formations. Over 70% of all new nonagricultural jobs has fallen within the service-performing sector. For every new job in goods production, 2.5 new service jobs have been created. Service growth, however, is not a simple function of expansion in manufacturing and related pursuits. Much of the service growth does not directly serve goods producers. Expansion in goods production, however, may stimulate growth in capital surpluses, some of which is then spent by households and busi-nesses in purchasing services, and some of which is captured by government through taxation and then applied to generate additional expansion in service industries. Since 1960, 0.6 new service jobs have been created for every person-increase in total population.

The expansion of service-performing industries relative to the goods-producing industries cannot continue indefinitely. The relative decline of manufacturing and related industries will surely slow as capital intensive production technologies reach their peak effectiveness. Worker productivity will then stabilize and further expansion will later be possible only as employment is increased. Much of the gain in value added through manufacturing in recent years, of course, has occurred by harnessing advanced technologies which have displaced many workers. Since population was increasing rapidly, and the fraction of total work-age population actually seeking employment was also increasing, the services sector became the employer of last resort. Its expansion has been critical in holding down unemploy-ment rates. The infusion of large federal, state, and local outlays within the service industries has therefore been as essential for generating jobs as for supplying the services which these industries perform. In the near future perhaps the most im-portant factor motivating change in manufacturing will be foreign competition. Given slowing rates of population growth, foreign markets will become even more critical if American manufacturing is to maintain its position.

Historically, national and sub-national developing regions have propelled them-selves through a succession of evolutionary transformations by securing external capital through the export of agricultural and other natural resources and, later, manufactured goods. Simultaneously, they gradually substituted local goods for ones which were previously imported. The emergence of services tended to accelerate once manufacturing was securely established. This condition, however, may be changing. Service industries, many of which have traditionally been founded on local resources and have served local service demands, are now selectively becoming interregional in character. Not only do they export to satisfy external demands, consequently drawing new capital to the region as a result of "foreign" sales, but they also are in varying degrees subsidized by the federal government through intergovernmental transfers and other related means. Let us now consider the pattern of change in service employment among the major regions and divisions of the U.S. since 1960, within the context of the whole space-economy.

REGIONAL ECONOMIC SHIFTS

National economic trends conceal substantial variation among U.S. regions. Whatever the aggregate shape and scale of national employment and the national product, individual regions have retained a degree of individuality due to differences in economic evolution, regional resources, urban structure, and relative location.

The magnitude of national growth and regional transformation since 1960 is substantial.[10] In the interval from 1960 to 1977, total national employment increased by about 55% while employment in service industries increased by 164%, even as goods-producing industries grew by about 21% (Table 26). This growth was not shared equally among regions. Both the South and West experienced employment gains of around 80%, with the non-coastal western Mountain states being especially prosperous (having a 101% gain in total employment). The remaining regions fared far worse. The Northeast (New England and Middle Atlantic states) realized a 23% gain from 1960 to 1977, while the North Central states (the Dakotas, Nebraska and Kansas, eastward to Ohio and Michigan) did slightly better, gaining 47% (Table 26). Overall, the combined gain of the South and West amounted to 53% of total national growth in the period between 1960 and 1970, but, from 1970 to 1977, 79% of all national growth occurred in these two regions, indicating an accelerating trend in relative Sunbelt prosperity.

The role of service-producing employment in regional shift since 1960 is particularly noteworthy. During the 1960s, all regions except the Northeast and West experienced rates of growth in service industries approaching the national average. The Northeast, however, lagged substantially behind while the West was well ahead. From 1970 to 1977, the South and West maintained growth rates in service production appreciably higher than the national average while the North Central states saw their rate of service production employment increase fall to the level of the Northeast.

Overall, then, the most rapid rates of total employment growth occurred in the South and West between 1960 and 1977. These regions had substantially lower goods-to-service production employment ratios in 1960 than the Northeast and North Central states. By 1977, however, the South's goods-to-services employment ratio had fallen to approximate the ratio of the Northeast and North Central states. At the same time, the West's goods-to-services ratio was substantially lower than those of the other major regions in 1977.

Table 26. Nonagricultural Employment by Major Sector,[a] Region and Division,[b] 1970-1977[c]

Sector, region, division	Employment[d] (thou.)			Change 1960-70		Change 1970-77		Regional growth as % of U.S.[d]	
	1960	1970	1977	N	%	N	%	1960-70	1970-77
NORTHEAST									
Total	15,584.4	18,653.0	19,212.1	3,068.6	19.7	559.1	3.0	17.3	5.0
New England	3,656.3	4,523.8	4,965.6	867.5	23.7	441.8	9.8	4.9	4.0
Middle Atlantic	11,928.1	14,129.8	14,246.6	2,201.8	18.5	116.8	12.4	12.4	1.0
Goods production	6,377.1	6,450.1	5,713.9	73.0	1.1	-736.2	-11.4		
Service production	9,207.3	12,202.9	13,498.2	2,995.6	32.5	1,295.3	10.4		
NORTH CENTRAL									
Total	14,718.6	19,918.9	21,654.4	5,200.3	35.3	1,735.5	8.7	29.4	15.5
East North Central	11,464.6	14,578.3	16,319.4	3,113.7	27.2	1,741.1	11.9	17.6	15.6
West North Central	3,253.6	5,339.9	5,336.1	2,086.3	64.1	-3.8	-0.1	11.8	(loss)
Goods production	6,045.7	7,215.5	7,122.5	1,169.8	19.3	-93.0	-1.3		
Service production	8,672.9	12,703.4	14,531.9	4,030.5	46.5	1,828.5	14.4		
SOUTH									
Total	14,047.6	20,279.0	25,852.7	6,231.4	44.4	5,573.7	27.5	35.2	49.9
South Atlantic	7,122.6	10,465.2	13,020.9	3,342.6	46.9	2,555.7	24.4	18.9	22.9
East South Central	2,687.8	3,825.0	4,901.9	1,137.3	42.3	1,076.9	28.2	6.4	9.6
West South Central	4,237.0	5,988.7	7,930.0	1,751.7	41.3	1,941.3	32.4	9.9	17.4
Goods production	4,938.6	6,649.5	7,810.6	1,710.9	34.6	1,161.1	17.5		
Service production	9,109.0	13,629.5	18,042.1	4,520.5	49.6	4,412.6	32.4		
WEST									
Total	8,251.0	11,444.7	14,742.2	3,193.7	38.7	3,297.7	28.8	18.0	29.5
Mountain	1,887.5	2,649.2	3,790.4	761.7	40.4	1,141.2	43.1	4.3	10.2
Pacific	6,362.5	8,795.5	10,952.0	2,433.0	38.2	2,156.6	24.5	13.7	19.3
Goods production	2,669.4	2,999.3	3,560.0	329.9	12.4	560.7	18.7		
Service production	5,581.6	8,445.4	11,182.4	2,863.8	51.3	2,737.0	32.4		
UNITED STATES[e]									
Total	52,601.6	70,295.6	81,461.7	17,694.0	33.6	11,166.1	15.9	100.0	100.0
Goods production	20,030.8	23,314.4	24,207.0	3,283.6	16.4	892.6	3.8		
Service production	32,570.8	46,981.2	57,254.7	14,410.4	44.2	10,273.5	21.9		

Notes:
[a]Major sectors are goods production (mining, contract construction, and manufacturing) and service production (transportation and public utilities; wholesale and retail trade; finance, insurance and real estate; services; and government) according to the Standard Industrial Classification.
[b]The four primary regions (Northeast, North Central, South, and West) and their internal divisions are defined by the U.S. Bureau of the Census.
[c]Figures for 1960 and 1977 are for October, while those for 1970 are annual averages. [d]Figures in this and later tables may not sum due to rounding. [e]Excludes Alaska and Hawaii, as do all later tables, unless otherwise noted.
Source: U.S. Department of Labor, Bureau of Labor Statistics, *Employment and Earnings* (Washington, D.C.: U.S. GPO, monthly). Sectoral and regional tabulations, and shift rates calculated by the author.

Table 27. Service-Producing Employment, by Region, 1960–77

Region	Payroll employees (thou.)			% change	
	1960	1970	1977	1960–70	1970–77
NORTHEAST					
Total	15,584.4	18,653.0	19,212.1	19.7	3.0
Goods production	6,377.1	6,450.1	5,713.9	1.1	-11.4
Transport, utilities, trade[a]	4,170.2	4,920.3	5,150.1	18.0	4.7
F.I.R.E.[b]	906.2	1,156.5	1,221.8	27.6	5.6
Services	2,137.5	3,283.1	3,903.4	53.6	18.9
Government	1,993.4	2,843.0	3,222.9	42.6	13.4
NORTH CENTRAL					
Total	14,718.6	19,918.9	21,654.4	35.3	8.7
Goods production	6,045.7	7,215.5	7,122.5	19.3	-1.3
Transport, utilities, trade	4,167.4	5,487.6	6,052.6	31.7	10.3
F.I.R.E.	621.7	911.4	1,021.3	46.6	12.1
Services	1,738.3	2,993.6	3,758.3	71.6	26.0
Government	2,145.5	3,321.8	3,699.7	54.8	11.4
SOUTH					
Total	14,047.6	20,279.0	25,852.7	44.4	27.5
Goods production	4,938.6	6,649.5	7,810.6	34.6	17.5
Transport, utilities, trade	4,194.8	5,589.0	7,206.1	33.2	28.9
F.I.R.E.	598.3	958.9	1,268.9	60.3	32.3
Services	1,654.0	3,022.8	4,358.7	82.8	44.2
Government	2,661.9	4,058.8	5,208.4	52.5	28.3
WEST					
Total	8,251.0	11,444.7	14,742.4	38.7	28.8
Goods production	2,669.4	2,999.3	3,560.0	12.4	18.7
Transport, utilities, trade	2,477.1	3,315.8	4,321.0	33.9	30.3
F.I.R.E.	390.0	603.2	821.3	54.7	36.2
Services	1,140.6	2,061.2	2,904.8	80.7	40.9
Government	1,573.9	2,465.2	3,135.3	56.6	27.2
UNITED STATES					
Total	52,601.6	70,295.6	81,461.7	33.6	15.9
Goods production	20,030.8	23,314.4	24,207.0	16.4	3.8
Transport, utilities, trade	15,009.5	19,312.7	22,729.8	28.7	17.7
F.I.R.E.	2,516.2	3,630.0	4,333.3	44.3	19.4
Services	6,670.4	11,349.7	14,925.3	70.2	31.5
Government	8,374.7	12,688.8	15,266.3	51.5	20.3

Notes: [a]This category includes transportation and public utilities, and wholesale and retail trade. [b]Finance, insurance, and real estate.

Source: U.S. Department of Labor, Bureau of Labor Statistics, *Employment and Earnings* (Washington, D.C.: U.S. GPO, monthly).

Performance of the constituent industries within the service-performing sector has varied significantly among regions (Table 27). In every region the "services" subcategory has advanced more rapidly than any other service industry since 1960. In the South and West, however, this subcategory was exceedingly active, increasing by over 150% since 1960. This category, of course, includes business and personal services as well as entertainment and recreational activities. Growth in government employment has also favored the South and West, particularly since 1970, as has F.I.R.E. In all regions, transportation, utilities, and trade as a class have fared better than goods-producing industries, and often close to the overall regional growth rate.

REGIONAL SHIFT-SHARE ANALYSIS

To bring to clearer focus the dimensions of regional transformation, a "shift-share" analysis has been undertaken.[11] This descriptive device reveals the relative contribution of several distinct factors in the process of economic change. The objective of shift-share analysis is to account for the difference between the amount of growth (change) in total employment which a region would have experienced if each of its industries had grown at the same rate as overall national employment, and the amount of growth (change) actually experienced within the region. We characterize the level of growth which a region would have experienced, if it had grown at the same rate as the nation as a whole, as its "national share." The difference between this share and the amount of growth actually experienced is called "shift."

There are two distinct components of shift. The first is the "industry mix" component. This is the amount of growth which a region would realize if each of its industries were to grow at a rate equal to the difference between the growth rate of its national counterpart industry and the growth rate of total national employment. Consequently, if any industry, nationwide, were to grow more rapidly than overall national employment, then the "industry mix" shift component would be positive. It follows that any region endowed with industries which have prospered nationally will tend also to prosper, if these industries account for a significant portion of total regional employment. Any industry, of course, tends not to perform equally in all regions. For any given industry, some regions are more competitive than others. This reality is acknowledged in the second shift component called "competitive advantage." Numerically this is the difference between the regional and national growth rates of any industry. It follows, for any regional industry over any interval of time, that the sum of the national share, industry mix, and competitive advantage components will equal the actual level of employment change within the industry.[12]

Shift-share analysis has been applied to goods-producing and the major service-performing industries in each major U.S. region for 1960 to 1970 and 1970 to 1977 (Table 28). During the 1960 to 1970 period, the Northeast experienced an increase of over 3 million nonagricultural jobs. Its national share for this same period would have been 1.7 times greater. The difference between actual growth and the national share to which the region was "entitled" was over 2.1 million

Table 28. Regional Components of Change in Service-Producing Employment, 1960–77

Region	Employment change (thou.)		Components of change					
			1960–70			1970–77		
	1970–70	1970–77	National share	Industry mix	Competitive advantage	National share	Industry mix	Competitive advantage
NORTHEAST								
Total	3,068.6	559.1	5,236.4	-65.1	-2,102.7	2,965.8	-14.1	-2,392.6
Goods production	73.0	-736.2	2,142.7	-1,096.9	-972.8	1,025.6	-780.5	-981.3
Transport, utilities, trade	750.1	229.8	1,401.2	-204.3	-446.8	782.3	88.6	-641.1
F.I.R.E.	250.3	65.3	304.5	97.0	-151.2	183.9	40.5	-159.1
Services	1,145.6	620.3	718.2	782.3	-354.9	522.0	512.2	-413.9
Government	849.6	379.9	669.8	356.8	-177.0	452.0	125.1	-197.2
SOUTH								
Total	6,231.4	5,573.7	4,720.0	91.0	1,420.4	3,224.4	-20.2	2,369.5
Goods production	1,710.9	1,161.1	1,659.4	-849.4	900.9	1,057.3	-804.6	908.4
Transport, utilities, trade	1,394.2	1,617.1	1,409.5	-205.5	190.2	888.7	100.6	627.8
F.I.R.E.	360.6	310.0	201.0	64.0	95.6	152.5	33.6	123.9
Services	1,368.8	1,335.9	555.7	605.4	207.7	480.6	471.6	383.7
Government	1,396.9	1,149.6	894.4	476.5	26.0	645.3	178.6	325.7
NORTH CENTRAL								
Total	5,200.3	1,735.5	4,945.5	-157.4	412.2	3,167.1	-130.9	-1,300.7
Goods production	1,169.8	-93.0	2,031.4	-1,039.9	178.3	1,147.3	-873.1	-367.2
Transport, utilities, trade	1,320.2	565.0	1,400.2	-204.2	124.2	872.5	98.8	-406.3
F.I.R.E.	289.7	109.9	208.9	66.5	14.3	144.9	31.9	-66.9
Services	1,244.3	775.7	584.1	636.2	24.0	474.2	465.3	-163.8
Government	1,176.3	377.9	720.9	384.0	71.4	528.2	146.2	-296.5
WEST								
Total	3,193.7	3,297.7	2,772.2	160.4	261.1	1,819.7	147.9	1,330.1
Goods production	329.9	560.7	896.9	-459.1	-107.9	476.9	-362.9	446.7
Transport, utilities, trade	838.7	1,005.2	832.3	-121.4	127.8	527.2	59.7	418.3
F.I.R.E.	213.2	218.1	131.0	41.7	40.5	95.9	21.1	101.1
Services	920.6	843.6	383.2	417.5	119.9	327.7	321.5	194.4
Government	891.3	670.1	528.8	281.7	80.8	392.0	108.5	169.6

Source: U.S. Department of Labor, Bureau of Labor Statistics, *Employment and Earnings* (Washington, D.C.: GPO, monthly). All components

jobs, of which 97% pertained to negative competitive advantage. In this same period the North Central region earned 5% more jobs than its national share, due primarily to a modest competitive advantage in goods production (178,000 jobs) and transportation, public utilities, and trade (124,000 jobs). The remaining regions fared still better, however. The West exceeded its national share by 15%, despite a negative competitive advantage in goods production, while the South was a substantial gainer, realizing a total increase of more than 6.2 million jobs (32% more than its national share). The South's success between 1960 and 1970 was due largely to the exceptional performance of its manufacturing sector relative to other regions.

Since 1970, the North Central region has seen all of its industrial sectors falter. As in the Northeast, every sector experienced a negative competitive advantage. During this same interval of time, however, both the South and West saw total employment rise by nearly 30%. In both regions, the major portion of total gain was due not to the industry mix, but rather to the competitive advantage of their service industries. Not only did the presence of service industries offset the negative industry mix components of goods production, but the service industries also exceeded percentage gains of their national counterparts. Shift-share analysis, it is cautioned, extracts component shifts and shares using employment as a measure of activity which, of course, can be misleading since worker productivity varies among both regions and industries.

CORRELATES OF REGIONAL SHIFT

Though there are usually significant time lags separating cause from effect in regional development, it is nevertheless instructive to examine the correlates of regional shifts since 1970. At the scale of the major sub-national regions, this information may, of course, conceal significant internal variation. Certain regional and interregional processes, however, may only appear in these seemingly gross characteristics, including the redistributional effect of federal funding, population shift, and associated features of the national urban system.

Population is used here as the baseline perspective. During 1970, about one-quarter of the entire U.S. population was located in each of three regions: Northeast (24%), North Central (28%), and South (31%). Only 17% was located in the West. These figures, as all earlier ones, of course, pertain to regions which are quite diverse and somewhat arbitrarily delineated. From 1970 to 1976, growth rates bore no systematic relation to prior scale. The Northeast won just less than 4% of the total increment of new population growth while the other regions fared better: North Central (10%), South (53%), and West (33%). The interregional distribution of new service-performing employment corresponds quite closely to the comparable distribution of new population, suggesting an equilibrating relation between the two despite interregional differences in population composition and service orientation. At the same time, total federal aid, over the years 1970 to 1976, excluding procurements and direct investments, correlates more closely with the percentage distribution of population in 1970 than the percentage distribution of either new service-performing employment or new population. In these same years, rates of

Table 29. Regional Characteristics, Mid 1970s

Region	1975 population (thou.)	% of 1976 population[2] Under 18	% of 1976 population[2] Over 64	Net federal dollar flow, 1975[a] (millions)[3]	Per capita federal expenditures[3] 1975 ($) Welfare programs[b]	Per capita federal expenditures[3] 1975 ($) Retirement programs[c]	Personal income per capita[4] 1976[d] ($)	% below poverty level,[e] 1975[5] Persons	% below poverty level,[e] 1975[5] Families	% of blacks in total 1975 population	Labor union membership[f] as % of 1974 of nonagricultural employment[6]
NORTHEAST	49,461	28.9	11.4	-10,776	137	403	6,848	8.9	7.2	9.6	32.8
New England	12,198	29.3	11.5	762	118	402	6,590	7.8	NA	3.5	23.4
Middle Atlantic	37,263	28.8	11.4	-10,013	143	403	6,932	9.1	NA	11.5	36.0
NORTH CENTRAL	57,669	30.8	10.8	-20,074	96	372	6,600	9.4	7.4	9.3	31.2
East North Central	40,979	31.1	10.2	-18,618	101	359	6,793	9.1	NA	10.2	34.3
West North Central	16,690	30.2	12.3	-1,456	83	403	6,130	9.5	NA	4.5	23.3
SOUTH	67,115	31.0	10.9	11,522[g]	115	503	5,811	15.3	12.1	18.8	15.4
South Atlantic	33,715	30.0	10.9	4,986[g]	102	426	6,007	13.7	NA	20.6	14.7
East South Central	13,544	31.6	10.8	4,293	124	368	5,194	18.1	NA	19.7	19.4
West South Central	20,856	32.1	10.2	2,243			5,895	16.1	NA	15.4	14.2
WEST	36,661	30.4	9.6	9,122	119	392	6,803	10.4	8.1	5.3	26.3
Mountain	9,644	32.9	8.9	3,631	82[h]	385[h]	5,990	11.7	NA	2.3	18.0
Pacific	27,017	29.5	9.9	5,491	132[h]	395[h]	7,081	10.0	NA	6.3	29.1
UNITED STATES[b]	210,906	30.3	10.7	—	115[h]	392[h]	6,441	11.4[h]	9.0[h]	11.5	26.2

Notes: [a]This net flow is for the year ending June 30. It is the difference between federal taxes (with the federal deficit distributed as an added tax) and federal expenditures (aid, procurements including defense contracts by location of prime contractor, and federal installations and operations, but excluding interest payments). [b]Includes medicaid, ADC, food stamps, supplemental security income, grants to states for social service programs, and unemployment compensation. [c]Social security (OASDHI) old age, survivors, disability, and health insurance—and others. [d]Data exclude federal employees. Regional and national figures imputed using July 1, 1976 provisional population estimates. [e]Poverty criterion is a national standard unadjusted to regional cost of living levels. Subject to sampling variability. [f]Includes AFL-CIO affiliates, and single firm and local unaffiliated unions. [g]Excludes Washington, D.C. [h]Includes Alaska and Hawaii.

Sources: [1]U.S. Bureau of the Census, *Current Population Reports,* Series P-23; [2]*Current Population Reports,* Series P-25, No. 646; [3]Government Research Corp., Washington, D.C., "Federal Spending: the North's Loss is Sunbelt's Gain," *National Journal,* June 26, 1976, No. 26, pp. 878-91; [4]U.S. Bureau of Economic Analysis, *Survey of Current Business,* April, 1977; [5]*1976 Survey of Income and Education;* [6]U.S. Dept. of Labor, Bureau of Labor Statistics, *Directory of National Unions and Employee Associations,* 1975.

population change in metropolitan areas by region roughly correlate with the percentage distribution of new population growth, while percent change in personal per capita income from 1970 to 1976, by region, was apparently governed by an independent dynamic.

Though gross cumulative federal aid to regions between 1970 and 1976 seems to have been roughly correlated with total regional population, much of this aid was keyed to particular sub-populations which, themselves, are unevenly distributed. Among regions, the average percentage of total population over age 64 is about 11%, though the West is somewhat lower. Per capita federal retirement program funding, however, is not closely correlated with these percentages. Likewise, the federal allocation of welfare funds is not closely correlated with the proportion of each region's population living in poverty (Table 29).

An expanded picture of federal impacts on regional development is provided in estimates of net federal dollar flow. These data are available for 1975 (Table 29). If this net dollar flow is defined as the difference between federal taxes (with the federal deficit distributed as an added tax) and federal expenditures (aid, procurements including defense contracts by location of prime contractor, and federal installations and operations, but excluding interest payments), then the Northeast and North Central regions appear to run large deficits, whereas the South and West gain far more than they contribute. Thus, while federal "aid" appears to have been distributed in proportion to gross population from 1970 to 1976, net total federal dollar flow for at least one recent year (1975) rewarded the South and West at the expense of the Northeast and North Central regions.

Ultimately, the impact of federal expenditures distributes itself throughout the economy, impacting all industrial sectors. Service-performing industries, in particular, are stimulated several ways:

(1) Government employment, itself, is a service industry demanding still other private sector services while performing an increasingly generative role within the economy.

(2) Federal procurements represent both the purchase of services and the purchase of goods whose production consumes services.

(3) Federal investments in infrastructure likewise may stimulate service industries either directly or through their overall growth-generating potential.

METROPOLITAN AND NONMETROPOLITAN TRENDS

A different perspective on the spatial dimension of regional shift derives from the changing characteristics of both metropolitan areas and their nonmetropolitan counterparts. Of the 278 SMSAs identified by the U.S. Census Bureau in 1978, 225 reveal a strikingly similar employment structure in all major national sub-regions. SMSAs in both the Northeast and North Central regions in 1977 had appreciably larger goods-producing sectors than those of the South and West. Generally, goods-producing employment constituted as large if not a larger fraction of total nonmetropolitan as metropolitan employment.

Still more interesting is the pattern of change since 1970. During 1970 to 1977, nonmetropolitan employment has in every region increased appreciably more rapidly than its metropolitan counterpart. While SMSA boundaries may no longer adequately measure the spatial extent of urban commuter fields, they suffice for a general impression of this dynamic. Further, in the Northeast, North Central, and Southern regions, nonmetropolitan service-performing growth rates exceeded those of the metropolitan areas.[13] In the West, the pattern was reversed, with metropolitan service employment growing by about 33% and nonmetropolitan by just over 15%. In every private sector of service-performing industry, growth rates were higher in nonmetropolitan than in metropolitan areas, whereas government employment advanced more rapidly in nonmetropolitan areas only in the Northeast and West. In every region except the West, nonmetropolitan percentage service employment gains have exceeded nonmetropolitan goods-producing gains. In the Northeast and North Central regions, the dispersal of employment opportunity into nonmetropolitan areas has been due primarily to expansion in service industries since 1970. In the South a similar trend occurs, while in the West manufacturing has been the prime force in nonmetropolitan growth. Overall, then, the recent vigorous growth of service industries has been manifested in decidedly different development patterns among the major sub-national regions.

The 25 largest metropolitan areas in 1977 have been chosen for closer study (Table 30). In every region except the South, one of these areas is numerically predominant. New York accounts for 33% of all employment in the Northeast, while Chicago accounts for 16% in the North Central region, and Los Angeles-Long Beach 22% in the West. In the South no area has more than 6% of the total. Among metropolitan areas there has been no consistent relationship between total employment and growth rate between 1970 and 1977. As expected, areas of the South and West had appreciably higher growth rates, as previously observed. Finally, the internal employment structures of these areas did not appear to correlate with regional location or size.

SERVICES AND THE NATIONAL SPACE-ECONOMY

In recent years service-performing activities have played an increasingly important role in the wealth-accumulating processes at every level of regionalization. Many service industries appear to be relatively insensitive to the locational factors which have for long held sway over the evolving economic geography of the nation. These seemingly footloose industries represent a growing fraction of the total economy, fostering economic dispersion within and among the major national regions. Their locational dynamic is not well understood. The larger metropolitan areas may possibly be losing a measure of control over their regional economies precisely because the processes governing the allocation of new service-performing activity are less often urban-centered.[14] Further, while many service industries continue to seek the "agglomerative" advantages associated with higher density concentrations of population and capital, they are today far more selective regarding the mix of localized activities which is considered beneficial. Certain service

Table 30. Employment Structure and Correlates: 25 Largest[a] Metropolitan Areas,[b] 1977

| Region | Total employment (Oct. 1977) | % change, 1970-77 | Employment as % of region, 1977 | Goods production | Employment by industry as % of total,[c] 1977 | | | | | |
| | | | | | Total | Services production | | | | |
						Transport public utilities	Trade	F.I.R.E.	Services	Government
NORTHEAST	19,212.1	3.0	100.0	29.7	70.3	5.6	21.2	6.4	20.3	16.8
New York[d]	6,312.9	-5.8	32.9	24.3	75.7	7.0	21.3	9.2	21.6	16.6
Philadelphia[f]	1,805.3	-0.5	9.4	28.4	71.6	5.3	21.9	5.9	22.3	16.2
Boston[e]	1,282.4	-0.7	6.7	23.3	76.7	5.3	23.4	7.4	25.6	15.0
Pittsburgh	908.1	3.8	4.7	33.3	66.8	6.3	22.3	4.6	20.0	13.6
Baltimore	876.7	8.5	4.6	24.3	75.7	6.1	23.1	5.7	19.0	21.8
Buffalo	504.9	1.6	2.6	32.5	67.5	5.3	22.4	4.3	17.9	17.6
NORTH CENTRAL	21,654.4	8.7	100.0	32.9	67.1	5.3	21.9	4.7	17.4	17.1
Chicago[d]	3,353.5	4.7	15.5	32.2	67.8	6.1	23.4	6.1	18.8	13.5
Detroit[e]	1,719.6	16.0	7.9	37.7	62.3	4.7	19.9	4.7	18.2	14.8
Minneapolis-St. Paul[e]	958.0	21.3	4.4	26.9	73.1	6.2	25.5	6.1	20.3	15.0
St. Louis[e]	938.5	4.4	4.3	31.1	68.9	7.0	22.3	5.3	19.6	14.7
Cleveland	886.4	3.2	4.1	34.6	65.4	5.0	23.0	5.1	19.0	13.3
Milwaukee	630.2	10.5	2.9	35.8	64.2	5.2	21.7	5.3	20.0	12.0
Kansas City[e]	582.1	14.5	2.7	25.0	75.0	8.8	25.6	6.4	19.3	14.9
Cincinnati[f]	559.5	9.8	2.6	33.2	66.8	5.6	23.3	5.2	18.9	13.8
SOUTH	25,852.7	27.5	100.0	30.2	69.8	5.7	22.2	4.9	16.9	20.1
Washington, D.C.[e]	1,397.5	20.8	5.4	9.2	90.8	4.7	19.7	5.7	23.7	37.0
Dallas-Fort Worth[e]	1,179.6	27.2	4.6	27.3	72.7	6.7	27.6	7.5	17.7	13.2
Houston[e]	1,178.0	53.0	4.6	30.9	69.1	7.1	25.2	5.6	19.6	11.6
Atlanta[e]	796.8	30.8	3.1	20.6	79.4	9.0	28.2	7.2	18.3	16.7
Miami	592.5	17.4	2.3	19.0	81.0	10.0	25.5	7.3	23.8	14.4
WEST	14,742.4	28.8	100.0	24.1	75.9	5.7	23.5	5.6	19.7	21.4
Los Angeles-Long Beach	3,264.5	12.7	22.1	28.7	71.3	5.5	23.3	6.1	21.2	15.2
San Francisco-Oakland	1,403.8	11.1	9.5	18.1	81.9	8.6	22.6	8.4	20.5	21.8
Anaheim-Santa Ana-Garden Grove	653.7	53.6	4.4	32.7	67.3	3.1	24.4	5.7	18.5	15.6
Denver-Boulder[e]	639.0	33.0	4.3	23.6	76.4	6.8	24.5	7.1	19.6	18.4
Seattle-Everett	628.7	21.1	4.3	24.0	76.0	7.2	25.1	7.2	19.1	17.4
San Diego	529.4	36.8	3.6	20.6	79.4	4.6	23.3	5.4	20.1	26.0

Notes: [a] According to total nonagricultural employment in October, 1977. [b] Standard Metropolitan Statistical Areas and Standard Consolidated Statistical Areas. [c] Calculated by author. [d] Standard Consolidated Area: New York-Northeastern New Jersey, and Chicago-Gary. [e] Counties or towns have been added to the area during 1970-76. [f] Cincinnati and Philadelphia are partly in the South.
Source: U.S. Department of Labor, Bureau of Labor Statistics, *Employment and Earnings*, Vol. 25, No. 1, 1978.

industries, as well, are subsidized by government, and therefore less prone to optimize location.

Service-performing activities have become a major vehicle for the disbursement of federal and state revenues through transfers from one government to another. In this manner service industries act as "basic" industries, securing external resources for internal purposes. This dimension of resource allocation represents a facet of the space-economy virtually ignored by conventional location theory, and poorly explained by the heuristics of welfare maximization models.

Though many service industries are small in scale, employing few workers and oriented to local markets, a growing number are of substantial size. These larger service entities have corporate structures spanning extensive regions and channeling wealth over great distances. Many of these firms also act as "basic" industries, selling exports, while securing "foreign" wealth. Some service industries, of course, due to the nature of their activity, must locate near the users of their service. In such instances, the parent firm may spin off branch plants near its customers. Even these may act as basic industries since profits generated in one place may be channeled to another.

In overview, then, the service-performing sector has in recent years become an increasingly important contributor to the welfare of regions, not only through the service functions it performs, but also its generative role in the development of major urban centers as well as outlying places. This diverse sector, which was once largely derivative of needs and resources associated with manufacturing, is now itself a significant propulsive factor in regional development. Yet our knowledge of this sector's spatial dynamics remains essentially descriptive. Location theory, including central place theory, may be marginally helpful in advancing to a more analytic perspective. Regional development theory, pertaining not to individual locational decisions but rather aggregate regional evolution, may be somewhat more useful.[15]

NOTES

[1] For a detailed examination of employment shifts since 1939 when data were first available for all states under the U.S. Current Employment Statistics Program, see J. M. Kelley and K. W. Shipp, "Shifting Patterns in Employment, 1939-70," in the U.S. Department of Labor, Bureau of Labor Statistics, *Employment and Earnings*, Vol. 17, No. 11 (May 1971), pp. 11-16.

[2] Daniel Bell traces a fixed sequence of events within the service sector on the way to a "post-industrial society" in the United States. Initially occurs the development of goods-oriented services, followed by commercial institutions for mass consumption, then personal services (travel, entertainment et al.), and finally services generated by government. Daniel Bell, *The Coming of the Post-Industrial Society: A Venture in Social Forecasting* (N.Y.: Basic Books, 1973), p. 127.

[3] Factors governing the development of the various service industries are also discussed in G. J. Stigler, *Trends in Employment in the Service Industries* (Princeton, N.J.: Princeton University Press, 1956).

[4] These points are elaborated in R. Fuchs, *The Service Economy* (N.Y.: Columbia University Press, 1968).

[5]Ibid, Chap. 1.

[6]Services are generally valued according to the cost of labor, whereas goods are valued by their market price. See A. Gartner and F. Riessman, *The Service Society and the Consumer Vanguard* (N.Y.: Harper & Row, 1974), 39–42. See also R. Lekachman, "Humanizing GNP," *Social Policy*, II, 3 (Sept.–Oct., 1971).

[7]Bell, op. cit., note 2, p. 112.

[8]Gartner and Riessman, op. cit., note 6, p. 19.

[9]The census regions and divisions are as follows: (A) *Northeast*–(1) New England (ME, NH, MA, CT, VT, RI), (2) Middle Atlantic (NY, NJ, PA); (B) *South*–(1) South Atlantic (DE, MD, WV, NC, SC, GA, VA, FL), (2) East South Central (LA, AR, OK, TX); (C) *North Central*–(1) East North Central (OH, MI, IN, IL, WI), (2) West North Central (MN, IA, MO, KS, NE, SD, ND); (D) *West*–(1) Mountain (MT, WY, ID, NV, UT, CO, AZ, NM), (2) Pacific (WA, OR, CA).

[10]See note 9 for the states which are grouped into each census region and division.

[11]The first application of this technique was apparently D. Cramer, "Shifts of Manufacturing Industries," in *Industrial Location and National Resources* (Washington, D.C.: Natural Resources Planning Board, 1943). Recent applications include H. S. Perloff et al., *Regions, Resources and Economic Growth* (Baltimore: Johns Hopkins Press, 1960); L. D. Ashby, *Growth Patterns in Employment by County, 1940-50 and 1950-60* (Washington, D.C.: U.S. Government Printing Office, 1965); and C. C. Harris, Jr., *State and County Projections*, Occasional Paper Series, Bureau of Business and Economic Research, University of Maryland (Jan., 1969). The technique is elaborated in W. Z. Hirsh, *Urban Economic Analysis* (N.Y.: McGraw-Hill, 1973), pp. 221–32.

[12]The utility of this technique as a descriptive device is in no way diminished by its (as modified) shortcomings as a predictive tool. See H. J. Brown, "Shift and Share Projections of Regional Economic Growth," *Journal of Regional Science*, Vol. 9 (1969), pp. 1–18.

[13]For spatial trends prior to 1970, see J. R. Borchert, "America's Changing Metropolitan Regions," *Annals*, Association of American Geographers, Vol. 62 (1972), pp. 352–73.

[14]Locational prerequisites and propensities of large scale, multilocational organizations favoring nonmetropolitan urban places are discussed in A. R. Pred, *City-Systems in Advanced Economies* (N.Y.: John Wiley & Sons, 1977).

[15]Pertinent theories of regional development have been discussed in T. A. Clark "Regional Development: Strategy from Theory," in G. Sternlieb and J. Hughes, ed., *Revitalizing the Northeast* (New Brunswick, N.J.: Center for Urban Policy Research, Rutgers University, 1978).

Chapter 9

Science and Technology in the American Metropolitan System

Edward J. Malecki

A good example of changes occurring within the nation's economic system is the changing spatial structure of science and technology activities. Technological changes that occur within a system result from research and development activities; where these activities are concentrated is just as important as understanding the diffusion process for innovations. Most research and development (R and D) activities are conducted by large firms having national markets, for example, the auto, aerospace, office machines, and chemical firms and more recently environmental and energy related industries. The level and type of technology activities within a region often affect the economic health of a number of related firms in cities of varying size; two examples are the auto industry around Detroit and petrochemicals around Houston. The major concentrations of R and D activities, including laboratories, scientists, and engineers, are in or around the largest SMSAs, for example, New York City, Washington, D.C., and Los Angeles. These activities are conducted by scientists and engineers in colleges and universities, private industry, and the federal government. The largest regional concentration is in the Manufacturing Belt, an area where traditional industrial growth has been slowing down. Through a factor analysis of variables related to R and D activities, it is found that metropolitan size and the agglomeration of science and technology activities are most important; on a per capita basis some research institutes and university cities are more important than their size would indicate. Science and technology activities are an important component in current and future regional economic development policy, whether it is funded by industries or the federal government.

This chapter addresses the role and the location of scientific and technological activities in the American metropolitan system. Very little research has been carried out on this topic, despite its rapidly growing significance as a factor in metropolitan economies. Data on the location of scientists and engineers, for example, only recently have become available at the metropolitan scale as opposed to the state scale. More importantly, the role of technological change in a regional context is only beginning to be understood. Within that perspective, this chapter first briefly discusses the subject of technological change from both a conceptual and empirical viewpoint, with emphasis on recent trends in the U.S. The second section presents and analyzes data on the geographical patterns of science and technology in the U.S. The final section suggests areas in which further knowledge and study are needed on the topic.

TECHNOLOGICAL CHANGE

Technological change refers to the creation and application of new knowledge in economic activities. Science and technology are the inputs used to generate innovations, large or small, which generally diffuse to become commonplace in the economy. Several famous innovations come to mind, such as the steam engine, the telephone, and the television, but technological innovations also affect us indirectly in all aspects of our lives. Recent examples, such as new medical scanning instruments, space exploration vehicles, and defense technology, are perhaps larger but no more conspicuous than new food products, no-iron fabrics, and twin-blade razors, all of which also represent technological advances. In all of these cases, technological change tends to follow a sequence from research and development to innovation to diffusion. The R and D stage comprises all the efforts that go into the creation of a new invention or usable innovation. Innovation is the first availability of a usable or marketable technology or product, which then tends to diffuse among potential users. Diffusion may be relatively rapid and complete within a region and an economy, as in the case of television, or it may be incomplete and never actually become a part of the economy, as happened with the leather substitute Corfam.

Geographers have tended to study diffusion of innovations, such as new products and services, rather than technological innovations which indirectly affect individuals. Consequently, despite considerable work by economists on technological innovations, relatively little is known about the geographical diffusion patterns of these innovations.[1] In addition, technological innovation is a more complex topic, in which R and D is a major activity.

The process of R and D itself has considerable variation, in terms of the type of activity, the levels of effort, and the performers involved in each phase.[2] *Basic research* is the advance of scientific knowledge with little or no known application, and accounts for only about 12.5% of all R and D in the U.S. This research tends to require long-term commitment and is funded largely by the federal government, but is performed primarily by universities and colleges (Table 31). Industry's commitment to basic research has decreased considerably in recent years, largely

Table 31. R and D Funding and Performance in the U.S. by Research Sector, 1976

Funding and performance	Sector							
	Basic		Applied		Development		All R and D	
	million $	%	million $	%	million $	%	million $	%
Source of funds								
Federal government	3,210	67.6	4,825	54.1	12,095	49.5	20,130	52.8
Industry	715	15.1	3,645	40.8	12,190	49.9	16,550	43.4
Universities and colleges	525	11.1	250	2.8	40	0.2	815	2.1
Other nonprofit institutions	300	6.3	205	2.3	90	0.3	595	1.6
Total	4,750	100	8,925	100	24,415	100	38,090	100
Performer								
Federal government	750	15.8	2,250	25.2	2,600	10.6	5,600	14.7
Industry	775	16.3	4,800	53.8	20,925	85.7	26,500	69.6
Universities and colleges[a]	2,600	54.7	915	10.2	145	0.6	3,660	9.6
FFRDC's[b]	335	7.1	380	4.3	365	1.5	1,080	2.8
Other nonprofit institutions	290	6.1	580	6.5	380	1.6	1,250	3.3
Total	4,750	100	8,925	100	24,415	100	38,090	100

Notes:
[a]Includes state and local government funds for R and D.
[b]Federally-funded R and D centers administered by universities and colleges.
Source: National Science Foundation, *National Patterns of R and D Resources 1953–1976* (Washington, D.C.: GPO, 1976).

because of the uncertainty over commercial usefulness and the long-term commitment required, and now stands at about 15% of all basic research in the country. This decline has caused concern on the part of observers who note that basic research by industry in the past resulted in such innovations as the transistor and synthetic fibers.[3] *Applied research* is the activity concerned with technologies or processes proven through basic research as likely to lead to useful or marketable innovations. The industry share of applied research is about 41%, reflecting the lower uncertainty at this stage. *Development* is the translation of research into products and processes that are known to be technologically feasible. At this stage, in which most R and D is concentrated, industry's commitment is greatest (50%) and surpasses federal funding.

The federal role in American R and D has been principally in the area of national defense, which accounts for over one-third of all federal R and D outlays, and a large portion of the federal funding in the applied research and development categories.[4] In defense, space, energy, and medical research, federally funded R and D is performed primarily by private industry. In fact, nearly 70% of all American R and D is conducted by industry, principally in the applied research and development areas. Universities, on the other hand, do well over half of all basic research, for which the federal government supplies over two-thirds of the funding. Development, by contrast, is almost exclusively performed by industry.

Why Is Technological Change Important?

The question of the importance of technological change is easiest to answer with regard to private industry, which has the greatest incentives to innovate. Firms must perform R and D, generate new products and processes, and imitate and improve the innovations developed by other firms to remain competitive regionally, nationally, and internationally. For both innovators and early adopters, who concentrate their efforts on improvements, any competitive advantage to the firm is quite short because of the nature of the product life cycle. This cycle refers to the pattern of demand and profits for any product, indicating growth potential only in the early years of an innovation's life. Consequently, those firms which support any R and D effort aimed toward "innovation streams" rather than a single innovation have the best long-term prospects for success.[5]

The interest of national governments in technological change is usually one or more national goals or missions, including national defense, space exploration, or a cure for cancer. Such national technological goals can change, as in the recent shifts from space research to energy and medical research. Considerable governmental emphasis and effort is addressed to basic research, in addition to goal-oriented R and D, much of which is of an applied or development nature, as indicated for the U.S. in Table 31. To a large extent, however, government R and D is allocated to the same sectors as private R and D.[6] These sectors, especially aerospace, electronics, and scientific instruments, are known as high-technology industries, reflecting an innovative and growth orientation typical of their stage in an industry life cycle.[7] Mature industries, such as textile, paper and wood products, and metals, have fewer opportunities for technology-based growth and, consequently, a relatively small innovative effort.

Table 32. R and D Expenditures by U.S. Industries, 1975 and 1977

Industry group[a]	R and D expenditures		R and D % of sales	
	1975	1977	1975	1977
Aerospace	825.3	971.5	3.1	3.5
Automotive	2,508.3	3,389.5	2.7	2.4
Building materials	208.4	167.2	1.2	1.0
Chemicals	1,317.4	1,665.3	2.6	2.5
Conglomerates	499.1	665.8	1.5	1.5
Drugs	1,157.6	1,257.4	4.7	4.9
Electrical and electronics	1,345.1	1,284.0	3.0	2.5
Food	243.2	348.4	0.5	0.5
General machinery	288.1	340.4	1.7	1.7
Instruments	695.6	435.8	5.4	4.7
Miscellaneous manufacturing	480.1	540.5	1.8	1.9
Natural resources and fuels	715.2	853.4	0.4	0.4
Office equipment and computers	1,707.0	2,312.5	5.6	5.5
Paper	98.2	94.5	0.8	0.9
Steel	105.9	137.4	0.6	0.6
Textiles and apparel	30.3	29.2	0.4	0.5
Tires and rubber	319.4	329.7	1.9	1.7
Other	1,971.6	3,225.1	1.4	1.9
ALL INDUSTRIES	14,515.8	18,047.6	1.8	1.9

[a]The firms comprising each industry differ somewhat between 1975 and 1977, but are roughly comparable for the two dates.

Sources: "Where Private Industry Puts Its Research Money," *Business Week* (June 28, 1976), pp. 62-84; "R and D Spending Patterns for 600 Companies," *Business Week* (July 3, 1978), pp. 58-77.

In the U.S., the sectors doing the greatest amount of R and D are (1) those with the largest firms and (2) those in which the technological opportunities are greatest. For example, in Table 32, the automobile industry accounts for the greatest expenditure on R and D, but over 42% of it is done by a single firm, General Motors. Similarly, IBM is responsible for 48% of the R and D in the office machine and computers sector. When examined in relative amounts, such as R and D expenditures as a percentage of sales, the effect of large firms is reduced. Neither General Motors nor IBM allocates the highest percentage of its sales to R and D, although both are above their industry averages. Technological opportunities, or the ability to improve productivity and to generate new products, are a major incentive to perform R and D. Likewise, in some industries, R and D is essential to defensively compete with innovative competitors. These conditions prevail in the office equipment, drug, instrument, aerospace, chemical, and electrical industries, all of which are above average in terms of relative allocations to R and D. The R and D intensity of an industry tends to be rather stable over time, reflecting more the opportunities for successful innovation at an industry's life cycle stage than any wide fluctuations.[8] A recent trend away from technological opportunities to technological requirements is affecting many industries, such as automobiles, chemicals, and steel. Government regulations have begun to channel R and D away from commercial innovations toward meeting environmental and energy objectives.[9]

Why Is the Location of Science and Technology Important?

The economic activities that occur in any location have a number of short- and long-term consequences. Most of these can be captured in the concept of *comparative advantage*. Locations, like people, firms, and organizations, tend to specialize in an activity which can be performed there more cheaply or more productively. For locations, the types of specialization tend to be related to industry and product life cycles. For example, the Detroit area specializes in automobiles, Houston in petrochemicals, and the San Francisco Bay area in electronics. Even within industries, some locations attract high-technology, innovation and R and D activities, whereas more routine production activities are done in other, lower-cost locations. This concept of regional life cycles, reflecting the type and level of technological activities in a region, has been recognized for some time, but emphasized in the context of technological change only recently.[10] The significance of localized complexes of science and technology is that their attraction and generation of further high-technology activities tend to be maintained and even to increase over time.[11] Consequently, the comparative advantage of scientific and technological regions becomes greater relative to other regions corresponding to theories of cumulative urban and regional growth.[12]

The regional growth implications of R and D have received considerable theoretical attention from geographers.[13] Of particular concern are the decisions within large multi-product, multi-locational corporations that determine the location of administration, research, and various levels of production activity. As a firm's strategy results in an emphasis on different products and lines of business, each typically in a different stage in its product life cycle, the regions where the firm is located are affected. Consequently, the operations of a firm have distinct regional specialization and life cycle characteristics.[14] Headquarters functions, R and D, and high-technology manufacturing are activities that require highly skilled labor. Other activities, such as manufacturing standardized products which are in the later stages of their product life cycle, can be performed equally well in locations with low wages and low level of technological capability.[15] The locational decisions of individual firms, weighing skilled-labor requirements, costs, productivity, and other factors, cumulatively result in regional specialization in specific stages of the product life cycle.[16]

The remainder of this chapter focuses on the location of R and D and high-technology activities. These activities, which are more involved in the generation and production of new products and processes, are perhaps the most important indicators of the economic health of a region. Any conclusions about regional economic development, however, require considerable knowledge about the tendencies of economic activities with respect to their locations.

THE METROPOLITAN LOCATION OF SCIENCE AND
TECHNOLOGY IN THE U.S.

Available studies of the geography of science, technology, or R and D in the U.S. have been done at either the state or multistate regional scale. The SMSA, although generally considered the most appropriate designation of an urban economic region, is a difficult scale at which to study such data. Most federal data are compiled for states and regions, and these indicate a notable concentration of scientific and technological activities in a small number of states.[17] California, Maryland, Massachusetts, New Jersey, New York, and Virginia are consistently among the states most involved in R and D and related work. These areas of concentration, however, disguise the much more concentrated pattern found at the SMSA level.

Agglomeration Effects

The orientation of R and D to centers of population has intrigued analysts of the U.S. science and technology base.[18] As is the case for most, but not all, urban functions, larger cities tend to have more of nearly everything. This certainly appears to be the case for various measures of science and technology. Table 33 lists the top 10 SMSAs according to four measures of science and technology: (1) the number of industrial research laboratories; (2) the number of scientists and engineers employed in the federal government; (3) the amount of R and D performed by the colleges and universities in an SMSA; (4) the number of scientists and engineers employed in R and D work.[19] A comparison with population rank shows that the 7 largest metropolitan areas are among the top 10 in all listings except federal government scientific employees. In industrial R and D, in university research, and in overall location of scientists and engineers, the largest SMSAs are also the largest concentration of scientific activity. Federal scientific research, which is largely in defense and aerospace, is less concentrated in large metropolitan regions. The greatest concentration is in the Washington SMSA, where over 23% of all federal scientists and engineers in the country are located. No similar agglomeration occurs for any of the other science and technology indicators, for which the New York or Los Angeles regions are dominant.

In order to capture the effects of a range of science and technology variables and some determinants of their location in the 177 SMSAs, a factor analysis of 12 variables was performed (Table 34). The variables include measures of population, corporate headquarters location, scientists and engineers employed in various fields, such as business, colleges and universities, federal government, and R and D, university R and D, manufacturing base, and industrial R and D laboratories. As expected, the dominant dimension of the data reflects the effect of metropolitan area size and the corresponding agglomeration of scientific and technological activities in large urban regions. This factor accounts for 73.5% of the variance in the 12 variables. A second factor, accounting for 9.7% of the variance, combines industrial employment with an absence of federal science and technology or a doctoral labor force. Table 35 lists the 12 SMSAs which have factor scores

Table 33. Top 10 U.S. Metropolitan Areas Ranked by Indicators of Science and Technology and by Population[a]

Rank	Industrial research laboratories, 1975[b]	Scientists and engineers in federal government, 1974[c]	R & D performed by colleges and universities, 1976[d]	Scientists and engineers in R & D, 1974[c]	Population, 1970
1	New York SCSA	Washington	New York SCSA	Los Angeles SCSA	New York SCSA
2	Los Angeles SCSA	Huntsville	Boston SCSA	New York SCSA	Los Angeles SCSA
3	Chicago SCSA	Los Angeles SCSA	San Francisco SCSA	Washington	Chicago SCSA
4	Philadelphia SCSA	Philadelphia SCSA	Los Angeles SCSA	Philadelphia SCSA	Philadelphia SCSA
5	Boston SCSA	San Francisco SCSA	Philadelphia SCSA	San Francisco SCSA	Detroit SCSA
6	Washington	Dayton	Chicago SCSA	Chicago SCSA	San Francisco SCSA
7	San Francisco SCSA	Baltimore	Madison	Boston SCSA	Boston SCSA
8	Cleveland SCSA	New York SCSA	Detroit SCSA	Detroit SCSA	Cleveland SCSA
9	Detroit SCSA	Denver	San Diego	Seattle SCSA	Washington
10	Pittsburgh	Boston SCSA	Minneapolis-St. Paul	Cleveland SCSA	St. Louis

[a]SMSA unless designated; see Office of Management and Budget, *Standard Metropolitan Statistical Areas 1975* (Washington, D.C.: GPO, 1975). *Sources:* [b]Jacques Cattell Press, eds. *Industrial Research Laboratories of the United States*, 14th ed. (N.Y.: Bowker, 1975). [c]National Science Foundation, *Characteristics of the National Sample of Scientists and Engineers, 1974: Part 3: Geographic* (Washington, D.C.: GPO, 1976). [d]National Science Foundation, *Expenditures for Scientific Activities at Universities and Colleges, Fiscal Year 1976, Detailed Statistical Tables* (Washington, D.C.: NSF, 1976).

Table 34. Rotated Factor Loadings for Science and Technology Variables

Variables[a]	Factor 1 (aggolmeration)	Factor 2 (Federal/industrial)
S and E in business and industry, 1974[b]	.970	–
SMSA population, 1970[c]	.965	–
Industrial R and D laboratories, 1975[d]	.949	–
S and E in R and D employment, 1974[b]	.945	–
Corporate administrative offices, 1972[e]	.942	–
S and E in 4-year colleges and universities, 1974[b]	.939	–
S and E with doctorates, 1974[b]	.930	-.301
Research universities, 1976[f]	.920	–
Total university R and D, 1976[f]	.903	–
Business-funded university R and D, 1976[f]	.749	–
Percent labor force in manufacturing, 1970[g]	–	.793
S and E in federal government, 1974[b]	.358	-.679
Eigenvalues	8.666	1.312
Variance explained	73.5%	9.7%

– = less than .250. [a]S and E = scientists and engineers.

Sources: [b]National Science Foundation, *Characteristics of the National Sample of Scientists and Engineers*; see Table 33. [c]Office of Management and Budget; see Table 33. [d]Cattell Press; see Table 33. [e]U.S. Bureau of the Census, *Enterprise Statistics: 1972, Part 2, Central Administrative Offices and Auxiliaries* (Washington, D.C.: GPO, 1976). [f]National Science Foundation, *Expenditures for Scientific Activities at Universities and Colleges*; see Table 33. [g]U.S. Bureau of the Census, *County and City Data Book, 1972* (Washington, D.C.: GPO, 1973).

Table 35. SMSAs with Large Loadings on Agglomeration Factor

Agglomerations of science and technology
New York SCSA
Los Angeles SCSA
Philadelphia SCSA
Chicago SCSA
Boston SCSA
San Francisco SCSA
Detroit SCSA
Washington
Pittsburgh
Houston SCSA
Cleveland SCSA
Dallas-Forth Worth

greater than 1.0 on the agglomeration factor. They are generally the largest metropolitan areas in the country, although the Pittsburgh, Houston, and Dallas-Fort Worth regions have larger scores than several larger SMSAs. Scores for the second factor seemed to confound several influences and could not be interpreted readily in the context of science and technology.

Specialized Concentrations of Science and Technology

As illustrated above, a large portion of the location pattern of science and technology is directly related to urban area size. Consequently, controlling for population would eliminate simple size-ordered patterns and identify SMSAs which have relatively greater activity in science and technology. The standardized ranking (Table 36) is considerably different from that in Table 33. With a few exceptions, the large SMSAs do not have a large per capita science and technology base. To the extent that the standardized data give us different information from

Table 36. Top 10 U.S. Metropolitan Areas Ranked by Science and Technology Indicators Standardized by Population

Rank	Industrial research laboratories, 1975	Scientists and engineers in federal government, 1974
1	Boston SCSA	Huntsville
2	Washington	Washington
3	Lafayette-W. Lafayette	Newport News-Hampton
4	New York SCSA	Bakersfield
5	Worcester-Fitchburg	Dayton
6	Bridgeport-New Haven	Billings
7	Milwaukee SCSA	Knoxville
8	Austin	Davenport-Rock Island-Moline
9	Hartford-Springfield	Boise
10	Madison	Denver-Boulder
Rank	R and D performed by colleges and universities, 1976	Scientists and engineers in R and D, 1974
1	Lafayette-W. Lafayette	Huntsville
2	Champaign-Urbana	Washington
3	Madison	Albuquerque
4	Austin	Newport News-Hampton
5	Lincoln	Cedar Rapids
6	Lansing-E. Lansing	Champaign-Urbana
7	Tucson	Madison
8	Fargo-Moorhead	Pittsfield
9	Baton Rouge	Rochester
10	San Diego	Knoxville

Sources: See Table 33.

the agglomeration effect that was dominant in the unstandardized data, a more detailed examination of Table 36 is warranted.

The exceptions to the lack of large SMSAs are exhibited mainly in industrial R and D laboratories, where the Boston, Washington, and New York areas also have among the highest per capita figures. Two other types of SMSA appear in the top 10. First, some smaller SMSAs with major research universities (Purdue in Lafayette-West Lafayette, Yale in Bridgeport-New Haven, University of Texas in Austin, and University of Wisconsin in Madison) have attracted a relatively large number of industrial research facilities. Second, industrial centers such as Worcester-Fitchburg, Milwaukee, and Harford-Springfield have research facilities associated with manufacturing plants. Thus, in per capita terms, several different factors appear to affect the relative importance of industrial science and technology. It is interesting to observe that, with the exception of Austin, all of the top SMSAs in industrial research are located in the Manufacturing Belt of northeastern U.S. This region has been increasing its concentration of research activity despite declines in other economic indicators.[20]

Concentrations of federal scientists and engineers include only three SMSAs with over 500,000 population (Washington, Dayton, and Denver-Boulder). The other metropolitan areas have federal scientific facilities that are large relative to small urban population. For example, Huntsville, the largest such complex in the U.S., is the site of a major NASA installation in a SMSA of about 282,000 people. The federal science complexes, unlike the industrial R and D centers, tend to be located outside the Manufacturing Belt, with Dayton a major exception. In federal and industrial science and technology, then, two quite different location patterns are evident, in terms of both city size and region.

Colleges and universities perform most basic research in the U.S. and play an important part in the training and education of all scientists and engineers. The largest amount of university research takes place in the largest SMSAs and in the locations of major institutions such as Wisconsin and Minnesota (Table 33). However, in per capita terms (Table 36) the largest urban areas appear insignificant in comparison with small urban areas with large state research universities. The influence of large Middle West schools in small SMSAs, such as Purdue, Illinois, Wisconsin, and Michigan State, is joined by other small SMSA institutions, including Texas, Nebraska, Arizona, and North Dakota State. A per capita evaluation may overstate the importance of such institutions in small cities as centers of science and research.

Location of all scientists and engineers in R and D work combines the three previous types of science and technology. On a per capita basis, federal government facilities generate the largest complexes (Huntsville, Washington, Albuquerque, Newport News, and Knoxville). Two major university SMSAs (Champaign-Urbana and Madison) and three industrial research complexes (Cedar Rapids, Pittsfield, and Rochester) also generate large-scale R and D concentration. Again, one notes a regional differentiation between industrial and university centers of science and technology in the northeastern U.S. and federal facilities in the South.

The contributions apparent from the various influences of per capita science and technology indicators can be distinguished statistically by means of factor

Table 37. Rotated Factor Loadings for Per Capita Variables

Variables[a]	Factor 1 (university)	Factor 2 (federal)	Factor 3 (industry)
PC S and E in 4-year colleges and universities	.986	–	–
PC S and E in education	.984	–	–
PC university R and D	.951	–	–
PC S and E with doctorates	.926	.272	–
PC S and E in federal government	–	.908	–
PC S and E in R and D work	.289	.786	.477
PC total employed S and E	.468	.746	.419
PC S and E in business and industry	–	.350	.791
Percent labor force in manufacturing	–	-.345	.741
PC industrial R and D laboratories	–	–	.714
Eigenvalues	4.117	2.372	2.102
Variance explained	48.3%	24.1%	13.5%

– = less than .250.

[a]PC = per capita: values for SMSA per thousand population; S and E = scientists and engineers.

Sources: See Table 34.

analysis. The analysis of the unstandardized data indicated an agglomeration factor that dominated all other indentifiable effects. When population is controlled, the separate influences are much clearer, with three factors accounting for 85.9% of the variance (Table 37). The first factor, which explains 48.3% of the variance, is most closely associated with university research and education. The second factor, accounting for one-fourth of the variance, primarily measures federal and overall science and technology employment. The third factor is an industry dimension, with large loadings for science and technology indicators in business and industry as well as relative manufacturing base.

The locational pattern of the three dimensions allows a classification of SMSAs according to their dominant scientific and technological orientation (Table 38). The per capita data minimize the effect of R and D agglomeration; the metropolitan areas in Table 35 comprise the fourth category of orientation in science and technology. SMSAs which have a significant university dimension, on a per capita basis, are the locations of the universities of Illinois and Wisconsin, Purdue, and the Research Triangle institutions in North Carolina, in addition to Nebraska, Arizona, Texas, and Michigan State. All of these SMSAs have major state universities.[21]

Metropolitan locations of federal science and technology concentrations include Huntsville, Orlando, and Dayton (aerospace), Washington and Denver-Boulder (administration), Newport News (naval facilities), and Albuquerque and Knoxville (energy research). Of this group, only Dayton is located in the industrial Northeast; most federal concentrations are found in Sunbelt and western SMSAs.

Table 38. SMSAs with Large Loadings on University, Federal, and Industry Factors[a]

University	Federal	Industry	
Champaign-Urbana	Huntsville	Pittsfield	Mansfield
Lafayette-W. Lafayette	Washington	Cedar Rapids	Lynchburg
Madison	Newport News	Rochester	Pittsburgh
Raleigh-Durham	Albuquerque	Binghamton	Anderson
Lincoln	Knoxville	Boston SCSA	Worcester-Fitchburg
Tucson	Orlando	Hartford-Springfield	Milwaukee SCSA
Austin	Denver-Boulder	Reading	Lancaster
Lansing-E. Lansing	Dayton	Rockford	Cincinnati SCSA
	Billings	Allentown-Bethlehem	Chicago SCSA
	Boise	Jackson (Mich.)	Lafayette
		Bridgeport-New Haven	Los Angeles SCSA
		Cleveland SCSA	Muskegon
		Houston SCSA	Buffalo
		Philadelphia SCSA	York
		Erie	

[a]Loadings greater than +1.0, ranked by size of loading.

Concentrations of industrial science and technology contrast strongly with the federal pattern above. Of 29 SMSAs with loadings greater than +1.0 on the third factor, only 3 are found outside the Manufacturing Belt (Houston, Lynchburg, and Los Angeles). The predominance of northeastern cities on this factor illustrates the persistent concentration of science, technology, and high-skill manufacturing in the region, despite recent publicity about the area's economic decline. The results of this classification reinforce findings that the Northeast is not declining in science and technology (especially in industry) relative to other regions.[22]

The four types of metropolitan concentration of science and technology (agglomerations, university cities, federal concentrations, and industry centers) exhibit nearly mutually exclusive locational patterns. Science and technology agglomerations are generally the largest American metropolitan areas and, with few exceptions, are located in the Northeast and California. University concentrations tend to be small SMSAs with major state universities, and tend to be outside the core of the Manufacturing Belt. Federal science concentrations are all located outside the Northeast, representing a major commitment of federal spending on science and technology in the South and West. Finally, industry centers, several of which are also major agglomerations, are almost exclusively located in the Northeast, especially in the New England and Middle Atlantic states.

What can be said of metropolitan areas which are not concentrations of science and technology? They are of all sizes, have no major federal facilities or state universities, and they tend to be located in the South or the West. For example, Kansas City, Phoenix, Seattle, New Orleans, Miami, Atlanta, and Memphis are among the large (over 500,000 population) metropolitan areas that do not fall into any of the four categories. In all, 127 of the 177 SMSAs analyzed are not classified as significant concentrations of science and technology.

INFLUENCES ON THE LOCATION OF SCIENCE AND TECHNOLOGY

Science and technology, whether utilized in research, development, or the production of new products, rely heavily on an educated and skilled labor force. The locational preferences of scientists and engineers, therefore, play an important part in the location of research and high-technology operations. A recent survey of R and D scientists showed that climate, recreation, cultural aspects, good college or university, and adequate transportation are among the regional attributes most preferred.[23] Local or community-specific attributes considered most important included good schools, taxes and municipal services, and community attitudes. These attributes are most likely to be available in the suburbs of large metropolitan areas, which also tend to have a wide range of recreation, cultural, and educational amenities. This preference for urban areas with their range of services, on the one hand, and for noneconomic amenities on the other, characterizes a large portion of the location pattern of scientific and technical employment. The 12 science and technology agglomerations identified in the previous section, for example, are the locations of over 54% of all the scientists and engineers involved in R and D work in the U.S. In addition, as noted by Ullman over 25 years ago, the role of amenities is especially important in the location of footloose activities such as research and technology.[24] Thus, the favorable locations of universities and federal facilities have attracted industrial and other components of science and technology to the Research Triangle area (Raleigh-Durham), Austin, Dallas-Fort Worth, Denver-Boulder, and Tucson. The important role of the California metropolises, Los Angeles and San Francisco, is at least in part attributable to the climate and other amenities of the West Coast. The location of this technical labor force acts as a significant comparative advantage with respect to other regions in the conduct of further technological activities. First, agglomerations of skilled labor attract new performers of R and D. The technical personnel in universities and in government and private R and D form a labor pool which can be a resource for other research performers. Second, spin-offs or new enterprises can be formed out of research-intensive firms or organizations by entrepreneurs who decide to make use of their technical skills in a new business.

Two demand factors also influence the location of science and technology, especially the R and D laboratories of major corporate research performers. For many companies, R and D facilities tend to be located within or in close proximity to the corporate headquarters complex. Most companies with large R and D commitments tend to have at least one facility with scientific capabilities in the same metropolitan area as the headquarters. The second locational influence related to corporate demand or need for science and technology is a linkage with production or manufacturing units of the firm, i.e., R and D performed may be used and tested in production processes, thereby resulting in a tendency for R and D to be

Table 39. Influences on Location of Scientists and Engineers,
Total and in R and D Work

Independent variables[a]	Total scientists and engineers per 1,000 population	β	Scientists and engineers in R and D work per 1,000 population	β
S and E in business	0.802 (0.058)	.435	0.568 (0.030)	.587
S and E in education	0.950 (0.052)	.416	0.384 (0.037)	.320
S and E in federal government	0.941 (0.080)	.363	0.773 (0.042)	.567
S and E in R and D work	0.507 (0.085)	.266	—[b]	
Constant	602.344		−306.599	
F	743.09		302.15	
R²	.944		.837	

Notes: [a]S and E = Scientists and engineers; all variables measured per 1,000 population.
[b]Note included. Standard errors are in parentheses. All coefficients are significant at the .01 level. β = Standardized regression coefficients.

associated locationally with manufacturing facilities. Linkage with both headquarters and production functions is consistent with available knowledge of corporate organization and innovation strategies.[25]

The relative effects of these supply and demand factors on the location of scientists and engineers can be determined by means of multiple regression analyses. The first analysis uses scientists and engineers per 1,000 population as the dependent variable; the second uses scientists and engineers in R and D work per 1,000 population. Both are analyzed in per capita terms to control for population effects which dominate in unstandardized analyses (Table 34). The independent variables are the same as those employed in the factor analysis in Table 37, with the exception of SMSA population. The results for both analyses indicate that the three principal dimensions found in the classification analysis of the previous section all contribute to the overall pattern for U.S. metropolitan areas.

The location of the total number of scientists and engineers reflects the contribution of the three research-performing sectors, as well as R and D work in all of these areas (Table 39).[26] The relative importance of the variables (indicated by the standardized regression coefficients, β) indicates that business, education, federal, and R and D variables contribute, in that order, to this location pattern. Thus, at the national scale, SMSAs with scientists and engineers in business contribute most to the overall pattern, followed by education and the federal government. Least important in the overall pattern is the location of such persons engaged in R and D work. This analysis merely serves to indicate the relative role of these employment types, and ignores the distribution of those scientists and engineers who may not be involved in work related to technological change.

This constraint is indicated by the influences on the location of only scientists and engineers in R and D work, data which exclude college teachers who are not primarily researchers, and federal and industry employees not involved in R and D.

The analysis (Table 39) indicates that the relative contributions of the three dimensions of science and technology in R and D location are quite different than for all scientists and engineers. The relative location of scientists and engineers in business and in federal government, in that order, influence the location of R and D employment. Those in education least affect the pattern of R and D. This would appear to correspond to the priorities of the three groups of employers. R and D is a more important function to business and industry and to the federal government than it is to colleges and universities, in which only a small number of personnel are heavily involved in research.

These analyses reinforce the findings of the classifications reported in the previous section. Business and industry are major employers of scientists and engineers, and a large number of SMSAs (29) are significant concentrations of such highly-skilled people. Federal employment of scientists and engineers, while on a smaller scale than in industry, takes place on a very large scale in a small number of SMSAs (10 of 177). On the other hand, scientists and engineers in education are largely involved in teaching rather than research and, therefore, contribute least to the location of R and D. Of variables not significant in these analyses, most are strongly correlated with the variables in Table 39. Scientists and engineers in 4-year institutions and with doctorates, the number of R and D labs, the number of research universities, and university R and D are all represented in the business populations of scientists and engineers. Two other measures, manufacturing labor force and corporate administrative offices, appear to have little influence on the location of scientific and engineering personnel in comparison with the employment types.

FURTHER RESEARCH DIRECTIONS

The location of science and technology is still a largely unknown area of research, but one with considerable importance for understanding the effect of science and technology on regional development, the interaction between public and private sector R and D, and policy-making in science and technology. The role of technological change in the context of regional development has been the focus of considerable conceptual work, but almost no empirical research.[27] We need considerably more knowledge of where, how, and why scientific and technological activities cluster in order to understand the extent of their effect on regional change. For example, are certain locations more efficient for R and D than other locations? Are the regional effects of science and technology generally the same as those of other economic activities?

In the area of public-private sector interaction in R and D, the magnitude and distribution (sectoral and spatial) of public R and D effort may affect the relative amount of private R and D, in some cases encouraging more private R and D in other cases supplanting industrial effort. The relationship between the two R and D sectors is critical in the light of new research goals, such as energy conservation and supply, and in the effects of government regulation on private R and D. Do environmental regulations necessarily reduce productive R and D in favor of research that responds to government standards? What are the effects of government regulation on technological change in different industries?

Policy-making in science and technology tends to favor industries which are already highly research-intensive to contribute to defense, energy, and other goals. These allocations have effects on industries and regions that may be unanticipated or unintended. Understanding of the effects of R and D on technological change requires better data on allocations both by firms and by the federal government according to area of research and location. As economic and technological competitiveness become more important, the use of R and D as an instrument of federal policy may have increasing importance in future national and regional economic development.

NOTES

[1] For reviews of this literature, see E. J. Malecki, "Firms and Innovation Diffusion: Examples from Banking," *Environment and Planning A*, Vol. 9 (1977), pp. 1291-1305, and M. D. Thomas and R. B. LeHeron, "Perspectives on Technological Change and the Process of Diffusion in the Manufacturing Sector," *Economic Geography*, Vol. 51 (1975), pp. 231-57.

[2] For a detailed look at R and D in the United States, see National Science Board, *Science Indicators 1976* (Washington, D.C.: U.S. Government Printing Office, 1977).

[3] "The Breaking of U.S. Innovation," *Business Week* (Feb. 16, 1976), pp. 56-68; "The Silent Crisis in R and D," *Business Week* (March 8, 1976), pp. 90-92; and "R and D Spending Patterns for 600 Companies," *Business Week* (July 3, 1978), pp. 58-60.

[4] W. H. Shapley and D. I. Phillips, *Research and Development AAAS Report III* (Washington, D.C.: American Association for the Advancement of Science, 1978).

[5] R. A. Erickson, "The 'Lead Firm' Concept: An Analysis of Theoretical Elements," *Tijdschrift voor Economische en Sociale Geografie*, Vol. 63 (1972), pp. 426-37.

[6] K. Pavitt and W. Walker, "Government Policies Toward Industrial Innovation: A Review," *Research Policy*, Vol. 5 (1976), pp. 11-97.

[7] J. J. van Duijn, "The Long Wave in Economic Life," *De Economist*, Vol. 125 (1977), pp. 544-76.

[8] Ibid.

[9] F. A. Long, "Technological Innovation for the U.S. Civilian Economy: The Role of Government," in W. Goldstein, ed., *Planning, Politics, and the Public Interest* (N.Y.: Columbia University Press, 1978), pp. 120-24.

[10] W. R. Thompson, "The Economic Base of Urban Problems," in N. W. Chamberlain, ed., *Contemporary Economic Issues*, (Homewood, Ill.: Richard D. Irwin, 1969), pp. 1-47, and M. D. Thomas, "Growth Pole Theory, Technological Change, and Regional Economic Development," *Papers of the Regional Science Association*, Vol. 34 (1975), pp. 3-25; Thomas and LeHeron, op. cit., note 1.

[11] N. G. Clark, "Science, Technology and Regional Economic Development," *Research Policy*, Vol. 1 (1972), pp. 296-319, and R. R. Nelson and V. D. Norman, "Technological Change and Factor Mix over the Product Cycle: A Model of Dynamic Comparative Advantage," *Journal of Development Economics*, Vol. 4 (1977), pp. 3-24.

[12] A. R. Pred, *City-Systems in Advanced Economies* (N.Y.: John Wiley & Sons, 1977).

[13] Thomas, op. cit., note 10; Thomas and LeHeron, op. cit., note 1.

[14] F. E. I. Hamilton, "The Changing Milieu of Spatial Industrial Research," in F. E. I. Hamilton, ed., *Contemporary Industrialization: Spatial Analysis and Regional Development*

(London: Longman, 1978), pp. 1–19, and G. Krumme and R. Hayter, "Implications of Corporate Strategies and Product Cycle Adjustments for Regional Employment Changes," in L. Collins and D. F. Walker, eds., *Locational Dynamics of Manufacturing Activity* (N.Y.: John Wiley & Sons, 1975), pp. 325–56.

[15]Thompson, op. cit., note 10.

[16]Krumme and Hayter, op. cit., note 14.

[17]T. P. Murphy, *Science, Geopolitics, and Federal Spending* (Lexington, Mass.: D. C. Heath, 1971); M. Ye. Polovitskaya, "The Geography of Research and Development in the United States," *Soviet Geography: Review and Translation*, Vol. 11 (1970), pp. 784–96; and N. E. Terleckyj, *State of Science and Research: Some New Indicators* (Washington, D.C.: National Planning Association, 1976).

[18]M. Ye. Polovitskaya, "Some Aspects of the Influence of Scientific and Technical Progress on the Formation of Economic Regions (with particular reference to the United States)," *Soviet Geography: Review and Translation*, Vol. 9 (1968), pp. 813–29, and Terleckyj, ibid.

[19]The designation SMSA is used here generically and includes Standard Consolidated Statistical Areas (SCSAs) designated by the Office of Management and Budget for large urban regions (40 SMSAs are included in 13 SCSAs). See Office of Management and Budget, *Standard Metropolitan Statistical Areas 1975* (Washington, D.C.: U.S. Government Printing Office, 1975). In addition, several SMSAs were combined for analysis with adjacent metropolitan areas: Santa Barbara with the Los Angeles-Long Beach Anaheim SCSA, Hartford-Springfield-Waterbury-Meriden-New Britain, Bridgeport-New Haven, and Worcester-Fitchburg. A total of 177 metropolitan areas were left with adequate data on science and technology.

[20]M. Ye. Polovitskaya, "The Linkage Between the Distribution of R and D Activities and Industry (with particular reference to the United States)," *Soviet Geography: Review and Translation*, Vol. 19 (1978), pp. 244–52.

[21]Colleges and universities located in nonmetropolitan areas, such as Cornell, Indiana, Iowa, and Pennsylvania State, are omitted from this analysis; included are 148 of the top 200 research universities in fiscal year 1976. National Science Foundation, *Expenditures for Scientific Activities at Universities and Colleges, Fiscal Year 1976, Detailed Statistical Tables* (Washington, D.C.: National Science Foundation, 1976).

[22]Polovitskaya, op. cit., note 20.

[23]R. R. Jones, "Sites for Scientists," *Industrial Research*, Vol. 17 (May, 1975), pp. 57–60.

[24]E. L. Ullman, "Amenities as a Factor in Regional Growth," *Geographical Review*, Vol. 44 (1954), pp. 119–32.

[25]E. J. Malecki, "Corporate Organization of R and D and the Location of Technological Activities," unpublished manuscript, and E. B. Roberts, "Generating Effective Corporate Innovation," *Technology Review*, 80 (Oct./Nov., 1977), pp. 27–33.

[26]The step shown is that at which further independent variables explained less than 1% additional variance.

[27]National Academy of Sciences and National Academy of Engineering, *The Impact of Science and Technology on Regional Economic Development* (Washington, D.C.: National Academy of Sciences, 1969), and Clark, op. cit., note 11.

Chapter 10

Usages of Communication Technology and Urban Growth

Susan R. Brooker-Gross

An example of the technology inventions Malecki addressed in Chapter 9 is provided in the effect of communication technology on urban form and functions. This chapter posits the major question of whether or not the diffusion of telecommunication advances, such as multiple cable television, teleconferencing, videophones, and interfacing telephone and computer systems, will spread rapidly throughout the entire urban hierarchy and result eventually in the substitution of communication for commuting. The costs of constructing and operating such schemes need to be weighed vis-a-vis the demand for communication technology as a substitute for travel and face-to-face business transactions. The impacts of this technology will probably not be available everywhere, at least for some time; there will likely be both polynuclear and mononuclear propagations of these innovations. Advances in communication and technology are unlikely to mean an end to the metropolis as we have known it. What may result is a continuation of sprawl and growth into metropolitan peripheries and medium-sized urban places.

One scenario of the future foresees humankind freed from the constraints of the city through the power of new communications technology. In this scenario, cities are seen as undesirable and no longer necessary. One forecaster, Dennis Gabor, has depicted the U.S. as "overurbanized," its trend to megalopolitan living as "against all reason." He has stated that the traditional reason for people to agglomerate in cities—accessibility to jobs—has disappeared. Transacting business face-to-face "has become an anachronism with the invention of the mail, let alone with the invention of the telephone, telex, facsimile transmission, and the Picturephone."[1]

Although Gabor's negative reaction to the metropolis as a place to live is not shared by everyone, anti-urbanism has a long tradition in American culture.[2] If one predicts an end to the ties which bind people to the metropolis, if one foresees an increase in economic freedom to choose a residence outside metropolitan areas, then the anti-urban tradition could well find a greater expression in reality, and promise the eventual demise of the metropolis. Recent increases in migration to exurban environments, with people escaping the city while maintaining ties to urban jobs, support the notion that the metropolis is not a preferred environment.[3] There are, of course, reasons other than employment for maintaining ties to urban settings. People's reasons for living in cities are varied and complex. Even someone taking such an extreme position as Gabor's acknowledges that access to cultural amenities may encourage and maintain urban agglomeration. Gabor, however, did not attach much significance to the role of amenities. He stated that access to jobs has been the primary reason for living in cities, and that this reason is outmoded.

While recognizing the fact that employment may not be the *only* significant cause for agglomeration, for the purposes of discussion, let us accept Gabor's claim that it is the primary cause. Will communications technology break these employment ties to the city? Probably not. The prognosis of the doomed metropolis, the replacement of commuting to work by "communicating to work," and the realization of the ideal small-town or rural environment for rearing children and other worthy pursuits is based on several other unarticulated assumptions.[4] These underlying assumptions are not entirely correct. To get a better grasp of the potential effect of communications technology on the metropolis, this chapter will make explicit and critique two of these assumptions: (1) that communications technologies will become available everywhere at once and (2) that use of communications technology is in fact substitutable for face-to-face contact.

SPATIAL PATTERNS OF SUPPLY

The first assumption is that the new technologies will become available everywhere at once. This assumption is rarely explicitly articulated, but it is equally rare to find a discussion of the process of spatial diffusion of these new systems of communications. Emphasis is usually placed on the willingness of potential users to adopt the new technologies, without much discussion of how these technologies will become available for adoption. In short, the spatial components of provision and adoption have been largely ignored.

Most published research has emphasized the social acceptability of new means of communications, asking whether potential users could be trained or convinced to adopt the technology. More will be said of this research under discussion of the second assumption (substitutability). But even in adopter decision research, the problem is rarely couched as a spatial diffusion process. Perhaps the spatial components of adoption are too uncertain to enter into the forecasts. If current research and propaganda are successful, potential adopters may be sufficiently informed and persuaded such that the adoption sequence is nearly instantaneous. But before adoption can occur, the facilities must be available. The spatial components of the diffusion of availability are far less likely to be trivial.

Patterns of supply can be inferred, to some extent, from the diffusion of past innovations in communications technology. In most of the forecast technologies, a complex infrastructure is required. Innovations such as cable television, videotelephone, and computer communications require networks of distribution, just as do television and radio networks and the telephone. Even the mail must be picked up, sorted, routed, and delivered. Radio and television stations need transmitting equipment, and broadcasting networks require inter-connecting linkages among stations. Telephone lines must be strung and provisions made for switching between customers and for tapping into a long-distance system for a local system. The technological requirements of the futuristic technologies involve the upgrading of existing routes of communication, or adding new routes. In the U.S., these routes have traditionally been either government maintained (the mail, the roadways) or managed by private enterprises subject to government regulation (radio, television, telephone). Because most of the new technologies have greater similarity to the current electronic media, they are likely to be provided by private enterprise. Emphasis needs to be placed on the willingness and ability of private enterprise to provide the innovation infrastructure, as well as on the businessman's or consumer's willingness to use the technologies.

The nature of the required infrastructure will vary somewhat with the technology in question. The next section outlines some of the devices forecast for future use, and the kind of infrastructure each requires.

The Technological Opportunities

One technology widely cited for the future is interactive cable television. Although cable television is now largely a one-way, one-to-many medium, it already has the capacity to be much more. First, channel capacity is being expanded, with new systems required to carry a minimum of 20 channels by the FCC. Some systems have the capacity to carry 30 channels or more. Thirty channels is the approximate number of television channels that one coaxial cable can now transmit clearly, but a given cable television system can use more than one coaxial cable in its system to double or triple its capacity. Systems existing in Seattle and San Francisco have reported capacities for 30 channels, while a system in San Jose has reported the technical capacity to carry 75 channels.[5] In the future, technological improvements in cables may increase capabilities to over 100 channels per cable, allowing even greater variety in channels.

Second, some channels may be used for viewer feedback. This feedback would enable "instant" public opinion polls, or even voting via one's cable television. The two-way capacity would also enable the householder to conduct financial transfers or to order consumer goods through a "video catalog." Television could potentially replace many banking and shopping trips.[6] Many cable television systems have plans to implement two-way capabilities, and some systems already have two-way capacity—for example, in Flagstaff, Ariz.; Frostburg, Md.; and in part of Manhattan.[7]

Cables need to be wired directly into the facilities of the potential users. For the most part, predicted use of cable television centers about home usage. Complete adoption must be preceded by complete wiring. Lines extended to dispersed settlements are expensive—there are no customers to pay for the extention along the way, while lines in more densely settled areas are tapped into and paid for by a continuous line of customers. Another infrastructural factor is the ease with which the wiring can be accomplished. Newly developed areas facilitate laying of underground cables during construction, while older, established areas present more problems.

A second technology of the present and future is the videotelephone. Unlike interactive cable television, the videotelephone's primary uses are assumed to be in business. Conducting routine business over the telephone has long been a way of life. But less routinized operations require greater interpersonal information, some visual as well as aural input. The videotelephone is seen as a mechanism to fill this gap. If meetings between more than two people in more than two places are required, a videoconference system may be employed.[8] A network similar to the present switched telephone network would be required if mass coverage and flexibility were to be built into the system.

Bell Telephone's version of the videotelephone requires use of existing telephone lines to transmit the audio portion of the communication link. The video portion requires a greater bandwidth, but regular telephone lines can still be used over fairly short distances. Widespread use of videotelephone, however, would require expensive upgrading of the lines. The videotelephone's future would seem to be an extension and repetition of the history of the telephone, at least in the nature of the supplier and paths of extension.

Another option for videotelephone usage is a non-switched system unique to one business firm. The firm may install permanent lines between each of its fixed installations to facilitate communication, or perhaps only between its headquarters location and its branch facilities.

A third type of technology is data transmission, and the use of computers as communications devices.[9] Data transmission has already witnessed phenomenal growth, and likely will continue to do so. The efficiency of data transmission is relatively low, however, with a small proportion of capacity usually used. Computers themselves are used on a time-shared basis, but the transmission lines are less often shared.[10] Kimbel cites other problems with the present-day interfacing of computer transmissions and the telephone transmission lines. The two systems are not inherently compatible, so that the most efficient uses of the computing systems are not being made. Problems include inappropriate pricing philosophy, the need for costly modems, low transmission speeds, and saturation of existing telephone lines. If computer transmissions are to become "as abundant and as effortless to employ as electric power is today," then upgrading of transmission lines will become necessary.[11]

Many other types of innovations already exist that are forecast to become important in the future, but these three are among those already used to some extent, and are most tangible to the user. Other types of improvements in technologies include systems to improve the speed and capacity of the network of interconnection, such as wave guides and lasers.

Possible Futures vs. a Probable Future

The recitation of possibilities and technical realities in communications systems incites the more extreme of futurists to predict great social upheavals. Certainly these technologies have potential to upturn society if instantly implemented. A more probable prediction would include gradual change as some of these innovations diffuse across the country.

To view the implementation of new systems as a diffusion process, we need to return to the idea that the infrastructure for each system will be provided by an entrepreneur or set of entrepreneurs. The corporations providing the infrastructure function are essentially diffusion propagators.

One important constraint these diffusion propagators face is the profitability of installing infrastructure in a given place. Given this constraint, what is the spatial pattern of the diffusion of infrastructure likely to be? In fact, will a particular device be installed at all? Initial implementation will depend on the communication entrepreneur's risk-taking decisions. The entrepreneur must be fairly certain of a sufficient number of early clients. He will thus be interested in the social acceptance of the innovation, and may try to persuade potential users that the new system is indeed valuable. This situation of persuasion seems to be the state of the art at present, with interests such as AT&T and GTE researching the social acceptability of some of the new technologies.

If a new communications system does get started, how will it diffuse? A look at Brown's analysis of spatial patterns of the diffusion of the *supply* of innovations in general is helpful at this point. Brown cites two polar types of suppliers. One is the "polynuclear propagator," the other, the "mononuclear propagator." In the case of the "polynuclear propagator," an innovation is supplied by a "diffusion agency" whose location is coincident with a local entrepreneur.[12] In past communications innovations, many local radio and television stations fall into this category. In the case of the "mononuclear propagator," a centralized authority plans the location of multiple facilities for the provision of the innovation.[13] In the past, private concerns of the telegraph, telephone, and parcel delivery services fit this category, as does the public service of the mail.

The strategies for the implementation of innovation supply vary between two types. A "polynuclear propagator" decision maker is likely to be located in a fixed location, and analyze the alternate business opportunities in that location. Thus a diffusion agency of this type could be located in nearly any place, or any sized city, as long as the place met the threshold size required for the diffusion agency to stay in business.[14]

In the mononuclear propagation situation, one would expect the centralized decision maker to choose among several locations to install a diffusion agency. The most lucrative alternative would usually be chosen first. Thus, the market with the greatest potential would be first to have the innovation available. In most cases, these "best" markets would be the largest cities.[15]

Brown cautions against using city size as an invariable surrogate for market potential, however, He cites factors such as institutional constraints in larger cities and the organizational structure of the centralized propagator as limiting factors. Nonetheless, city size would be an important consideration.[16]

Which of these two polar types are most likely to be the case with the predicted new technologies in communications? Once again, we may find the past to be the key to the future. As mentioned above, both types have been present in the past. As larger corporations increase their economic dominance, and as the communications technology becomes ever more sophisticated and requires increasing amounts of initial capital, it becomes all the more likely that companies will account for the bulk of the innovations supply.

The case of cable television is a good example. The earliest cable systems were of the polynuclear type. Individual entrepreneurs set up an antenna and wired customers' television sets into it. As the sophistication of cable increased, an increasing proportion of the systems was begun or bought by centralized propagators. In Pennsylvania, the state with the first cable systems and one of the states with the most systems today, "group" ownership controls 80% of the cable systems (group ownership implies a company owning several systems, a mononuclear propagator). In addition, these groups control an even larger proportion of systems within large city market areas ("Top 100" are the largest 100 markets in the nation, as designed by the FCC) (Table 40).

The more sophisticated the system, the more likely it is to be owned by a group as well (Tables 41 and 42). Group ownership of systems having more than the traditional 12 channels is 90%, while their overall ownership is only 80%. Similarly, although the correlation between group ownership and two-way systems is small ($C = 0.03$), groups still dominate the two-way installations (Table 42).

In the case of videotelephone and computer networks, again we are likely to see the predominant influence of large corporations, inasmuch as these networks

Table 40. Group Ownership by Market Size, Pennsylvania[a]

Market size	Group ownership	Not group ownership	Total
Top 100 markets:			
Number	266	41	307
Row %	87	13	
Column %	71	44	65
Not top 100 markets:			
Number	111	53	164
Row %	68	32	
Column %	29	56	35
Total	377	94	471
Row %	80	20	

[a]Contingency coefficient, $C = 0.22$.

Source: Television-Factbook, Services Volume, No. 45, (Washington, D.C., Television Digest, Inc., 1976).

Table 41. Ownership by Channel Capacity, Pennsylvania[a]

Channel capacity	Group ownership	Not group ownership	Total
Twelve or fewer channels			
Number	288	84	372
Row %	77	23	
Column %	76	89	79
More than 12 channels			
Number	89	10	99
Row %	90	10	
Column %	24	11	21
Total	377	94	471
Row %	80	20	

[a]Contingency coefficient, C = 0.13.
Source: See Table 40.

are intimately linked with the telephone network. Already, the telephone companies have experimented with the systems, with the largest markets being used.

The spatial pattern of diffusion is likely to be downward through the urban hierarchy, until a minimum population size for profitability is met. Past diffusion sequences support this prediction. Even the diffusion of polynuclear-propagated commercial television stations in the United States was largely hierarchical.[17] The diffusion of long-distance telephone lines, controlled primarily by the Bell system,

Table 42. Ownership by One-way/Two-way Systems, Pennsylvania[a]

System	Group ownership	Not group ownership	Total
One-way systems:			
Number	341	87	428
Row %	80	20	
Column %	90	93	91
Two-way systems:			
Number	36	7	43
Row %	84	16	
Column %	10	7	9
Total	377	94	471
Row %	80	20	

[a]Contingency coefficient, C = 0.03.
Source: See Table 40.

Table 43. Comparison of Two Cable Television Systems
(Channel capacity[a])

California cable television system (1976)				
Community population	<12	12	13–30	31–75
0–5,000	11	65	26	1
5,001–50,000	0	94	55	6
50,001–2,000,000	0	20	33	5
Wyoming cable television systems (1976)				
Community population	<12	12	13–30	31–75
0–5,000	0	14	0	0
5,001–50,000	0	12	12	0
50,001–2,000,000	0	0	0	0

[a]"Channel capacity" indicates the number of channels the cable system was designed to carry, and is often greater than the number of channels actually utilized. Channel capacity may be used as an indication of the technological sophistication of the system. Overall, there are more sophisticated systems in California than there are in Wyoming, and larger cities have more sophisticated systems than do smaller cities. Few very small settlements (less than 1,000 population) have access to cable television at all.

Source: See Table 40.

expanded through the interconnection of major cities first.[18] One-way cable television is sometimes said to be an exception to the diffusion down the urban hierarchy, but if one analyzes its functions separately, it is not an exception. Initial cable systems were a continuation of the diffusion of television down the urban hierarchy, with polynuclear propagators making television signals available in areas too small for their own broadcasting station, and too distant to receive signals from larger cities. Later cable systems, increasingly group-owned, continued the diffusion of *variety* in television far down the urban hierarchy to cities too small to have several local broadcasting stations. Future cable systems will diffuse two new functions—two-way capability and community access to television broadcasting through the even greater number of channels available. It is likely that the basic sequence of diffusion will continue to be down the urban hierarchy. Channel capacity may be the best indicator of the future of cable at present. Greater channel capacities are already more likely to be found in larger urban places (Table 43).

Heeding Brown's caution that city size is not the only measure of market potential, one should note that ease of "wiring" will play an important role in the diffusion sequence. New towns and new suburbs and other places of rapid growth and physical change will most easily accommodate the construction of the requisite infrastructure. In some places, construction problems and political barriers may be sufficiently less in smaller cities to offset a smaller population size.

A final question in predicting the likely diffusion sequence is how far down the hierarchy of settlements will these innovations go? The telephone and the mail are presently ubiquitous, and radio and television nearly so. Will the future systems also become ubiquitous? It would be wise to first ask how the present-day systems achieved nearly complete dispersion. The answers are more political and technological than economic.

The telephone and the mail systems gained complete dispersal largely through government subsidization. Belief that all persons should have access to a communications system is the foundation of the U.S. postal services, a monopoly service. Mail delivery in densely settled areas can subsidize more costly delivery to thinly settled areas. Private companies have so far not succeeded in changing this argument. The Postal Service continues its monopoly, claiming that private mail carriers would skim off the "cream"—the large cities—and the postal deficit would climb higher yet, trying to maintain equitable service to rural areas.[19]

The telephone's downward diffusion to rural areas was likewise aided by the governmental Rural Electrification Administration.[20] The price structure is not subsidized in the same way as the mail system, and rural customer charges are often based on distance ranges from a central office. Technological improvements in telephone service, common in cities and towns, are often still unavailable in rural areas.

The near ubiquitousness of radio and television does not stem from any direct government subsidy, although subsidized rural electrification was a prerequisite, and government regulations on radio transmissions at least are designed to afford access to powerful city stations even in isolated country areas. Technology is more important in explaining small town and rural access to radio and television. Broadcasting systems do not have to be delivered directly (by wires or postmen) to a consumer's home. Even at considerable distance, signals can be picked up from the airwaves. The distance can be augmented either by cable television systems, if population size and density makes that economical, or by individual antenna systems.

The systems proposed for the future do require physical networks rather than use of the airwaves. For a long time to come, they are also more likely to be considered luxuries than necessities, and, as such, will not gain public subsidization to extend them to isolated small towns and rural areas. Thus the systems will reach some threshold of minimum population size and minimum population density.

THE DEMAND FOR COMMUNICATIONS: SUBSTITUTABILITY

The second underlying assumption is that use of communications technology can be substituted for face-to-face contact, and thus for transportation. If we are to envision the futurist's scenario of a defunct metropolis with people communicating to work instead of commuting, with consumers shopping and banking and being entertained on their home cable TV console, and with businessmen teleconferencing instead of physically conferencing, then we must accept that people are willing to substitute communication for travel. Certainly some would-be trips can be replaced by communication. The telephone now carries routine messages, inquiries, and arrangements that would otherwise have required a trip. Interactive cable television may well replace a routine trip to the bank. Videotelephone may replace routine conferences. And computer linkages can accomplish transportation of various sorts of information. It has been estimated that only 16% of urban vehicle-miles are for the purpose of transporting goods and therefore not replaceable by communication.[21] Some of the remaining 84% of urban vehicle-miles are travel for pleasure, but most are business-oriented, largely journey to work. Some proportion of work trips are not substitutable, but many managerial and clerical work trips may eventually be eliminated by the substitution of communications.

These managerial and clerical workers are the people who may communicate to work. One forecast sees communication replacing travel to work in a sequence of four stages.[22] In the first stage, we have a totally centralized corporation. All operations of the corporation occur at the same site. In the second stage, segments or branches of a corporation are physically removed from the main location. While this fragmentation does decentralize activity, it does not lead to any reduction in urban travel. Workers still need to commute to the outlying facility, and some physical as well as telecommunication contacts must be maintained between the outlying facility and the main office. The third stage is far more decentralized, and may in fact cause some reduction in work trip mileage. Workers would report to their employer's local work center closest to their home, regardless of their specific job. There they would "communicate" to their jobs through a computer communication system. Although each person still would travel to work, the trip would be shorter. In the final stage, the worker need not travel at all. In a "wired city," each person's home may have access to a switched network of coaxial cables, enabling a mix of a videotelephone communication, two-way cable television, and access to a computer data transmission network. The worker could perform his job through his home "communication center."[23]

For both economic and cultural reasons, realization of all stages of this forecast seems unlikely. Disperson of activity into segmented and branched facilities has already taken place, increasing the necessity for both communication and travel. Dedicated substitutionists would suppose that increased use of videoconferencing would eliminate the need for travel between main and branch office. They maintain that the businessman can be persuaded to accept videoconferencing as a substitute for conferences, and that initial resistance is overcome by usage.[24] Others have stated that social and psychological resistances are too strong to achieve much substitution.[25] A more moderate view is that the substitutability is task-dependent—that the medium of communication does not affect tasks involving coordination of facts or exchange of information, but that face-to-face contact is necessary for situations involving conflict or situations where a personal judgment needs to be made.[26] Indeed, surveys show that present tasks are accomplished in this manner, with the telephone calls dominantly used for single-purpose contacts involving exchanges of information. Face-to-face contacts are employed for general discussions, bargaining, and multi-subject contacts.[27]

The costs of communication vs. travel must also be taken into consideration. While communication costs may not be as sensitive to distance as are transportation costs, communication costs are far more sensitive to the use of time. Of course, there are costs incurred by the loss of time spent in travel to a conference, or to oversee operations in one branch facility or another, but once the conference

Table 44. Conference Costs with Origin at Los Angeles

Destination	Duration of conference	Costs[a]	
		Travel	Common carrier
San Francisco	2 hours	$ 72.50	$ *53.70*
	4 hours	*72.50*	117.10
Chicago	1 day	$370.53	$*214.94*
	2 days	*395.53*	429.88
New York	2 days	$498.23	$*450.42*
	3 days	*523.23*	675.63

[a]Lower costs in italics.
Source: Nilles et al., note 28, p. 133.

participant or the business supervisor has arrived, the costs of talking are negligible. Communication links, on the other hand, incur costs in the reverse order. Connection costs are small but costs of communicating increases with the amount of time spent. Estimates of costs of travel vs. costs of telecommunicating for business purposes show travel often to be the less expensive mode. Conferences of short duration and long distances may be cheaper if completed via presently available communications systems, but the longer the duration and the shorter the distance, the more economical travel becomes (Table 44).[28] If other technologies become more widely implemented, they still may not change the cost relationship between travel and communications. Dickson and Bowers have estimated costs of travel vs. costs of videophone conferencing. In order to justify (on the basis of cost) a videophone call between New York and Chicago lasting 6.6 hours, a participant would have to value his own time at $125 per hour or more.[29] Of course, considerations other than cost may make videoconferences feasible under special conditions. Widespread use, however, would await economic justification. Thus communication systems may be appropriate for some uses but highly inefficient for others.

For intraurban communication, new technologies may have only a moderate impact on decentralizing business activity. Current geographic distributions of telecommunication and travel contacts are similar. Comparing office workers' telephone contacts with face-to-face meetings in London, Goddard found very similar distribution of destinations (Table 45). Contact patterns of telephone calls and meetings reinforce one another more than they complement one another. The telephone has a slight edge in maintaining contacts at intermediate distances (Greater London to the entire U.K.), while face-to-face meetings predominate by a small margin at either extreme (within Central London and in overseas contacts).[30]

Communication Systems and Increases in Travel

The substitution argument does not take into account the *increase* in travel encouraged by communications technology.[31] As it becomes easier, more personally

Table 45. Geographical Distribution of Telephone and Face-to-Face Contacts

Destination	% of telephone contacts	% of meetings	N respondents
Within Central London[a]	58	64	705
Within Greater London[a]	19	15	
Within Southeast region	8	5	
Within U.K.	12	9	
Overseas	3	7	

[a]Mutually exclusive categories.
Source: Goddard, note 27, p. 164.

rewarding, and cheaper to maintain contacts at a distance, it is likely that trips will be made to those distance places. As decentralization occurs, trips will be made between increasingly removed places. Face-to-face contact will periodically supplement communication over distance. The transportation linkages between cities and between nodes within urban areas must be sufficiently efficient to sustain the contacts. Once again, some minimum nodality would be the prerequisite for efficient linkages between places, and upper levels of the urban hierarchy will be favored over lower levels, as will major intraurban nodes over minor nodes.

In addition, there is another branch of communications innovations which encourage travel—mobile communications. These systems are designed both to facilitate and encourage transportation, and to communicate with people in moving vehicles. Ever since the telegraph was first used to enhance the safety and efficiency of the railroad, communications have benefitted mass transportation. Today, computerized systems are increasingly used in intraurban mass transit, to coordinate buses and rapid transit systems. Mobile communication improvements are also increasingly applied to private transportation systems.[32] Citizens' Band radio has made the motorist's journey faster and safer—not to mention more entertaining. Likewise the businessman no longer needs to sit at his desk to be near the telephone if he has a telephone in his automobile.

These mobile communications systems can help transportation become more efficient, and thus an even better supplement to communications over distance. Like other sophisticated communications technology, the more sophisticated transportation-related communications systems are likely to be first found in the largest markets. Even the relatively unsophisticated Citizens Band gives the motorist more and better information on high traffic volume routes than on lesser-traveled paths.

IMPLICATIONS FOR URBAN GROWTH

It should be evident that the new technologies do not spell the end of the metropolis, but neither do they propel us back into a compact, densely settled city with clear boundaries. Rather, they would seem to reinforce the trend to "middle-range urbanism," the continued sprawl of metropolises, and the growth of smaller cities and large "small towns."

The arguments presented here for a diffusionist perspective on availability of the communications technologies, and against a total substitution of communications for travel, roughly correspond to the interurban and intraurban effects of the innovations. The predicted sequence of spatial diffusion has implications for the growth of places in the urban system. Some minimum population size and density will be required to implement these new technologies. The systems will thus not encourage dispersion of the population (presumably the new technologies would be attractors of growth rather than repellers). Furthermore, the technologies are likely to be found first in the largest markets. Advantages in communication already possessed by larger metropolises will be reinforced before the advantages diffuse to smaller places. These advantages should facilitate growth of the metropolis. Decentralized clusters may be the first areas where technologies are implemented. Such decentralized clusters of either residences or businesses may be particularly attractive to the "diffusion propagator" if they are being newly built and thus facilitate installation of the required wiring infrastructure.

Networks linking city to city are also likely to be pairs of the larger metropolises. Such a prediction fits with Janelle's concept of "relative advantage."[33] Routes with the greatest potential for profit and volume of traffic will receive the first improvements, and thus in a pattern of circular reinforcement will continue to be the most utilized. The national importance of the upper levels of the urban hierarchy would initially be reinforced.

As the technologies diffuse down the urban system, smaller metropolitan centers would become increasingly accessible via communications to the larger metropolises, enhancing their viability as growth centers. Indeed the processes of (1) downward diffusion of the innovations, (2) continued preference for and migration to smaller urban places, and (3) presumed relative cost decreases in use of communications systems as the technology improves may all be mutually reinforcing and supportive of growth in the metropolitan peripheries and in nonmetropolitan cities and towns. The diffusion propagators, having established systems in the most profitable markets, would seek out the next most profitable set of markets. At the same time, these smaller markets may have been growing in size, making them more attractive markets. The communications technologies may also become more affordable, thus expanding all markets and lowering the thresholds of size and density for implementation. When thus combined with other trends, the spatial diffusion of the new technologies may favor growth in mid-sized urban places and in metropolitan peripheries.

The argument against complete substitution of travel by communications would likewise seem to favor a continuance of the trends to dispersed centralization within the metropolis, but would not favor total decentralization. Face-to-face contact will continue to be required for sensitive negotiations. Businessmen frequently involved in matters involving such judgments of other businessmen will continue to agglomerate near one another. Their agglomerated cluster may be free of other locational constraints, however, since nonsensitive matters can be handled through telecommunications. A pattern of decentralized clusters will be fostered, a pattern consistent with other locational trends in the metropolis.

In summary, the forecast new communications technologies will reinforce trends toward dispersal and decentralization, but not in the extreme manner predicted by Gabor and others. Clustering to achieve minimum population size and density will still be required, but, through time, this minimum size will decrease. The communication systems can maintain routine contacts among clusters, both among those clusters that are cities and among clusters within the metropolis.

But travel between clusters will still be required from time to time. As communications reinforce bonds over space, occasional face-to-face validation of those bonds would occur. Barring severely restrictive constraints from energy costs or regulation, the overall mobility of society is likely to increase.

NOTES

[1] Dennis Gabor, "Social Control Through Communications," Chap. 7, in *Communications Technology and Social Policy: Understanding the New "Cultural Revolution"*, George Gerbner, Larry P. Gross, and William H. Melody, eds. (New York: John Wiley & Sons, 1973), p. 86.

[2] Yi-Fu Tuan, *Topophilia* (Englewood Cliffs, N.J.: Prentice-Hall, 1974), pp. 193, 237.

[3] For example, see Curtis C. Roseman, *Changing Migration Patterns Within the United States* (Resource Papers for College Geography No. 77-2. Washington, D.C.: Association of American Geographers, 1977).

[4] William J. Bray and Alex S. L. Reid, "Telecommunications Developments in the United Kingdom and Their Social Implications," *IEEE Transactions on Communications*, Vol. 23 (1975), p. 1078.

[5] *Television Factbook*, Services Volume (Washington, D.C., 1976), "Directory of CATV Systems," pp. 397a–815a.

[6] Kas Kalba, "Telecommunications and Human Development: An Emerging Strategy," in *The Environment of Human Settlements: Human Well-being in Cities*, Vol. 2, Proceedings of the Conference held in Brussels, Belgium, April 1976 (Oxford: Pergamon Press, 1976); John W. Wentworth, "Broadcasting Technologies," Chap. 2 in Gerbner et al., op. cit., note 1, p. 34; and Richard C. Harkness, "Innovations in Telecommunications and Their Impact on Urban Life," Chap. 2 in *Innovations for Future Cities*, Gideon Golany, ed. (N.Y.: Praeger, 1976), pp. 21–28.

[7] *Television Factbook*, pp. 397a–815a, op. cit., note 5.

[8] Edward M. Dickson, "Potential Impacts of the Video Telephone," *IEEE Transactions on Communications*, Vol. Com-23 (1975), pp. 1172–1176; David Coll et al., "Multidisciplinary Applications of Communication Systems in Teleconferencing and Education," *IEEE Transaction on Communications*, Vol. Com-23 (1975), pp. 1104–1118; Michael G. Ryan, "The Influence of Teleconferencing Medium and Status on Participants' Perception of the Aestheticism, Evaluation, Privacy, Potency, and Activity of the Medium," *Human Communication Research*, Vol. 2 (1976), pp. 255–261.

[9] Arthur D. Hall, III, "Trends in Switched Services," Chap. 2 in Gerbner et al., op. cit., note 1, p. 16.

[10] James T. Martin, "Communication and Computers," Chap. 1 in Gerbner et al., op. cit., note 1, p. 10.

[11] Dieter Kimbel, "An Assessment of the Computer-Telecommunications Complex in Europe, Japan, and North America," Chap. 11 in Gerbner et al., op. cit., note 1, pp. 149-151.

[12] Lawrence A. Brown, "The Market and Infrastructure Context of Adoption: A Perspective on the Spatial Diffusion of Innovation," Studies in the Diffusion of Innovation Discussion Paper No. 1 (Columbus: Department of Geography, Ohio State University, 1974), p. 5.

[13] Ibid.

[14] Ibid.

[15] Ibid.

[16] Ibid.

[17] Brian J. L. Berry, "Hierarchical Diffusion: The Basis of Developmental Filtering and Spread in a System of Growth Centers," in Man, Space, and Environment, Paul Ward English and Robert C. Mayfield, eds. (N.Y.: Oxford University Press, 1972), pp. 340-359.

[18] John V. Langdale, "The Growth of Long-Distance Telephone in the Bell System: 1875-1907," Journal of Historical Geography, Vol. 4 (1978), pp. 145-159.

[19] Morton S. Baratz, The Economics of the Postal Service (Washington, D.C.: Public Affairs Press, 1962), pp. 50, 58-60.

[20] Arthur D. Hall, III, "Trends in Switched Services," Chap. 2 in Gerbner et al., op. cit., note 1, p. 20.

[21] Paul Polishuk, "Review of the Impact of Telecommunications Substitutes for Travel," IEEE Transactions on Communications, Vol. 23 (1975), p. 1090.

[22] Jack M. Nilles, "Telecommunications and Organizational Decentralization," IEEE Transactions on Communications, Vol. 23 (1975), p. 1145. The last two stages are described similarly as satellite and neighborhood centers by Harkness, op. cit., note 6, pp. 39-44.

[23] Nilles, op. cit., note 22, p. 1145.

[24] Kay Kohl, Thomas G. Newman, Jr., and Joseph F. Tomey, "Facilitating Organizational Decentralization Through Teleconferencing," IEEE Transactions on Communications, Vol. 23 (1975), pp. 1098-1104.

[25] Ronald Abler, "Effect of Space-Adjusting Technologies on the Human Geography of the Future," Chap. 3 in Human Geography in a Shrinking World, Ron Abler et al., eds. (North Scituate: Duxbury, 1975), p. 53.

[26] Kohl et al., op. cit., note 24, p. 1100.

[27] J. B. Goddard, Office Linkages and Location: A Study of Communications and Spatial Patterns in Central London, Progress in Planning, Vol. 1, Part 2 (Oxford: Pergamon Press, 1973), p. 185.

[28] Jack M. Nilles, F. Roy Carlson, Jr., Paul Gray, and Gerhard J. Hanneman, The Telecommunications-Transportation Tradeoff: Options for Tomorrow (N.Y.: John Wiley & Sons, 1976), pp. 132-134.

[29] Edward M. Dickson and Raymond Bowers, The Video Telephone: Impact of a New Era in Telecommunications (N.Y.: Praeger, 1974), p. 133.

[30] Goddard, op. cit., note 27, pp. 162-165.

[31] Lesley A. Albertson, "Telecommunications as a Travel Substitute: Some Psychological, Organizational, and Social Aspects," Journal of Communications, Vol. 27 (1977), pp. 40-42 and Peter Cowan, "Moving Information Instead of Mass: Transportation versus Communication," Chap. 21 in Gerbner et al., op. cit., note 1, pp. 339-352.

[32] John Cohn, "Communicating with Man on the Move," Chap. 4 in Gerbner et al., op. cit., note 1, pp. 37-48 and R. V. Mrozinski, "The Application of Telecommunications to City Services," IEEE Transactions on Communications, Vol. 23 (1975), p. 1083.

[33] Donald G. Janelle, "Spatial Reorganization and Time-Space Convergence," unpublished Ph.D. Dissertation, Michigan State University, 1966.

Chapter 11

The Changing Patterns of Industrial Corporate Control in the Metropolitan United States

John D. Stephens and Brian P. Holly

The changing spatial structure of corporation decision-making that Brooker-Gross attributes to communication technology is also related to the major locational changes in the control functions of the largest U.S. corporations from 1955 to 1975. These head offices or control points are integral components in post-industrial economic systems. The spatial structure operates at varying levels of the urban hierarchy, in much the same way that Clark and Malecki describe national systems. The major concentrations of headquarter offices are in and around New York, Detroit, Chicago, and Pittsburgh. Recent changes in the distribution reveal growth in Sunbelt cities and middle-sized metropolitan centers in the Northeast. The growth of Sunbelt cities illustrates the emergence of aerospace, energy, electronics, and telecommunication industries, all associated with post-industrial economies. The changing pattern of corporate control is tied both to mergers (more recently vertical rather than horizontal integration) and the trend toward highly diversified conglomerates to retain a competitive advantage. Despite a remarkable stability in the locational pattern of industrial corporate control over the past two decades, this chapter documents that the largest metropolitan areas are beginning to lose some of their attractiveness for these head offices while those in the South and West are registering major gains; Houston, Tulsa, and Dallas are examples. Also, metropolitan centers surrounding New York City are increasing their share of these office. Corporate Office Headquarters (CHOs) are important in tieing the urban centers together into a national system.

As the U.S. makes the transition from an industrial to a post-industrial economy, the number of jobs concerned with the processing, compiling, and communicating of information is increasing. Gottmann referred to these information-intensive jobs as "quaternary activities," which are concerned with and operate through abstract transactions and which direct the processes of production and distribution.[1] During the past quarter century, managerial, professional, technical, and clerical occupations have mushroomed. Within manufacturing firms the administrative job functions have experienced the greatest increases.[2] These activities fall into Gottmann's quaternary category and include routine office work, accounting, information-processing, product development, planning and decision-making. Such transactional functions rely heavily on contacts and communications and, therefore, will favor large metropolitan areas as locations for operation. For it is there where information, the commodity of administration, can readily be exchanged.

To the extent that metropolitan areas have become the locations of jobs and organizations concerned with the dissemination and processing of information and with economic decision-making, they can be characterized as "control points" in the nation's economic system. Over the past 70 years, and especially since World War II, large, complex, multi-locational organizations have been gaining an increasingly large share of the nation's economic assets and employment. This list includes manufacturing firms, utilities, banks, insurance and investment companies, and retailing organizations. Since the 1920s, the largest corporations in these categories (over 1,700 in number) have increased their ownership of the nation's economic assets from one-fifth to one-fourth of the total.[3] Between 1954 and 1974, the share of the total industrial sales of the 500 largest industrial corporations rose from one-half to two-thirds.[4] In terms of jobs controlled, between 1960 and 1973, the number of domestic and foreign jobs accounted for by the 500 largest industrials grew from 9.2 to over 15.5 million, a growth rate twice that of U.S. nonagricultural employment over the same period.[5]

Geographer John Borchert has commented on the geographical importance of large organizations:[6]

> The pattern of allocation of savings, production and resources is of special geographical importance. Either allocation decisions reinforce existing regions, routes, and nodes, or they promote change. Thus, large organizations shape the evolving settlement pattern of the nation....The products of creative entrepreneurship, these organizational headquarters have been major shapers of the images of downtown districts, cities, and regions. They have influenced regional differences in tax base and philanthropy. Their decisions are an essential part of any practical land use plan, and their headquarters expenditures reflect expansion or contraction in remote parts of their corporate networks.

The mounting economic power of large-scale business organizations has spurred an interest in their locational patterns and decision-making processes on the part of geographers and other social scientists. Particular emphasis is being placed on the spatial distribution and locational behavior of the national office headquarters of multi-locational firms. It is important to understand the relationship between head office functions of multi-locational firms and the spatial organization of the metropolitan system since decisions made at the highest level of corporate control directly influence the growth and development of city systems. Geographer Allan Pred sees this occurring in three interrelated ways: (1) through the generation of local and nonlocal multiplier effects; (2) by the diffusion of growth inducing or employment generating innovation impulses; and (3) through the accumulation of "operational" decisions affecting the survival and scale of subunits in the organization located in other cities. These processes share the feature of contributing to the growth and development of systems of cities by ultimately influencing at what locations new jobs are created.[7] This chapter continues the effort begun by others by investigating the locational trends and spatial concentration of headquarters of the largest U.S. industrial corporations for the 20-year period from 1955 to 1975.

THE SPATIAL STRUCTURE OF ADMINISTRATIVE FUNCTIONS

At a national scale, large multi-functional organizations are made up of a mix of units operating on a national basis, a regional basis, and a local basis.[8] Various functions tend to locate at different levels in the urban hierarchy: CHO in a nationally important metropolis, divisional head office in a regional center, and manufacturing and service operations in local centers. Figure 20 provides a simple graphic example of three hypothetical organizations with a rigidly hierarchical bureaucratic structure mapped into geographical space. In this example, various levels in the organization are located in cities all at different positions in the urban hierarchy. A complex set of linkages or interdependencies exists within and between the units of these organizations at different hierarchical levels. Internal linkages take the form of lines of administrative authority and ownership ties, while external linkages exist between different organizations, e.g., with service firms in particular urban centers.

Although this simple conceptual model may not apply to all corporate organizations, it does attempt to link the structure of organizations with that of the national system of cities. Usually, the controlling headquarters operation is located in an economically diversified metropolitan center at or near the apex of the urban hierarchy. In the case of the head offices coordinating the activities of semi-autonomous operating subdivisions, the national administrative office of each division will likely be situated in a large metropolis. The management offices of production, marketing, and service units, vested with more routine, programmed decision functions, are most commonly found in the subnational tier of metropolitan centers, while the most locally oriented units display a greater tendency to be footloose within the urban system. As a result, they can be found in or near cities of all sizes. The tendency, then, is for higher level functions of organizations to gravitate to larger urban complexes:[9]

> As a result of such behavior, major cities which are the loci of head offices of corporate organizations have naturally become the control or steering centers for the urban system. The increasing concentration of economic activity into a limited number of such organizations has tended to reinforce this process of spatial concentration of control and the resulting disparities in regional development.

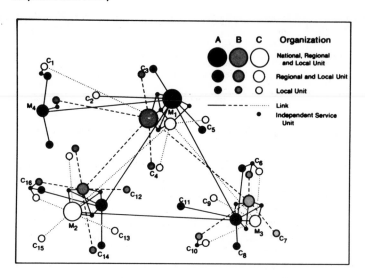

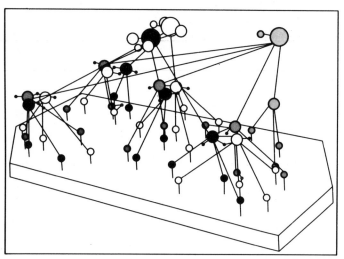

Fig. 20. Spatial arrangement and hierarchical level of units within three hypothetical organizations.

CHOs are normally concerned with control activities of an orientation nature.[10] Through these processes the firm searches the environment for new alternatives in terms of markets, products, services, locations, and societal values. In this way, the organization can make long-term adjustments to changes in economic, social, political, and technological conditions. Orientation processes are extremely contact dependent; therefore, the geographical environment best suited to meeting the firm's needs for face-to-face contacts is that of the large, economically diversified urban center. In the largest metropolises, the firms find the widest possible array of governmental, research, financial, legal, and other business services essential for the successful conduct of CHO functions. The CHOs and business services, together with such ancillary services as printing, hotels, restaurants, and entertainment, constitute the Corporate Headquarters Complex.[11]

SPATIAL CONCENTRATION OF CONTROL FUNCTIONS

An increasing amount of evidence supports the contention that large private sector organizations have become more concentrated in major metropolitan centers in recent decades, particularly in Western Europe and North America.[12] At least one study found that the distribution of corporate control, as measured by sales and assets, had become spatially less concentrated between 1956 and 1971.[13] However, the analysis was not based on location in metropolitan centers but on changes in distribution between census regions of the U.S.

In advanced economies, where the national economic system is dominated by one or a few large urban centers, the extreme concentration of CHOs is common (Fig. 21). In the less centralized, more log-normal, metropolitan system of the U.S., the largest metropolis, New York, does not dominate as do London, Paris, or Stockholm over their respective national economies. Although New York City dominates the U.S. in terms of the absolute number of CHOs, Chicago, the second ranking metropolitan center in terms of CHOs, has a far higher percentage of the total than the second ranking centers in most other industrial nations. Earlier studies have emphasized the extreme concentration of CHOs in the New York metropolitan area and other large cities within the Manufacturing Belt.[14] In recent years, New York and some older industrial cities of the Northeast have experienced both an absolute and a relative decrease in their share of CHOs while gains have occurred in some Sunbelt cities and middle-sized metropolitan complexes in the Northeast.[15] In recent years, New York City has fallen victim to a massive outflow of CHOs. As recently as 1957, metropolitan New York could boast of 144 CHOs. By 1974, this total had dropped to 107, with only 90 headquartered within the city limits.

This change in the distribution of head offices cannot be attributed to relocations alone. In fact, of the 40 actual departures of "Fortune 500" headquarters from New York between 1968 and 1974, only 6 went to Sunbelt cities. Most moved to suburban Connecticut, New Jersey, or New York; General Dynamics departed for St. Louis and Johns Manville went to Denver. Although Sunbelt cities registered a net gain of 24 headquarters between 1970 and 1975, not all occurred as a direct result of relocations.

RELOCATION OF CONTROL FUNCTIONS FOLLOWING MERGER OR ACQUISITION

The redistribution of corporate control in the U.S. cannot be attributed simply to physical relocations of individual CHOs. More often than not, changes in the

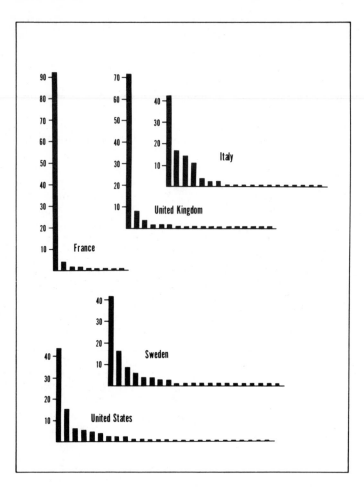

Fig. 21. Aggregate sales of the 100 largest industrial companies in 1965 by place of headquarters.

distribution of CHOs occur due to merger and acquisition activity. While organizational growth often occurs through internal expansion, the strategy of external expansion, achieved through combination with other enterprises by merger or acquisition, is more common to the already large, multi-locational organizations. The following review of the history of business take-overs in the U.S. provides necessary background with which to access the redistribution of corporate control.

The first wave of merger activity in the U.S. began shortly before the turn of the century (1897 to 1905), followed by two increasingly high peaks (1925 to 1929 and the 1960s) separated by troughs of relatively less merger activity. The upsurge of mergers between 1897 and 1905 fostered the emergence of "oligopolistic" structure, or the horizontal consolidation of many producers and suppliers of the same industrial sub-sector into relatively large enterprises that controlled a large share of the market. Another important development that occurred during this period was the spatial separation of management from production or marketing and the appearance of specialized establishments possessing only control functions—the CHOs that have come to dominate some cities' skylines.

The second period of merger activity was noteworthy for the vertical integration of firms. Enterprises expanded vertically by involving themselves further in the production or marketing sequence in two directions: backward and forward linkages. Vertical integration in some cases meant the acquisition of formerly independent marketing and distribution operations.

Another important development during the second wave of mergers was the appearance of large, multi-functional organizations of the "conglomerate" type. A conglomerate is a multi-functional organization composed of several production units, some of which act neither as suppliers nor consumers to the major production or service activities of the firm. Diversification, which has produced this new breed of enterprise, "spreads the risk," thereby reducing a firm's dependence on one or a few products. Through diversification, conglomerates and vertically integrated firms have gained competitive advantages over smaller competitors by being able to (1) limits their supplies, (2) acquire ownership of their principal buyers, and (3) realize economies of national advertising as well as a variety of other scale economies.[16]

The peak of mergers that occurred during the 1960s was clearly the greatest of the three in terms of both the number and the value of mergers. This most recent wave has been dominated by the creation and further expansion of highly diversified conglomerates. The growth in size of some of the largest organizations accelerated through the acquisition of other, already large corporations. Thus, the conglomerates were rapidly piecing together vast empires of astonishing diversity and, in the process, were taking over scores of well-known companies.

The emergence of the national, multi-locational corporation has involved a horizontal division of management into specialist departments, e.g., finance, personnel, purchasing, and sales, and a vertical system of control devised to connect and coordinate departments. The head office's responsibility, in particular, has been to coordinate, evaluate, and plan for the survival and growth of the entire corporation. Almost by definition, take-over implies the transfer of managerial control from the acquired to the acquiring company. Growth of corporations through mergers and take-overs often leads to a considerable concentration of administrative employment as duplicated functions that existed in the separate organizlations before amalgamation are eliminated. Moreover, external services that smaller organizations had to contract out are internalized because they can now be economically provided for the larger group.

From a spatial viewpoint, merger and acquisition activity can mean that control of a metropolitan region's productive resources can be transferred to another region upon acquisition, if the acquirer is headquartered elsewhere. Thus, acquisition can be part of a process leading to the growth of "external control" of local industry for some regions and consolidation of ownership into other regions.[17] However, there are important post-acquisition differences of degree in the transfer of control functions.[18] Complications also arise because not all acquired companies are independent prior to acquisition: Some take-overs consist of the transfer of subsidiary companies from one group to another.

Clearly, not enough is known about the relationship between the geography of mergers and acquisitions and the redistribution of corporate control. But, the preceding discussion demonstrates that we cannot consider the majority of CHO relocations as planned, physical relocations (i.e., as analogous to migration decision).

REDISTRIBUTION OF CORPORATE CONTROL

Employing data on the relocation of CHOs of the 500 largest industrial corporations over a 20-year period and using an analysis of the urban rank-size hierarchy in the U.S. for the same time interval, the remainder of this chapter focuses on both metropolitan deconcentration and the redistribution of corporate control.[19] We postulate that there is a trend toward a less spatially concentrated distribution of corporate control in the U.S. This proposition can be tested by analyzing changes in corporate headquarters location associated with changes in the urban rank-size hierarchy. Although there appears to have been a major shift in the location of CHOs of the largest industrial corporations, this has not taken form primarily as actual relocations but is mainly associated with regional changes in the rank size of metropolitan areas and with changes owing to mergers and acquisitions. The net gain of 24 CHOs by Sunbelt cities from 1970 to 1975 cannot be attributed solely to relocations. It is not enough to suggest that CHOs are relocating to the South and West because of climatic, recreational, taxation, or labor cost advantages. The locational requirements of these organizations are such that receiving cities must be of sufficient size, diversity, and national economic importance so that head office functions can be carried out effectively. Headquarter offices favor those locations which facilitate the generation, processing, exchange, and consumption of information. Position in the rank-size hierarchy is one means of measuring a city's attractiveness as a head office location.

A suitable example to demonstrate this point is that of Houston. In 1950, Houston was the 20th ranked SMSA in terms of population. In 1975 it had moved up to number 13. In 1955, the earliest year for which the "Fortune 500" data were compiled, Houston could boast of only one company on the list, for 67th ranked Continental Oil. By 1960, as Houston moved up to the 17th ranked SMSA, it had gained one additional "500" company, the 466th ranked United Texas Natural Gas. The firm did not relocate but had had insufficient sales to make the list in 1955. In 1975, Houston could count the headquarters of 11 "Fortune 500" companies within the SMSA boundaries.

Corporate Headquarter Data

Data pertaining to the pattern of headquarters location in the U.S. are scarce. Available data sources are problematic due to irregularities in method of reporting, insufficient detail, lack of comparability over time, and other ambiguities owing to mergers and acquisitions. The primary source of information on the characteristics and location of CHOs in the U.S. is Fortune's annual listings of the 500 and, more recently, of the 1,000 largest industrial corporations and the 50 largest organizations in each of six nonindustrial categories: retailing, utilities, transportation, commercial banking, insurance, and diversified financial.

CHO location by city can be summarized from the Fortune listings. However, the number of headquarter units located in a particular city is inadequate as a measure of headquarters importance since the head office units differ substantially in organizational size. Better weighted measures of headquarters importance include total sales, assets, and jobs controlled, all of which are reported in the Fortune listings.

Inconsistencies in the Fortune data make time comparisons difficult. Trends of the 1,000 largest organizations between 1955 and 1975, for example, are impossible to trace since the listings prior to 1972 are limited to the largest 500. Similar comparisons of the 50 largest nonindustrials in each of the several categories suffer from changes in the classification of these categories. The directories of the 500 largest industrials published annually by Fortune since 1956, however, permit the development of a relatively rich time series with which to evaluate the trends of CHO location by city.

The Fortune data permit the aggregation of organizations by city of headquarters location. With data for at least two different years organized in this way, one can evaluate the changing pattern of head office location. Such comparisons, however, can be misleading since relatively few headquarters losses and gains actually involve locational shifts. Entry into the "Fortune 500" list depends primarily on total sales. Thus, many organizations which failed to qualify in, say, 1965 entered the 1975 listing due to a rapid expansion in sales or the acquisition of other firms. Alternately, some organizations were dropped from this list because of a relative or absolute decline in sales. In both cases, it is quite possible that the organizations retained their headquarters location.

Comparisons over time in the pattern of CHO location can be misleading for yet another reason. Organizations appear and disappear erratically among the 500 largest industrials. Between 1962 and 1969, for example, 80 head offices disappeared because of merger and absorption into another already existing organization. Among the 10 corporations with the largest percentage gains in sales during 1955 and 1975, not one had enough sales to make the first Fortune list published in 1956. All 10 powered their sales drives with mergers. Together the 10 have acquired about 550 smaller firms, with the leader acquiring more than 120.

Another effect of the merger explosions, making comparisons difficult, has been the rash of name changes. Typically, the change involved an effort to overcome the one-industry connotation of its original name. Of the 79 name changes that occurred during 1966 to 1970 alone, examples include Automatic Sprinkler which became A-T-O and Pittsburgh Plate Glass which adopted the PPG industries. Interestingly, all 70 organizations changing names retained their head office locations.[20]

Metropolitan Dominance and Corporate Dominance

Since the functions associated with CHOs are conducted most successfully in the information rich environments of large cities, we should except to find the greatest concentration of corporate control in the largest metropolitan areas. One means of examining this relationship is to fit a rank-size function to metropolitan areas by both population size and by degree of corporate dominance. A logarithmic rank-size function was fitted to population data for the 268 SMSAs defined in 1975 for the years 1950, 1960, 1970, and 1975.[21] On the basis of significance tests on the parameters of the model, it can be concluded that all metropolitan centers have grown at the same rate over the 25-year period and that the change in population is statistically significant. This trend in allometric growth may be generalized by a series of nearly parallel rank-size curves that shift outward over time (Fig. 22).

Upon closer examination it may be seen that the presently most important metropolitan complexes have experienced either no shift in population rank or an upward or downward shift of only a few ranks. However, in some cases significant adjustments have occurred to their population ratios. While rank stability

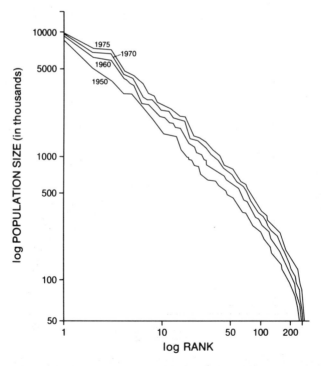

Fig. 22. Metropolitan rank size distributions, 1955–1975.

characterized the largest metropolitan complexes of the U.S. during the 25-year interval, this is generally not true for either intermediate- or small-sized metropolitan areas. Instead, evidence for a number of advanced economies, including the data analyzed here, consistently indicates that the probability of size-rank change is inversely proportional to population.

The rank stability of large metropolitan complexes over the relatively brief interval considered here is but a continuation of a long-term trend that has been observed in the U.S. since 1790.[22] There is much evidence to indicate that once a few urban centers rise to the highest population ranks of a national or regional city-system, they are unlikely to be displaced from these positions of dominance.

Total population of metropolitan areas represents one measure of city size. Other measures relevant to this study include the volume of sales, amount of assets, and the number of employees controlled by corporations. When these data for the 500 largest industrial corporations are aggregated by city of head office location, they offer alternative definitions of the rank-size distribution of cities. Inasmuch as the three measures of corporate size are highly intercorrelated, we will refer to the aggregate of assets held by corporations of a given city as the index of the degree of corporate dominance of that city. The rank-size model was applied to the corporate assets by city for the period 1955 to 1975. Figure 23 illustrates the change in the rank-size distribution for metropolitan areas, using the amount of assets as a surrogate for population size.

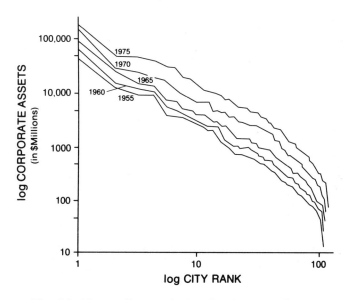

Fig. 23. Metropolitan rank-size distributions of corporate assets, 1955–1975.

The results indicate that, in terms of industrial corporate assets, all metropolitan centers having headquarters grew at approximately the same rate, and the increase in total assets is statistically significant. Changes in the slope of the rank-size distributions are not statistically different. The results appear to support the assertion that, regardless of the measure used, the key aspect of metropolitan dominance is stability. Individual places rise and fall within the hierarchy, but at a national scale rank-size distributions of corporate influence maintain a stable equilibrium.

The highest ranking metropolitan areas, as defined by the amount of corporate assets controlled, retain the same rank order in 1975 as they did in 1955. However, the evidence indicates that since 1955 major forces have been operating to lessen the attractiveness of the largest metropolitan areas as locations for CHOs. In 1955, the 10 leading metropolitan areas accounted for 3 out of 5 of the Fortune 500 firms; by 1975 they accounted for less than half. New York, Detroit, Chicago, and Pittsburgh controlled a noticeably smaller share of the total assets of the 500 largest industrial corporations in 1975 than they did in 1955 (Fig. 24). Houston, Dallas-Ft. Worth, Atlanta, Los Angeles, and metropolitan areas on the periphery of the New York urban field registered the most impressive gains in assets controlled.

A breakdown of the number of corporate headquarters and percent sales, assets, and employees by census region demonstrates that a spatially less concentrated pattern of corporate control is emerging. This deconcentration is indicated by the gains in the West, South Central, Pacific, and New England regions, while the Middle Atlantic and East North Central regions show up as losers (Table 46). Gains

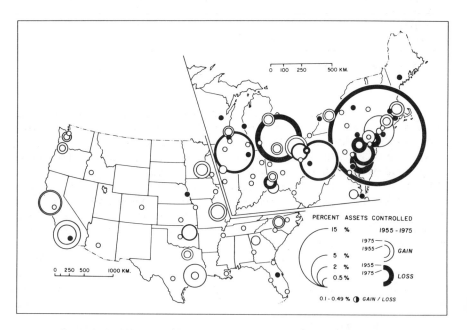

Fig. 24. Largest 500 industrial corporations headquarters, 1955–1975.

Table 46. Characteristics and Distribution of the 500 Largest Industrial
Corporations, by Region of Headquarters Location, 1955 and 1975

Census region	CHOs (N)	Sales (%)	Assets (%)	Employees (%)
		1955		
New England	22	2.05	1.66	2.78
Middle Atlantic	218	49.36	53.66	48.85
South Atlantic	23	3.83	5.59	4.00
East South Central	2	0.18	0.15	0.26
West South Central	14	1.90	2.59	1.21
East North Central	151	32.89	27.71	32.65
West North Central	30	3.39	2.35	3.23
Mountain	4	0.34	0.33	0.34
Pacific	32	6.07	5.96	6.69
		1975		
New England	43	7.30	7.43	9.86
Middle Atlantic	165	39.77	42.08	37.32
South Atlantic	33	4.60	4.90	5.18
East South Central	4	0.28	0.24	0.45
West South Central	26	5.15	5.74	3.34
East North Central	137	27.87	25.53	30.74
West North Central	34	4.84	3.94	5.42
Mountain	8	0.97	0.85	0.95
Pacific	46	9.22	9.30	6.71

Sources: Fortune, 1956; 1976.

in the West South Central region are due primarily to the relative growth of the
Houston, Dallas, and Tulsa metropolitan complexes. The suburbanization of CHOs
from New York City to Bridgeport-Stamford-Norwalk accounts for most of the
growth in New England. The 20-year trend toward a less concentrated distribution
is supported by the data on sales, assets, and employees. Those regions having lost
CHOs also show declines in their relative share of these measures of corporate
control. Likewise, gains were experienced by those regions adding to their total
of CHOs over the interval. To what extent these changes were due to actual relocations as opposed to changes in the makeup of the "Fortune 500" list has not been
investigated. Both factors are probably operating here.

From an examination of Table 47 it could be concluded that locational shifts
are taking place from smaller to larger places. This may be more apparent than
real, however. As SMSAs move into a larger size class, they take with them their
corporate sales, assets, and employment. From 1955 to 1975, the greatest losses
were sustained by the very largest and smallest SMSAs, whereas the most dramatic
increases are reflected in the 500,000 to 999,999 and 1,000,000 to 2,499,999
size categories for all measures of corporate influence. Tables 48 and 49 demonstrate

Table 47. Characteristics and Distribution of the 500 Largest Industrial
Corporations, by Size of SMSA of Headquarters Location, 1955 and 1975

SMSA size	CHOs (N)	Sales (%)	Assets (%)	Employees (%)
		1955		
2,500,000+	255	64.41	62.79	62.15
1,000,000-2,499,999	100	15.25	16.37	15.56
500,000- 999,999	49	5.81	4.82	7.19
250,000- 499,999	51	10.30	12.36	10.95
100,000- 249,999	31	3.24	2.74	3.29
50,000- 99,999	10	0.99	0.93	0.86
		1975		
2,500,000+	218	55.57	54.45	50.46
1,000,000-2,499,999	134	21.67	22.24	23.48
500,000- 999,999	85	15.01	15.98	18.57
250,000- 499,999	36	4.79	4.54	5.13
100,000- 249,999	17	2.52	2.41	1.77
50,000- 99,999	6	0.44	0.38	0.59

Sources: Fortune, 1956; 1976.

this trend for individual places. For metropolitan areas with more than 1% of total sales, Table 48 shows the dominance of the industrial Northeast in 1955, whereas Table 49 indicates a slightly more geographically balanced distribution in 1975.

CONCLUSIONS

Two major findings result from the analysis of the locational pattern of CHOs over the 20-year period from 1955 to 1975. The first conclusion, and one that is supported by both the popular and scholarly literature in recent years, refers to a more geographically balanced distribution of corporate control on an inter-regional basis. This redistribution can only be partially attributed to actual reloca-tions of corporate headquarters from the previously dominant North and East to the emerging South and West. Our analysis lends support to Semple's findings on the deconcentration of sales, assets, and employees for the Fortune 500 largest industrials.[23] This situation has occurred primarily as a result of significant gains in the size and importance of major urban centers in the South and West. Spec-tacular growth has also been registered by industries traditionally identified with these areas (e.g., aerospace, energy, telecommunications, and electronics) resulting in entry to the Fortune 500 list by many corporations already headquartered in Sunbelt cities. An analysis of changes in the membership of the Fortune 500 by industry code would shed light on the extent of this trend. Therefore, differentials

Table 48. Characteristics and Distribution of the 500 Largest Industrial
Corporations by SMSA of Headquarters Location, 1955

Rank	Metropolitan area[a]	CHOs (N)	Sales (%)	Assets (%)	Employees (%)
1	New York	156	38.078	40.864	36.925
	Bridgeport-Stamford-Norwalk-Danbury CMA	3	0.203	0.184	0.260
	Jersey City SMSA	2	0.096	0.061	0.083
	Nassau-Suffolk SMSA	4	0.470	0.219	0.550
	New Brunswick-Perth Amboy-Sayreville SMSA	1	0.140	0.105	0.143
	New York SMSA	142	36.909	40.048	35.530
	Newark SMSA	2	0.136	0.150	0.182
	Paterson-Clifton-Passaic SMSA	2	0.124	0.097	0.177
2	Detroit	21	12.333	10.018	12.644
	Ann Arbor SMSA	1	0.091	0.037	0.057
	Detroit SMSA	20	12.242	9.981	12.587
3	Chicago	51	9.411	7.467	7.650
	Chicago SMSA	50	9.373	7.434	7.596
	Rockford SMSA	1	0.038	0.033	0.054
4	Pittsburgh	25	5.851	7.052	6.067
5	Philadelphia	24	3.937	5.461	3.585
	Philadelphia SMSA	20	2.467	2.575	2.208
	Wilmington SMSA	4	1.470	2.886	1.377
6	Cleveland	20	4.044	3.562	4.903
	Akron SMSA	4	2.064	1.715	2.904
	Cleveland SMSA	16	1,980	1.847	1.999
7	Los Angeles	15	2.960	2.243	3.529
	Los Angeles-Long Beach SMSA	14	2.775	2.190	3.279
	Anaheim-Santa Ana-Garden Grove SMSA	1	0.185	0.053	0.250
8	San Francisco-Oakland SMSA	12	2.318	3.231	2.096
	San Francisco-Oakland SMSA	11	2.144	3.041	1.919
	San Jose SMSA	1	0.174	0.190	0.177
9	St. Louis SMSA	12	1.417	1.219	1.500
10	Allentown-Bethlehem-Easton SMSA	2	1.382	1.591	1.749
11	Cincinnati	6	1.317	1.151	1.032
	Cincinnati SMSA	4	0.790	0.600	0.555
	Hamilton-Middletown SMSA	2	0.527	0.551	0.477
12	Minneapolis-St. Paul SMSA	8	1.086	0.797	0.994

[a]Metropolitan areas ranked according to total corporate sales.
Source: Fortune, 1956.

Table 49. Characteristics and Distribution of the 500 Largest Industrial
Corporations by SMSA of Headquarters Location, 1975

Rank	Metropolitan area[a]	CHOs (N)	Sales (%)	Assets (%)	Employees (%)
1	New York	136	35.140	36.742	33.144
	Bridgeport-Stamford-Norwalk-Danburg CMA	19	4.662	5.067	5.816
	Jersey City SMSA	1	0.037	0.038	0.080
	Nassau-Suffolk SMSA	1	0.154	0.078	0.195
	New Brunswick-Perth Amboy-Sayreville SMSA	2	0.376	0.299	0.490
	New York SMSA	98	27.694	28.874	23.761
	Newark SMSA	5	1.015	1.110	1.256
	Paterson-Clifton-Passaic SMSA	10	1.242	1.276	1.546
2	Detroit	14	9.512	7.482	10.830
	Ann Arbor SMSA	1	0.046	0.035	0.052
	Detroit SMSA	35	9.466	7.447	10.778
3	Chicago	47	7.580	7.223	7.747
	Chicago SMSA	45	7.484	7.114	7.611
	Kankakee SMSA	1	0.037	0.031	0.042
	Rockford SMSA	1	0.059	0.078	0.094
4	Pittsburgh SMSA	15	5.296	6.040	5.141
5	Los Angeles	23	4.847	4.759	3.567
	Los Angeles-Long Beach SMSA	22	4.182	4.743	3.525
	Riverside-San Bernardino-Ontario SMSA	1	0.035	0.016	0.042
6	Cleveland	20	3.474	3.844	4.893
	Akron SMSA	4	1,486	1.556	2.388
	Cleveland SMSA	16	1.988	2.288	2.505
7	San Francisco	13	3.177	3.387	1.754
	San Francisco-Oakland SMSA	10	2.985	3.199	1.415
	San Jose	3	0.192	0.188	0.339
8	Philadelphia	18	2.674	2.955	2.554
	Philadelphia SMSA	15	1.635	1.746	1.430
	Wilmington SMSA	3	1.039	1.209	1.124
9	St. Louis SMSA	11	2.185	1.886	2.716
10	Houston SMSA	11	2.144	2.790	1.217
11	Minneapolis-St. Paul SMSA	13	1.747	1.724	2.292
12	Boston SMSA	12	1.186	1.043	1.560
13	Dallas-Fort Worth SMSA	6	1.152	0.833	1.386
14	Cincinnati	4	1.147	1.028	0.841
	Cincinnati SMSA	3	0.796	0.637	0.502
	Hamilton-Middletown SMSA	1	0.353	0.391	0.339
15	Tulsa SMSA	4	1.131	1.459	0.393

[a]Metropolitan areas ranked according to total corporate sales.
Source: Fortune, 1976.

in regional growth processes, associated with a shift from industrial to post-industrial employment patterns, have resulted in a more balanced distribution of CHOs and associated indices of economic control.

Examination of the distribution of corporate control within the urban system leads to a slightly different interpretation of the behavior of large business organizations. At a national scale, the head offices of industrial corporations display a marked conservatism in their locational behavior. Just as the urban hierarchy displays a tendency toward long-term stability, so also does the distribution of corporate influence. City systems in advanced economies have historically maintained stability in the national population rank of their leading metropolitan areas. According to Pred, these metropolitan "complexes" offer CHOs and other high-level administrative activities three specialized information advantages usually not available in smaller urban centers: (1) greater propensity for interorganizational face-to-face contacts, (2) availability of specialized business services, and (3) high levels of intermetropolitan accessibility.[24] These advantages tend to be self-reinforcing, thereby contributing to the long-term stability of both metropolitan rank and degree of corporate concentration. Forces currently operating to the advantage of newer metropolitan areas at the expense of older, higher-ranking complexes have distributed the rank order of some extent. The rank ordering of corporate assets shows no statistically significant change over the 20 years covered by this study. Thus, corporate influence as measured by the Fortune data has been more stable than the urban rank-size hierarchy. Data on the distribution of corporate influence even suggest a slight increase in concentration in large metropolitan areas since 1955.

When changing scale to the local level of analysis, we find CHOs to be more geographically footloose. The trend toward suburbanization of CHOs and other office entities has been the subject of some research and is the primary result of actual relocations.[25] This fact, together with the increased concentration of CHOs in the largest metropolitan areas, results in what may be termed a concentrated dispersal of CHO functions. While, the largest metropolitan areas remain the home of most CHOs, they may be found in a variety of locations from the Central Business District of the core city to suburban counties and even in recently designated contiguous SMSAs (Tables 48 and 49). Location within these "urban fields"[26] allows CHOs to maintain their established contact networks and ties to ancillary services as well as to retain their proximity to intermetropolitan transportation networks.

The results of empirical analysis in this chapter support the research findings of others on the locational behavior of the headquarters of large industrial corporations. The importance of these units in steering the national economy and in influencing urban and regional development cannot be understated. Their addresses can be considered control points in the national economic system, thereby linking their fortunes inexorably to those of the urban system and the entire economy.[27]

NOTES

[1] J. Gottmann, "Urban Centrality and the Interweaving of Quaternary Function," *Ekistics*, Vol. 29 (1970), pp. 322–31.

178   Stephens and Holly

[2] R. B. Armstrong, *The Office Industry: Patterns of Growth and Location* (Cambridge: MIT Press, 1972).

[3] J. R. Borchert, "Major Control Points in American Economic Geography," *Annals*, Association of American Geographers, Vol. 68 (1978), pp. 214–32.

[4] L. G. Martin, "The 500: A Report on Two Decades," *Fortune*, Vol. 41 (1975), pp. 238–41.

[5] A. R. Pred, *City Systems in Advanced Economies: Past Growth, Present Processes, and Future Development Options* (N.Y.: Halsted Press, 1977), p. 99.

[6] Borchert, op. cit., note 3, p. 215.

[7] A. R. Pred, *Major Job Providing Organizations and Systems of Cities* (Washington, D.C.: Association of American Geographers, 1974), p. 9.

[8] Pred, op. cit., note 7, p. 8.

[9] J. B. Goddard, *Office Location in Urban and Regional Development* (London: Oxford University Press, 1975), p. 13.

[10] B. Thorngren, "How Do Contact Systems Affect Regional Development?" *Environment and Planning*, Vol. 2 (1970), pp. 409–27.

[11] The Conservation of Human Resources Project, *The Corporate Headquarters Complex in New York City* (N.Y.: Columbia University, 1977).

[12] See L. Ahnstrom, *Styrande och ledande Verksamhet i Vasteuropa: en ekonomisk-geografisk studie* (Stockholm: Almquist & Wiksell, 1973); Borchert, op. cit., note 3; L. S. Burns, "The Location of the Headquarters of Industrial Companies: A Comment," *Urban Studies*, Vol. 14 (1977), pp. 211–14; A. Evans, "The Location of the Headquarters of Industrial Companies," *Urban Studies*, Vol. 10 (1973), pp. 387–96; J. B. Goddard and I. J. Smith, "Changes in Corporate Control in the British Urban System, 1972–77," *Environment and Planning A*, Vol. 10 (1978), pp. 1073–84; and Pred, op. cit., note 7.

[13] R. K. Semple, "Recent Trends in the Spatial Concentration of Corporate Headquarters," *Economic Geography*, Vol. 49 (1973), pp. 309–318.

[14] E. L. Ullman, "Regional Development and the Geography of Concentration," *Papers and Proceedings of the Regional Science Association*, Vol. 4 (1959), pp. 179–98 and W. Goodwin, "The Management Center in the United States," *Geographical Review*, Vol. 55 (1965), pp. 1–16.

[15] See Armstrong, op. cit., note 2, pp. 33–44; Pred, op. cit., note 7, pp. 18–22; and Borchert, op. cit., note 3.

[16] Pred, op. cit., note 7, p. 11.

[17] P. Dicken, "The Multiplant Enterprise and Geographical Space: Some Issues in the Study of External Control and Regional Development," *Regional Studies*, Vol. 10 (1976), pp. 401–412.

[18] R. Leigh and D. J. North, "The Potential of the Microbehavioural Approach to Regional Analysis," in P. W. J. Batey, ed., *Theory and Method in Urban and Regional Analysis*, London Papers in Regional Science 8 (London: Pion Ltd., 1978), pp. 54–63.

[19] The Editors of Fortune, "The 500 Largest Industrial Corporations," *Fortune*, Vol. 54 (1956) Supplement; "The Fortune Directory: The 500 Largest U.S. Industrial Corporations," *Fortune*, Vol. 64 (Jan., 1961), pp. 167–185; Vol. 74 (Feb., 1966), pp. 230–249; Vol. 83 (May, 1971), pp. 170–189; Vol. 93 (May, 1976), pp. 316–337. Population total for SMSAs were drawn from the U.S. Bureau of the Census, *United States Census of Population* for the years 1950, 1960, and 1970. Population estimates for 1975 were obtained from *Estimates of the Population of Counties and Metropolitan Areas: July 1, 1974 and 1975.* Current Population Reports: P-25, No. 709 (Washington, D.C.: U.S. Government Printing Office, 1977).

[20] Martin, op. cit., note 4.

[21] The standard rank-size distributions may be expressed in logarithmic form as
$\log P_i = \log C - q \log r_i$

where:

P_i = population of center of rank r;

r_i = rank of center i;

C = the intercept value, a constant approximately equal to the population of the center of rank 1; and

q = the slope coefficient, expressing the degree of concentration or dispersion of population within the urban system.

Following a method proposed by Casetti and later extended by Malecki, the parameters of the logarithmic form of the rank-size function may be expanded to account for changes in the rank-size structure over time. Since log C and q vary temporally, they can be expressed as linear function of time. Hence, the expanded logarithmic rank-size model, and the one used in this analysis, becomes:

$$P_i = \log C_o + \log C_1 \, t - q_o \log r_i - q_1 \, t \log r_i$$

where t is time.

See: E. Casetti, "Generating Models by the Expansion Method: Applications to Geographic Research," *Geographical Analysis*, Vol. 4 (1970), pp. 81–91; and E. J. Malecki, "Examining Change in Rank-Size Systems of Cities," *The Professional Geographer*, Vol. 27 (1975), pp. 43–47.

[22] Pred, op. cit., note 5.

[23] Semple, op. cit., note 13.

[24] Pred, op. cit., note 5.

[25] J. R. O'Meara, *Corporate Moves to the Suburbs: Problems and Opportunities* (N.Y.: The Conference Board, 1972); W. Quante, *The Exodus of Corporate Headquarters from New York City* (N.Y.: Praeger, 1976); W. H. Whyte, "End of the Exodus: The Logic of Headquarters City," *New York*, Vol. 9 (1976), pp. 88–99; G. Manners, "The Office in Metropolis: An Opportunity for Shaping Metropolitan America," *Economic Geography*, Vol. 50 (1974), pp. 93–110; and Burns, op. cit., note 12.

[26] J. Freidmann, "The Urban Field as Human Habitat," in L. S. Bourne and J. W. Simmons, eds., *Systems of Cities* (N.Y.: Oxford University Press, 1978).

[27] Borchert, op. cit., note 3.

Chapter 12

Energy and its Effect on Regional Metropolitan Growth in the United States

Frank J. Calzonetti

A vital ingredient in the present and future of the American metropolitan system is the impact energy availability and pricing will have on spatial forms and structures. It is not only that energy problems exist but that energy problems vary regionally. The effects of energy supplies and pricing on regional metropolitan growth, which will exist for some time, are discussed in this chapter. The purpose is not only to identify the major energy-producing and deficit states but also to discuss the impact higher prices and diminished supplies (of fossil fuels) are likely to have at interregional and intrametropolitan scales. That Frostbelt states are growing less rapidly than a decade earlier but in many areas are experiencing slow growth, high unemployment, and fiscal problems compared to the energy-producing Sunbelt states is likely to see a continuing shift of industries to energy-surplus states. Energy will become a more important factor in industrial location as price increases favor those energy-endowed states where distribution costs are less; expanding markets and regional multiplier effects in the Sunbelt will likely result in an interregional shift of old industries to Texas, Louisiana, Oklahoma, and Kentucky. At the intrametropolitan level, higher energy prices and higher automobile costs may change commuting patterns and the form of cities. More compact housing patterns (even in suburbs) and downtown growth are likely. The greatest adverse effect of higher energy prices will be in those deficit states and surplus states dependent on the automobile and that have a dispersed population. In summary, one must recognize that energy issues affect the growth, financing, and form of cities—now and in the future. Quite possibly public policies made regarding energy will have a greater impact on cities and metropolitan areas than any other urban problems dealt with.

A discussion of American metropolitan systems would hardly be complete without recognizing the influence of energy availability, price and use on urban growth, economic well-being, and relationships among cities. Energy has been abundant and inexpensive throughout most of the 20th century and was not a major factor in the industrialization or urbanization of the nation.[1] Recent years, however, have shown that energy may be a limiting factor controlling economic activities. The impact of energy shortages on urban areas, for example, was forcefully demonstrated in the winter of 1975–76 when natural gas shortages closed many schools, industries, and offices in the Northeast and Middle West.[2] Some cities, in effect, were almost completely closed during this time. Future energy supply problems, rising energy prices, the shift to new energy-producing regions, and the commercialization of new energy supply technologies have begun and will continue to affect metropolitan growth throughout the remainder of this century.

This chapter explores ways in which energy availability and price are likely to affect metropolitan growth in the U.S. on both an interregional and intraurban scale. Before examining these considerations, though, it is necessary to show that energy supply problems do indeed exist in this country and will continue to exist into the near future. In addition, it is shown that energy supply problems will vary regionally throughout the nation in intensity and scope.

ENERGY AVAILABILITY: NOT A TEMPORARY "CRISIS"

Although the "energy crisis" of long service station lines and "gasless Sundays" may have lost its intensity, a persistent erosion of national economic strength is the product of the nation's energy situation. A national trade deficit is not surprising considering that in 1977 alone the U.S. imported $45 billion worth of foreign oil. Some technological optimists view current energy supply problems as a temporary aberration in a trend toward continuous and abundant energy supplies and unmetered electricity.[3] Others profess faith that the market system will assure adequate supplies of energy for the future.[4]

A more accurate description of the U.S. energy situation is that a potential does exist to increase domestic energy supplies substantially, but capital requirements and uncertainties are impeding development. Thus, the nation should prepare for an extended period of tight energy supplies and rising energy prices.

Table 50 summarizes the anticipated "shortfalls" between domestic energy production and national energy demand through 1990. These figures were derived from an analysis of energy demand-supply scenarios compiled by the Congressional Research Service (CRS). It is shown that the energy shortfall continues to increase throughout the latter part of this century. CRS acknowledges that even if domestic energy supplies are increased dramatically energy availability problems will still remain a significant national problem:[5]

Table 50. U.S. Energy Demand and Supply Projections and Anticipated
Shortfalls
(in million barrels per day oil equivalent)

Supply	1977	1980	1985	1990
Oil and NGL	9.6	10.0	10.5	11.0
Natural gas	9.2	8.5	8.1	8.3
Shale oil	–	–	.1	.2
Nuclear power	1.5	2.3	3.4	5.0
Coal	6.7	6.8	7.7	10.5
Hydro/solar, geothermal	1.3	1.7	1.9	2.4
Total U.S. supply	28.8	29.3	32.3	37.4
Demand	36.9	40.4	45.1	51.5
Shortfall	-8.6	-11.1	-12.8	-14.1

Source: Congressional Research Service, *Project Interdependence: U.S. and World Energy Outlook Through 1990* (Washington, D.C.: GPO, 1977), p. 6.

Even with a combination of low energy demand coupled with high coal use and nuclear capacity expansion, and an increase of about 50% in natural gas reserve additions...the Nation would still have to import close to nine million barrels per day.

Any effort to increase domestic energy production requires the construction of new energy supply facilities. Although national goals clearly call for increased domestic energy production, no mechanisms now exist to insure that the requisite energy supply facilities will be sited.[6] National plans for increasing domestic energy production rely on indirect methods such as regulations and incentives to motivate the private sector. Systematic long-range plans are formulated by private enterprise establishments, but these are considered proprietary and are not publicly disclosed. Therefore, a serious lack of coordination exists in achieving stated national goals of increased domestic energy production.

Energy facilities are characterized by long lead times. Once a decision is made to construct an energy facility at a given location, it may take from 5 to 10 years before that facility is actually operating.[7] Similar lead times also exist in energy conservation efforts. For instance, it takes approximately 7 years to turn over the existing stock of automobiles.[8]

Thus, it appears that energy availability problems will remain with us at least for the next few decades. In that energy is a driving force behind our economy, it is essential that geographers attempt to discern some of the impacts likely to result from its scarcity and inequitable regional concentration, as these impacts will surely be expressed differently in different locations.[9] Ideally, anticipating problems may enable one to suggest alternative solutions.

REGIONAL VARIATIONS IN ENERGY SUPPLY AND DEMAND

Fossil fuels, namely oil, natural gas, and goal, comprise over 90% of the nation's total energy consumption.[10] These resources, however, are not uniformly distributed throughout the nation, as some regions register a diverse and abundant reserve base whereas others are rather devoid of such resources. In addition, since the demand for energy is often highest in those regions lacking a sufficient reserve base, one can identify energy surplus and deficit regions. The degree to which a region is relatively energy self-sufficient provides one cornerstone of economic growth and fiscal health.

Figure 25 shows states that registered a fossil fuel surplus in 1975.[11] This information was compiled by totaling the BTU equivalents of oil, natural gas, and coal produced by each state compared to the total BTUs consumed. The principal fossil fuel exported for each of these states is also shown. Figure 26 shows the location of the 10 principal energy deficit states along with their relative consumption of oil, natural gas, and coal. Although this figure is certainly affected by the population size of the state, it does show those regions where the largest absolute fuel deficits exists. This information is tabulated in Table 51 along with the fuel balance for oil, natural gas, and coal.

It is immediately obvious that the major energy deficit states occupy the traditional Manufacturing Belt, whereas the energy surplus states, for the most part,

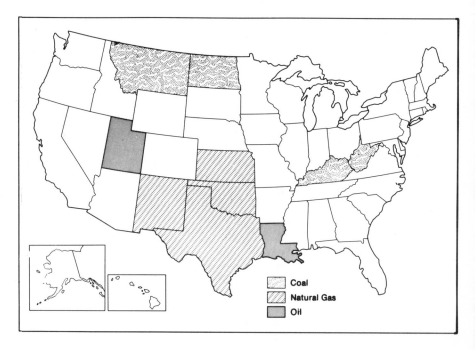

Fig. 25. Fossil fuel surplus states.

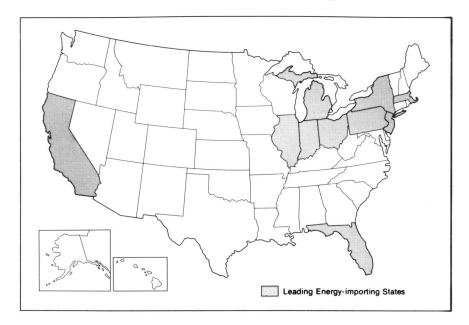

Fig. 26. Leading energy-importing states.

are more recently expanding in both population and industrial capacity. Except for Kentucky and West Virginia, traditional coal producing states, the principal energy exports are in the Southwest, Western Plains, and Rocky Mountain regions. Thus, it appears that distinct energy "producing" and energy "consuming" states exist in terms of their net balance of fuel trade.

Some energy-consuming states in the Northeast and Middle West do produce substantial quantities of coal. Illinois and Pennsylvania, for instance, actually produce more coal than they consume. In addition, Ohio is the nation's fifth largest producer of this fuel but also leads the nation in coal consumption, thus registering a net coal deficit. The Northeast does not have sufficient quantities of onshore oil and gas and must rely upon other regions or foreign imports to satisfy demand requirements. The West does hold great promise for increased energy production.[12]

What are some of the implications of this discrepancy in regional energy supply and demand on the American Metropolitan System? First, it appears that the areas of the country enjoying a better energy supply-energy demand ratio have been faring better, or even improving their situation, since the energy crisis first broke in 1973, compared to other less fortunate regions of the country. Much has been written on the Sunbelt-Frostbelt phenomenon in which regional growth rates in the South and Southwest are gaining while the Northeast and Middle Western states are stagnating (Fig. 27).[13] The Northeast and Middle West have been facing serious fiscal problems, an out-migration of firms and people and chronically high unemployment rates. The fiscal problems are most clearly

Table 51. Energy Deficit–Surplus, 1975 by States
(10^{13} BTU's)

State	Oil[a]	Natural gas[b]	Coal[c]	Total
	Energy Deficit States			
1. New York	-226.8	-62.3	-27.8	-316.9
2. Michigan	-80.2	-80.3	-73.5	-233.0
3. Ohio	-99.4	-85.9	-49.9	-225.2
4. California	-37.4	-155.2	-5.0	-197.7
5. Illinois	-96.7	-177.3	+41.3	-172.7
6. Indiana	-60.7	-45.7	-51.2	-157.7
7. New Jersey	-106.3	-28.3	-5.6	-140.1
8. Pennsylvania	-121.2	-61.1	+48.8	-133.5
9. Florida	-92.1	-22.5	-12.9	-127.5
10. Massachusetts	-104.0	-16.0	-0.9	-120.9
11. Georgia	-50.3	-33.2	-35.1	-118.7
12. N. Carolina	-52.3	-11.9	-50.1	-114.9
13. Missouri	-45.2	-36.4	-33.1	-114.8
14. Wisconsin	-44.0	-36.1	-33.1	-113.9
15. Tennessee	-39.1	-22.8	-43.3	-105.2
16. Minnesota	-43.0	-32.6	-25.9	-101.5
17. Iowa	-29.5	-34.7	-14.4	-78.5
18. Maryland	-51.3	-13.8	-12.3	-77.2
19. Alabama	-32.9	-24.4	-13.1	-70.4
20. Connecticut	-49.7	-6.7	-0.1	-56.5
21. Washington	-36.7	-16.6	-0.9	-54.2
22. S. Carolina	-28.1	-12.3	-13.3	-55.7
23. Nebraska	-13.0	-20.6	-4.1	-37.7
24. Oregon	-25.8	-9.5	-0.3	-35.6
25. Arkansas	-19.2	-16.5	+1.1	-34.6
26. Arizona	-24.4	-15.9	+7.1	-33.2
27. Nevada	-7.4	-6.0	-10.6	-24.0
28. Mississippi	-1.0	-18.3	-3.7	-23.0
29. Idaho	-10.8	-5.4	-1.2	-17.4
30. Delaware	-12.6	-2.1	-2.3	-17.0
31. S. Dakota	-8.3	-3.4	-5.2	-16.9
32. Colorado	-2.1	-14.7	+0.1	-16.7
33. New Hampshire	-12.2	-.8	-2.5	-15.5
34. Rhode Island	-12.2	-2.2	–	-14.4
35. Virginia	-70.7	-11.5	+68.0	-14.2
36. District of Columbia	-7.5	-2.6	-0.9	-11.0
37. Vermont	-5.9	-0.4	–	-6.3
	Energy Surplus States			
1. Louisiana	+323.7	+547.5	–	+871.2
2. Texas	+557.5	+273.8	-3.2	+828.1
3. Kentucky	-25.4	-15.9	+270.6	+229.3
4. Oklahoma	+66.7	+90.5	+6.7	+163.9

Table 51. (cont'd.)

State	Oil[a]	Natural gas[b]	Coal[c]	Total
Energy Surplus States				
5. W. Virginia	-13.4	-1.3	+176.1	+161.4
6. N. Mexico	+40.6	+85.1	+3.2	+128.9
7. Wyoming	+69.2	-17.5	+37.5	+124.2
8. Montana	+7.6	-4.0	+48.9	+52.5
9. Kansas	6.7	+23.3	-6.7	+23.3
10. N. Dakota	3.2	-1.3	+18.7	+20.6
11. Utah	8.3	-8.4	5.8	+5.7

Sources: [a]American Petroleum Institute. *Basic Petroleum Data Fact Book* (Washington, D.C.: API, 1978). [b]Federal Power Commission. *National Gas Flow Patterns 1975* (Washington, D.C.: FPC, Table 12, 1977). [c]U.S. Bureau of Mines. *Minerals Yearbook 1975* (Washington, D.C.: GPO, 1977), p. 446.

demonstrated by the financial crises of the major cities in the region, notably New York and Cleveland.[14] While there are numerous explanations for the relative decline of the region, the energy problem must be viewed as an important contributing factor. In contrast, part of the growth of energy-producing states can be traced to regional multiplier effects.

Compare the energy-producing to the energy-importing states. The average unemployment rate for the 10 leading energy-importing states was 8.6 in 1976, compared to 5.2 in 1973 (the year in which the "energy crisis" first arose), a rise of 3.4% in 4 years. In the 11 energy-exporting states, by contrast, the unemployment rate rose from an average 4.5 in 1973 to 5.8 in 1976, an increase of only 1.3%[15] The number of employees on manufacturing payrolls in 1973 and 1976 is also markedly different according to whether a state was a net energy producer or a net energy consumer. The 10 largest energy-importing states registered an average 8.9% decline in such jobs from 1973 to 1976, whereas energy-exporting states showed an average 2.9% increase in jobs.[16]

In terms of *value-added*, energy-exporting states also appear to be benefiting from higher energy prices. An analysis of the U.S. input-output table by Miernyk suggests that energy-producing sectors of the economy registered the highest value-added increase from 1967 to 1974.[17] Miernyk found that the change in value-added for coal mining increased about 450%, that of petroleum refining and related industries about 220%, and that of crude oil and natural gas about 160%. The states with the largest value-added were Texas ($5.8 billion), Louisiana ($3.1 billion), West Virginia ($2.9 billion), Kentucky ($1.5 billion), and Oklahoma ($1.4 billion).[18]

These figures are also likely to grow with increases in the price of energy. Even prices of those energy forms not controlled by OPEC will increase in relation to OPEC oil price increases.[19] The price of coal, for instance, has demonstrated a

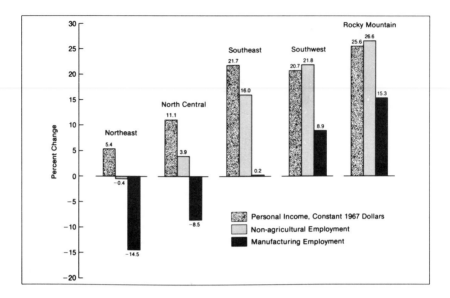

Fig. 27. Changes in real personal income and nonagricultural and manufacturing employment: 1970 and 1975.

close correlation to increases in the price of oil.[20] In 1973, the average U.S. value of coal (F.O.B.) was $8.42 per ton, but increased to $19.43 per ton by 1976.[21] Additional increases in the price of coal are expected.

It appears that there may continue to be a shift in real income from energy-consuming states to energy-producing states. Part of this shift will be reflected in the increased tax revenues in energy-producing states. Severance taxes on fuel is one way in which energy-producing states will benefit by higher energy prices. Table 52 compares the energy severance tax collections from oil, gas, and coal for 1973, 1975, and 1978 for the energy-exporting states. These revenues are a substantial addition to the budgets to these states. In Texas, these taxes provide over one-fourth of the state's total tax collections. Since 1973, all of the energy-exporting states increased their severance tax collections to a significant degree. Texas and Louisiana, for instance, increased their collections by $620 and $207 million, respectively. Kentucky increased its collections by $91 million to over $128 million over the 5-year period, almost entirely on coal taxes.

The role of state severance taxes is likely to increase the discrepancy between energy-consuming and energy-producing states, as some states have increased their taxes in the past few years and have added energy conversion taxes. Montana, for instance, has increased its coal severance tax to 30% in anticipation of increased coal production.[22] Over 50% of this tax is to be allocated to the state's general fund, much of which will be used for education. Over one-third of these revenues are to be used to mitigate coal development impacts.[23] This severance

Table 52. State Energy Severance Tax Collections, 1973, 1975, and 1978
(in thousands of dollars)

Energy exporting state	1973			1975			1978			1973–1978
	oil/gas	coal	total	oil/gas	coal	total	oil/gas	coal	total	
Louisiana	259,455	—	259,455	539,571	—	539,571	466,346	—	466,346	206,891
Texas	334,798	—	334,798	662,089	—	662,089	955,050	—	955,050	620,252
Kentucky	159	37,226	37,385	349	98,740	99,089	395	127,765	128,160	90,775
Oklahoma	71,456	—	71,456	128,096	—	128,096	230,368	—	230,368	158,912
West Virginia[a]	—	—	—	—	—	—	—	—	—	—
New Mexico	36,116	—	36,116	140,226	—	140,226	128,678	—	128,678	92,562
Wyoming	5,307	—	5,307	18,176	—	18,176	—	—	—	66,021
Montana	694	2,693	3,387	6,180	5,396	11,576	6,808	33,624	40,432	37,045
Kansas	711	—	711	700	—	700	841	—	841	130
N. Dakota	3,140	—	3,140	6,880	—	6,880	10,730	7,889	18,619	15,479
Utah	1,530	—	1,530	5,896	—	5,896	6,643	2,283	8,926	7,396

Sources: U.S. Department of Commerce, Bureau of the Census, State Tax Collections in 1973, 1975, and 1978. Washington, D.C.: GPO, 1978, 1976, and 1974.

[a]Some states, such as West Virginia, tax the energy industry through other mechanisms.

tax will pump additional millions of dollars into the state as new coal mines begin operation and existing mines are upgraded. Even if Montana coal sells at the 1976 price of $4.90 a ton (a highly improbable event), the state can expect to collect an additional $170 million annually in coal severance tax revenues.[24] This anticipated increase in collections alone is over twice that which is currently collected by the state from all other sources.[25] While these taxes are viewed as usurious to many outside the region, Montana stands firm in its determination not to be exploited by outside energy developers.[26]

Application fees for energy facilities will also add revenues to energy-producing states. North Dakota, for instance, requires an application fee of $150,000 for a large energy facility.[27] Montana requires about $2 million for a $1 billion energy facility.[28] Thus, it appears that the energy-producing states will likely get richer as they tax energy leaving the state, as well as through additional value-added. Energy-consuming states will continue to pay higher prices for energy, whether domestically produced or imported, and a flow of revenues from energy-consuming to energy-producing states should continue.

It is logical to assume, then, that those cities in energy-producing states and states likely to increase their energy output will be in a better position than cities in states which are not benefiting from energy production and exportation revenues but are paying higher energy prices. Of course, states which do not tax energy production capabilities effectively, such as West Virginia in the past, will not benefit as much as those states with more vigorous tax policies. States such as Texas and, in the near future, Montana will not be in such a financial pinch, and will be able to invest in infrastructural improvements and be better able to endow universities, libraries, parks, and other social services. It is likely that cities in these states will reflect the investments made in them in terms of human resources as well, and will be more attractive for industry and people alike. Furthermore, with such investments and population growth many of these cities will become self-sustaining entities.

IMPACTS UPON METROPOLITAN SYSTEMS

It appears that the metropolitan system will be affected by the energy situation in important and long-lasting ways. These impacts can be discerned at both the interregional and intrametropolitan scale. At the interregional scale, differential rates of growth, regional multipliers, and the degree to which an area is attractive for new industries will depend upon relative energy self-sufficiency. At the intrametropolitan scale, energy availability and price are likely to alter commuter behavior and the spatial form of cities. This section briefly notes some of the ways that the energy situation may affect industrial location decisions and the form of American cities.

IMPACT ON INDUSTRIAL LOCATION DECISIONS

The importance of energy in influencing industrial location decisions has long been recognized. Weber found that "power supplies" can be an important material input for some industries.[29] More importantly, he argued that a primary goal in determining the optimum plant location was to minimize overall transportation costs, upon which energy prices have a profound influence.[30] These two roles of energy in industrial location decision making are still important. Energy can be viewed as a material input or as a factor influencing transportation costs.

As the costs of transportation decreased throughout the 20th century because of declining energy prices and competition among transportation modes, many location theorists downplayed the significance of transportation costs as a crucial factor in industrial location decisions. Indeed, throughout the 1960s and early 1970s conventional wisdom held that the "friction of distance" would follow historical trends and continue to decrease in importance as a determinant of industrial location. The impacts of declining transport costs on industries, for instance, are detailed by Lloyd and Dicken:[31]

> A universal decline in transportation costs combined with the changes. . .toward a more efficient use of raw materials in production processes and the substitution of one material for another (for example, electricity for coal) means that transportation has become a relatively less important factor in the overall cost structure of many industries.

However, higher energy prices are resulting in higher transport costs which may once again make the minimization of transportation costs a significant goal in choosing plant locations. Higher energy prices affect the transportation economics of a firm by altering the relative optimality of plant location vis-a-vis the markets and raw materials. Higher transport costs may not allow the location decision maker the luxury of considering other factors (e.g., personal preference, climate) in the plant location decision.

Rising transportation costs also increase distribution costs, making market locations attractive for some firms. The change in the distribution of industrial facilities toward the South and Southwest may reflect the fact that the region has experienced gains in people and personal income. Giarratani and Socher, for instance, show that the income potential of the region has increased substantially over the gain exhibited in energy-consuming states from 1970 to 1974.[32] The energy-producing states are emerging as important markets attracting industrial establishments who desire to offset the rising distribution costs for their products.

As transportation costs increase, external economies may also rise in significance as locating adjacent to linked industries reduces overall transport costs.[33] Those industries in proximity to closely linked industries or services may not suffer so much from rising transportation costs as those firms located at more remote regions.

Energy also can be an attractive force as a material input. A trend has been recognized showing the attraction of industries to better energy endowed areas of the country.[34] It does not appear, however, that energy availability factors have become fully recognized as an explicit motive behind such a move. Firms mention nonunion labor; lower land, labor, and construction costs; tax advantages; favorable climate; and proximity to growing markets as being more important than energy supplies and as the primary motivation behind the expansion of new operations in the South.[35] Another advantage of choosing sites in energy rich states is the potential security of energy supplies. It has been argued that modern corporations aim to reduce uncertainties so that they can plan for a changing future.[36] Planning efforts are thwarted by energy curtailments or "brown-outs" that may interfere with project scheduling. An entrepreneur who is assured adequate energy supplies needs not worry about halting operations because of local energy shortages even though the energy price advantage from one region to the next may not be so significant.

However, because many new industries and offices are being located in the metropolitan areas of many energy-producing states (e.g., Houston, Oklahoma City), future prospects for growth in the region seem bright. As new establishments are sited, the employment multiplier effects contribute to a circular and cumulative process of local growth. This process has been identified by Pred in terms of leading to the rank stability of cities in advanced economies, and by Thompson as providing fertile ground for the development of entrepreneurial talent.[37] This growth process will further increase the income potential of emerging metropolitan areas.

INTRAMETROPOLITAN IMPACTS

The proliferation of suburbs in the U.S., a crucial aspect of urban form, owes its existence to inexpensive individual transportation more than to any other factor.[38] The dispersed, low-density nature of American cities springs from the automobile. The pervasive influence exerted by the automobile on the form of our cities has been noted by many geographers. Rugg, for example, described the role of the automobile in altering the face of American cities:[39]

> The only thing that made the suburbs possible for so many American people is mobility via the automobile. . . .It became possible to live 5, 10, 15 miles from the center of the city, depending on access roads, and still spend less than an hour commuting. Therefore, more and more people were able to live in a single agglomerated settlement and the settlements covered larger and larger areas, while densities of population decreased on the periphery of the city.

Many writers did not envision that the forces driving suburban growth would be undermined so quickly. Johnson, for instance, writing in 1974, remarked that "in the long run, the growth of dispersed cities is likely, as increased affluence almost everywhere brings a parallel increase in car ownership and encourages a quest for the private space associated with low-density housing."[40] The energy situation may have drastically reversed this trend.

Rising energy prices are reflected in higher gasoline prices and higher prices for automobiles. Thus, higher energy prices increase the cost of commuting by raising the daily travel expenses involved. These factors should work to discourage long-distance commuting, hence modifying the form of our cities. A preliminary study by Henderson and Voiland suggested, for instance, that higher energy prices reduce the desirability of residing in suburban locations.[41]

The energy situation should have the most significant impact on the form of those metropolitan areas that are most dependent upon the automobile, despite the relative abundance of energy in the region. This relationship has been observed by Romanos who notes that "If energy prices are allowed to continue their upward trend, some radical changes in the structure of American cities could be conceivable, and [that] such changes would be directly related to the dependence of these cities upon the use of private automobile."[42] Thus, individuals in automobile dependent cities in the energy surplus states will be as hard hit by rising gasoline prices as their counterparts in the Northeast and Middle West. A survey of 55 cities by Platt's Oilgram Price Service found that the prices ranged from 58.8¢ in Miami, Fla. to 66.4¢ in Fargo, N.D., a range of only 7.6¢.[43] No real spatial patterns in the price of gasoline were detected. The price of gasoline at the pumps depends more upon local marketing characteristics and state and local taxes than upon the regional energy situation.

The effect of higher gasoline prices on the form and structure of American cities has been discussed by some writers. Romanos maintains that "Energy effects should be expected to reinforce the steady trends of business and industry relocation from the central city to the suburbs simply because this move is likely to produce transportation energy savings for the suburban labor pool."[44] He envisions that:[45]

> more compact and dense future residential areas are likely to develop around semi-independent suburban centers of economic activity and employment. The future metropolitan configuration therefore could be one of compact urban clusters each consisting of a suburban employment center and a relatively dense residential area around it.

In some cities, however, there appears to be a resurgence of the downtown area as suburbanites migrate back in to the city from surrounding communities. This could reflect the increased undesirability of commuting or the impact of intercity transportation. It is clear that some cities are more dependent on the automobile because of low density development and the lack of mass transit facilities. A comparison of the effect of energy price increases on the form of cities could be made for those metropolitan areas heavily committed to the automobile (e.g., Detroit, Los Angeles) with those which have other transportation possibilities (e.g., Philadelphia, Washington, D.C.).

CONCLUSIONS

It appears that energy availability problems and higher energy prices will affect metropolitan areas in at least four ways. First, as energy prices and energy demand continues to rise, the dependency of energy deficit regions on energy surplus regions and imports will solidify. Some regions of the country, such as New England,

194   Frank J. Calzonetti

are critically short of essential energy resources. Indeed, variations in energy supply and demand have already spawned regional friction.[46]

Second, energy availability and cost will alter the comparative advantage of cities in some regions over cities elsewhere in terms of the attractiveness to industry. This will be particularly the case where energy expenditures assume a large share of a company's total expenses and if energy supply interruptions are unacceptable for the continued profitability of a firm. Such regional distinctions in energy availability and price may encourage the migration of industrial facilities to locations with less expensive or more secure energy supplies, with economic benefits occurring as a result of regional multiplier effects and self-sustaining growth.

Except for minor centers in the Rocky Moutain-Northern Great Plains states (such as Gillette, Wyo.), the major metropolitan areas in the energy-exporting states have already expanded beyond the growth predicted by export base theory and are as important as consumption centers as they are in their role as sites for basic industries. Thompson argued that once metropolitan areas reach the size of 500,000 inhabitants they begin to become self-sustaining entities.[47] Usually cities of this size have an educated population, a skilled work force, and provide fertile ground for rising entrepreneurial talent. They become sophisticated centers.[48] In this role, the larger metropolitan areas in the energy-producing states (e.g., Houston) should not be viewed as transitory economic "hot-beds" tied exclusively to fossil fuels, but as important permanent centers in the economic landscape of the U.S.

In addition, the future of these cities may even be more promising if they learn from the mistakes made in other metropolitan areas. As these cities grow they can benefit from the experiences faced by New York, Chicago, and Los Angeles in coping with several million people. The point is emphasized by Thompson:[49]

> Thus, New York was the first to have to learn how to handle 10 million people, and must soon be the first to master the problems posed by 20 million. Each successively smaller city, roughly in its rank order, has one more example from which to profit, whether the examples be good or bad....Chicago finds the path a little easier because New York has gone before, and Detroit profits from the pioneering of both.

Efforts by the Southern Growth Policies Board to take cognizance of the problems in the North demonstrate this theme.[50]

Third, energy-producing states are likely to become more financially sound than their energy-deficit counterparts. The degree of such financial soundness depends upon how energy production and exportation is taxed. The contingency funds of energy-producing states are likely to be much higher than in states importing most of their energy needs.[51] Many energy-exporting states impose high energy excise taxes and invest tax dollars into social overhead capital. These states may be able to provide the sound infrastructure that is essential to metropolitan development.

Fourth, the availability and price of energy are likely to influence urban form. It is anticipated that rising energy prices will encourage compact urban clusters over the typical decentralized, dispersed cities of today. Escalating gasoline prices will undoubtedly deter long-distance commuting to some degree.

In sum, it appears that the energy situation will affect the American metropolitan system in pervasive and contradictory ways. On one hand, it appears that those metropolitan areas in energy rich regions will benefit from the increased value of their energy resources and will be favorable sites for certain establishments. This trend would lead to further regional specializations. On the other hand, rising energy prices will increase transfer costs and work to discourage regional specialization, particularly for vital commodities that are generally transported by truck (e.g., milk).[52] If energy prices continue to increase, transportation costs will comprise a larger share of the costs of many products. The result may be a trend away from regional specialization as smaller producers may be able to compete with national organizations at the local level. The outcome could be a return of the local brewery and bakery to the local scene, reminiscent of pre-World War II days.

ADDENDUM

It is not an overstatement to say that energy may be one of the most important factors affecting the American metropolitan system but is so fast-breaking that no printed form, save the daily newspapers, can keep abreast of current developments. Public policy decisions concerning energy may have more ramifications for the relationships among cities and metropolitan growth than public policy decisions made in other problem areas, and these important decisions are difficult to prognosticate. A few examples show how recent public policy decisions could affect the American metropolitan system.

The effects of the Clean Air Act Amendments of 1977, for example, have raised serious issues relating to regional energy development, have spurred conflicts between eastern and western interest, and have demonstrated the importance of public policy considerations to the American metropolitan system. In May, 1979, the U.S. Environmental Protection Agency issued regulations requiring low-scrubbing of lower-sulfur western coals, partial scrubbing of higher sulfur midwestern coals, and full scrubbing of the highest sulfur eastern coal. Although many eastern utilities and coal operators feared that EPA would lower the emissions ceiling of 1.2 pounds of sulfur dioxide per million BTU's, EPA kept the previous ceiling. Before the new rules were released, an intense debate ensured with eastern interests claiming that a lower ceiling would close most eastern mines. One estimate released by the National Coal Association showed that if the ceiling were lowered to 0.55 pounds per million BTU's, almost no coal from either Ohio or Northern West Virginia could be burned.[53] The implications of this to regional employment and metropolitan growth are obvious.

The resulting "sliding scale" rules represent a public policy decision based upon the premise that a marginal increase in air pollution in the West is more damaging to that environment than an equivalent increase in pollution in the East. This is because the present air quality in the West is much cleaner than that in the East and even a slight deterioration would be noticeable. This decision reduces the attractiveness of western coal with respect to midwestern and eastern

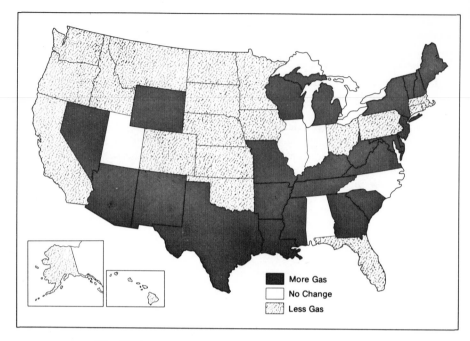

Fig. 28. Standby gas rationing plan: winners and losers.

coal and could slow the shift in energy production to the Rocky Mountain-Northern Great Plains states.

The President's standby gasoline rationing plan would also be adjusted to conform to regional differences in gasoline use. The essence of the plan is to allocate fuel on the basis of vehicle registration but according to the amount of monthly gasoline used in each state. In other words, it is believed that states which consume more gas per capita represent those where per capita gasoline use is less, as shown in Figure 28. This plan has been subject to many criticisms, notably from states with a low per capita consumption which complain that they are being punished for being frugal, and from Great Plains and western states which complain that they export the fuel to other states but are forced to conserve at home.[54] In addition, the dependence upon the automobile varies within each state among cities, suburbs, and occupations. The implications of gas rationing to urban sprawl are enormous, as it may abruptly force patterns of automobile use and perhaps urban development, that would otherwise slowly evolve in response to price increases.

NOTES

*I would like to express my gratitude to Graham D. Rowles and Harley Johansen for reviewing and commenting on earlier drafts of this chapter.
[1]William H. Miernyk, "Rising Energy Prices and Regional Development," *Growth and Change: A Journal of Regional Development*, Vol. 8 (1977), pp. 2-7.

[2]Stan Benjamin, "An Energy Primer," *Washington Post*, Jan. 30, 1977, p. 18. A general discussion of the impact of energy shortages in urban areas can be found in Richard L. Meier, *Planning for an Urban World: The Design of Resource Conserving Cities* (Cambridge, Mass.: MIT Press, 1974), pp. 99–101.

[3]For example, J. Edwin and L. D. Belzung, *World Resource Management: Key to Civilizations and Social Achievement* (Englewood Cliffs, N.J.: Prentice-Hall, Inc., 1975), pp. 214–15. Nuclear fusion, for instance, is touted as one technology that will eliminate our energy supply problems forever. Despite recent promising reports on nuclear fusion "breakthroughs," the technology is still elusive and will probably not be a significant factor in U.S. energy supply in this century. Furthermore, the deuterium-tritium reactor, which is the focus of present fusion research, will not be the panacea envisioned, as tritium is derived from lithium, the availability of which has already been questioned. See "Report of Fusion Breakthrough Proves to Be a Media Event," *Science*, Vol. 201 (1978), pp. 792–94; Denis Hayes, *Rays of Hope* (N.Y.: W. W. Norton & Co., 1977); and Congressional Research Service, *Project Interdependence: U.S. and World Energy Outlook Through 1970* (Washington, D.C.: U.S. Government Printing Office, 1977), p. 396. The more advanced deuterium-deuterium reactor receives much more press coverage but is farther from development than the deuterium-tritium process.

[4]Milton C. Weinstein and Richard J. Zeechauser, "The Optimal Consumption of Depletable Natural Resources," *Quarterly Journal of Economics*, Vol. 89 (1975), pp. 371–92. The authors state on page 390 that "Recent doomsday predictions about our inevitable bare cupboards seem overdrawn. It is powerful solace to know that underlying market forces will work to produce appropriate rates of resource consumption."

[5]Congressional Research Service, op. cit., note 3, p. 45.

[6]"President Carter's Energy Message to Joint Session of Congress," *Energy Users Report*, No. 193 (April, 1977), p. 28.

[7]J. R. Calvert, "Licensing Coal-Fired Power Plants," *Power Engineering*, (Jan., 1978), pp. 37–45.

[8]W. W. Rostow, *Energy, Full Employment, and Regional Development* (Austin, Texas: Council on Energy Resources, 1978), pp. 24–26.

[9]A good survey of ways in which geographers are making contributions to energy research is presented by Wilbanks. Thomas J. Wilbanks, "Geographic Research and Energy Policy Making," *Geographical Survey*, Vol. 7 (1978), pp. 11–18.

[10]Congressional Research Service, op. cit., note 3, p. 6.

[11]1975 data are used since more recent figures for all energy forms were not available at the time of compilation.

[12]U.S. Congress. House Committee on Science and Technology Subcommittee on Energy Research, *Energy Facts II*. 92nd Congress, 2nd Session, (Washington, D.C.: U.S. Government Printing Office, 1975).

[13]The relative growth of the Sunbelt was identified before energy problems were a consideration. See Edgar M. Hoover, *An Introduction to Regional Economics* (N.Y.: Alfred A. Knopf, 1971), pp. 200–10.

[14]More detail on this situation can be found in the following report. U.S. Congress. Joint Economic Committee, *The Future of State and Local Government Finances* (Washington, D.C.: U.S. Government Printing Office, 1977).

[15]Data compiled from the U.S. Bureau of the Census, *Statistical Abstract of the United States, 1977* (Washington, D.C.: U.S. Government Printing Office, 1978).

[16]U.S. Department of Labor, *Handbook of Labor Statistics, 1977*, Bulletin 1966 (Washington, D.C.: Bureau of Labor Statistics, 1977).

[17]William H. Miernyk, "Some Regional Impacts of the Rising Costs of Energy," *Papers of the Regional Science Association*, Vol. 37 (1976), pp. 213–27.

[18]Ibid., p. 222.

[19]Philip Windsor, *A Guide Through the Total Energy Jungle* (Boston: Gambit Press, 1976).

[20]William H. Miernyk, "Regional Consequences of High Energy Prices in the United States," in William H. Miernyk, Frank Giarratani, and Charles F. Socher, eds., *Regional Impacts of Rising Energy Prices* (Cambridge, Mass.: Ballinger, 1978), pp. 5-32.

[21]National Coal Association, *Coal Facts 1978-79* (Washington, D.C.: National Coal Association, 1978), p. 67.

[22]Leonard D. Bronder, *Severance Tax Comparisons Among WGREPO States* (Denver, Col.: Western Governors Regional Energy Policy Office, 1977).

[23]Irvin L. White et al., *Energy From the West: Draft Policy Analysis Report* (Washington, D.C.: U.S. Environmental Protection Agency, 1978), p. 384.

[24]National Coal Association, op. cit., note 21, p. 67. Information on expected coal production increases in Montana taken from Charles H. Rich, Jr., *Project to Expand Energy Sources in the Western States. An update of Information Circular 8719* (Washington, D.C.: U.S. Bureau of Mines, 1978), p. 104.

[25]U.S. Department of Commerce, *State Tax Collections in 1975* (Washington, D.C.: U.S. Government Printing Office, 1975), p. 28.

[26]Michael Billings, the state budget director, expressed the feelings well. "To my way of thinking, the Arabs are doing what they should have done long ago when they were exploited for years by the oil companies." He notes that similar exploitation has occurred in Montana. "We've made some people in other states and countries extraordinarily wealthy from our copper but there is nothing left for us. We're not going to let that happen again." Bill Richards, "The Stip-Mine Boom Windfall to Montana," *Washington Post*, May 22, 1977.

[27]North Dakota Century Code, Chap. 49-22 (1975).

[28]Montana Major Facility Siting Act of 1975. Montana Revised Lodes Annotated 70-801 through 70-823 (cumulative suppl., 1975).

[29]Alfred Weber, *Theory of the Location of Industries*, translated by Carl J. Friedrich (Chicago: University of Chicago Press, 1929), p. 39.

[30]Ibid., p. 41.

[31]Peter E. Lloyd and Peter Dicken, *Location in Space: A Theoretical Approach to Economic Geography*, 2nd ed. (London: Harper & Row, 1977), p. 189.

[32]Frank Giarratani and Charles F. Socher, "The Pattern of Industrial Location and Rising Energy Prices," in Miernyk, Giarratani, and Socher, ed., op. cit., note 20, pp. 103-16.

[33]William H. Latham, III, "Measures of Locational Orientation for 199 Manufacturing Industries," *Economic Geography*, Vol. 54 (1978), pp. 53-65.

[34]U.S. General Accounting Office, *Better Planning Needed to Deal with Shifting Regional Energy Demand* (Washington, D.C.: U.S. General Accounting Office, 1978), p. 4.

[35]John H. Sheridan, "Industry's View of the South—Fruitful but Flawed," *Industry Week* (Feb. 28, 1977). It has been cautioned that it is difficult to identify the most important factors in industrial location decisions from the decision makers themselves because they often attach more importance to emotional factors, such as high taxes or unionized labor, than to the factors which are more realistically important in the location decision. See Edgar M. Hoover, op. cit., note 13, pp. 16-17. This point is also discussed by Nishioka and Krumme who emphasized that site selection decisions are exceedingly complex and not adequately portrayed by conventional location surveys. The authors noted that "Due to a widespread lack of understanding of the relationships between location conditions, factors, and decision stages, location analysts and regional planners have tended to put undue emphasis on the site-selection stage as the focus of analysis or planning concern, without, moreover, clearly identifying the conditions and factors which are effective at this state." Hisao Nishioka and Gunter Krumme, "Location Conditions, Factors, and Decisions: An Evaluation of Selected Location Surveys," *Land Economics*, Vol. 69 (1973), pp. 195-205, quote p. 205.

[36] John Kenneth Galbraith, *The New Industrial State* (Boston: Houghton Mifflin, 1971).

[37] Allen Pred, *City Systems in Advanced Economics* (N.Y.: John Wiley & Sons, 1977). Pred discussed the role of multiplier effects (pp. 30–32) and acknowledged the role of growth in leading to "enhanced likelihood of invention or innovation" (p. 90). Wilbur R. Thompson, "Internal and External Factors in the Development of Urban Economics," in Harvey S. Perloff and Lowdon Wingo, Jr., eds., *Issues in Urban Economics* (Baltimore: The Johns Hopkins Press for Resources for the Future, 1968), pp. 43–80.

[38] Hoover argued that the growth of leisure and longer vacations also have encouraged the growth of suburbs as one's "appetite for spacious home sites and neighborhoods" is increased. Edgar M. Hoover, "The Evolving Form and Organization of the Metropolis," in Harvey S. Perloff and Lowdon Wingo, Jr., eds., op. cit., note 37.

[39] Dean S. Rugg, *Spatial Foundations of Urbanism* (Dubuque: William C. Brown Co., 1972), p. 63.

[40] James H. Johnson, "Geographical Processes at the Edge of the City," in James H. Johnson, ed., *Suburban Growth* (London: John Wiley & Sons, 1974), pp. 1–16, quote p. 12.

[41] Floyd H. Henderson and Michael P. Vailand, Jr., "Some Possible Effects of Energy Shortages on Residential Preferences," *Professional Geographer*, Vol. 27 (1975), pp. 323–26.

[42] M. C. Romanos, "Energy-Price Effects on Metropolitan Spatial Structure and Form," *Environment and Planning*, Vol. 10 (1978), pp. 93–104, quote p. 94.

[43] American Petroleum Institute, *Basic Petroleum Data Fact Book* (Washington, D.C.: American Petroleum Institute, 1978).

[44] M. C. Romanos, op. cit., note 42, p. 100.

[45] Ibid., p. 102.

[46] Neal R. Pierce, "Northeastern Governors Map Battle Plan for Fight over Federal Funds," *National Journal*, Vol. 27 (1976), p. 1699.

[47] Wilbur R. Thompson, op. cit., note 37.

[48] Galbraith offered a different interpretation of the usefulness of "entrepreneurial talent" in the context of an economy largely composed of large corporations. He argued that the application of advanced technology and specialization has eliminated the "need" for geniuses in the management of a major corporation as tasks are well-defined and narrow in scope within the organizational framework. The importance of "entrepreneurial genius" in directing a modern corporation is anachronistic. However, Thompson's argument on the importance of a large city to urban growth is still sound, as such metropolitan areas and their universities still produce armies of technicians, engineers, lawyers, and accountants which form the backbone of any large corporation. John Kenneth Galbraith, op. cit., note 36.

[49] Wilbur Thompson, op. cit., note 37.

[50] E. Evan Brunson and Thomas D. Bever, *Southern Growth Trends 1970-1976* (Research Triangle Park, N.C.: Southern Growth Policies Board, 1977).

[51] U.S. Congress, Joint Economic Committee, *The Current Fiscal Position of State and Local Governments* (Washington, D.C.: U.S. Government Printing Office, 1975).

[52] For a discussion of the importance of transportation innovations on regional specialization at a time when the impact of highway transportation was first being realized, see George T. Renner, "Geography of Industrial Localization," *Economic Geography*, Vol. 23 (1947), pp. 167–89.

[53] Dick Kirschten, "Politics at the Heart of the Clean Air Debate," *National Journal*, Vol. 11 (1979), p. 816.

[54] Seymour Zucker, "Why More People Are Thinking of Gasoline Rationing," *Business Week*, No. 2591 (June 25, 1979), p. 82.

Chapter 13

Alternative Prospects for America's Urban Future

Stephen S. Birdsall

Geographers and other social scientists examining urban futures need to study specific predictions and changes within metropolitan-based population and land use models and not only the problems likely to occur. Too often urban predictions are based on monocentric urban models such as those of Burgess and Hoyt. Their concepts are increasingly difficult to juxtapose with the most recent patterns that are currently characteristic of the expansive metropolitan areas of urban America. Future metropolitan areas will differ sharply from the past in that there will be multiple major commercial nodes, communities based on voluntary bases not limited to ethnicity, and a regional or metropolitan governmental organization. Other changes include population and income profiles that will tend to flatten out and travel behavior patterns reflecting higher energy costs. A major cornerstone of metropolitan systems in the future will be a form of political organization needed to accommodate the greater variety of social services demanded by metropolitan population. The chapter concludes that the transformations that will occur will generate a different, but possibly better, urban America.

If we were to rely on the popular media for our view of America's urban future, it would appear obvious that the nation's larger cities are dying. There are frequent reports of big city mayors petitioning the federal government for relief. Allocations of billions of dollars for inner city investment and rehabilitation projects are reported adjacent to other analyses of the persistence of urban deterioration and approaching municipal bankruptcy. The political Right blames government waste and "those people" for making cities unpleasant and dangerous. The political Left points an accusing finger at private enterprise and a different "those people" for seeking personal gain without recognizing the human damage done by central city abandonment. And the general conclusion from all this appears to be supported by academic analyses, as well.[1]

I have begun to suspect that this pessimistic conclusion is not inevitable and that we should consider our cities' obituaries "somewhat premature." America's urban landscape is changing; there can be no argument over that. However, it is important that we recognize that our large cities' problems, especially those of the older large cities, are not terminal, they are only transitional. If the study of urban problems is restricted to an essentially fatalistic paradigm, the resulting policy is likely to be specious and undoubtedly fruitless. With an alternative, more neutral view, the goal of urban research would be shifted toward easing the transformation from what is to what will be and toward making it as painless as possible. As Charles Leven recently told the House Select Committee on U.S. Population, we need a strategy that will "help New York grow old gracefully."[2]

In developing the following thoughts on America's urban future, intuition has been my guide among the labyrinth of others' efforts. To dare to consider such a large and exceedingly complex issue in so decidedly unscientific a manner is risky, of course, but the success of another in a similar approach, even though more able than I, has provided encouragement enough to quiet my misgivings.[3] While following this intuition, I consciously strove to remain neutral as long as possible. That is, I avoided imposing what I thought desirable and considered instead what actually seems to be happening in spite of the best efforts of various social and political groups. Berry has argued that there are deep-seated cultural impulses beneath America's urban transformation.[4] To ignore such fundamental trends is to be prematurely misled by personal conviction.

My purpose, therefore, is to present alternative views of America's urban future and to consider policy approaches relevant to one view that might ease the transition. As with any look toward the future, especially the several-decade period envisioned here, there is the additional risk that readers of scientific bent will discount the effort as meaningless or trivial because long-term predictions do not lend themselves to early verification. It is my hope, however, to stimulate alternative questions and subsequent investiations by those who will not accept the historically deterministic view that there is only one possible future from our single past.

THE BASIC PROBLEM: THE OLD PARADIGM

Pessimistic perceptions of the spatial character of major urban problems are rooted in models of urban structure that developed during the late 19th and early 20th centuries. Burgess offered his concentric model of urban structure when central business districts dominated much of the apparent urban form.[5] Hoyt's sectoral modification provided an alternative emphasis,[6] but it remained a single-center model. The nominally multi-nuclear model suggested by Harris and Ullman[7] does not seem to have altered the general perception of urban structure, perhaps in part because their model is more difficult to experience directly. In any case, it is more accurately multi-*zonal* with distinct functions dominating each zone. Whatever the reason, most dire predictions of our urban future continue to imply a monocentric structure.

The spread of urban population beyond the political limits of central cities, the enclosure of the large cities by politically independent suburbs, and the metropolitan imbalance between fiscal resources and service demand are at the base of many of our older central cities' current problems.[8] This dismal sequence has become familiar through its repetition: As the urban population grew through the early 20th century, those who were able to afford new homes and the long daily trip into the city moved to the outer edge of urban development. Those who needed to stay closer to work or who were less able to afford a "nicer place" remained in the central city. Gradually, the income distribution of the urban area reflected these shifts with higher average income among the suburban population, a dichotomy reinforced politically by municipal incorporation of the surrounding communities. Business and industry eventually moved beyond central city borders as well to lower taxes, more room for expansion, and proximity to an increasing share of their white collar employees. By 1975, for example, headquarters for 3 of the top 9 and nearly one-third of Fortune's top 1,000 companies were located in suburbs rather than central cities.[9] The central cities' tax base declined, which resulted in deterioration of services and further flight by residents who could move and by many of the remaining businesses. Most people migrating from metropolitan areas appear to be leaving for reasons that have little to do with employment.[10] With few exceptions, the pace of relocation away from the largest cities has increased since 1970[11] (Table 53).

Table 53. Population Loss Among Major U.S.
Cities, 1970–1978

1970 rank	City	Population decline	% decline
1	New York	-472,732	-6.0
2	Chicago	-295,273	-8.8
3	Los Angeles	-65,819	-2.0
4	Philadelphia	-152,593	-7.8
5	Detroit	-199,857	-13.2
6	Baltimore	-78,348	-8.6
9	Washington	-56,380	-7.4
10	Cleveland	-125,236	-17.0
11	Indianapolis	-37,435	-5.0
12	Milwaukee	-56,290	-7.8
13	San Francisco	-52,196	-7.0
16	Boston	-22,821	-3.6

Source: Population Reference Bureau, *Intercom*, Vol.
7, No. 1 (Jan. 1979), p. 15.

The changing social composition of the central cities has compounded this grim scenario. Excluded from most suburbs by lower average incomes and racial discrimination, blacks were much less able to relocate to the urban fringe than whites.[12] Until recently, the central cities gradually became more black while suburbs remained largely white. For example, Cleveland's central city was 39% black by 1970 while the balance of its metropolitan area was only 3% black. In the Detroit metropolitan area, the difference was 44% black within the city but 95% white in the suburban ring. Thus, the pattern of suburban affluence and central city poverty that probably would have developed even within a racially homogeneous population came to be seen primarily in racial terms.

By coasting along within the perspective provided by this sequence, the demise of America's larger central cities appears inevitable. The abandoned buildings, poorly repaired streets, choking pollution, reductions in police and fire personnel, and recurrent budgetary problems seem to be leading toward a time when inner city populations will be all but abandoned to lives of meagre survival.

AN ALTERNATIVE

The mechanistic inevitability of this perspective is unfortunate, for this sinister script offers only one of several likely futures and ignores changes already tentatively in evidence. As these changes have occurred—changes often only peripherally related to central city/suburban resource imbalance—the traditionally pessimistic view has become outmoded. If America's large cities continue to be seen in terms of "decaying cores" or "declining sectors," judgments and prescriptions for those cities remain bound by the Burgess or Hoyt conceptualizations of urban structure.

It is becoming easier to anticipate large cities with a rather different spatial organization in the future. Nearly equivalent in total population and economic energy to our present stumbling urban giants, future urbanized regions are likely to appear and function more like large dispersed clusters of smaller urban communities. Rather than a single dominant central core containing the locus of all major managerial functions, there will be many small cores. The smaller cores will each possess their own economic activities, but these will not necessarily be the same from core to core. One, for example, may be a theater-museum-restaurant cluster while another may be primarily financial and commercial, even if it too contains some activity sites for social recreation.

The smaller, distinct communities will be akin to congregations of mutual interest and mutual values.[13] While similar to ethnic enclaves in their largely voluntary congregate origins, these future mutual interest communities will not be limited by ethnicity. To permit administration of such an urban patchwork or mosaic, it will no longer be feasible to have an unwiedly bureaucracy that attempts to serve the entire sprawling urban area at all levels of government and is highly susceptible to lobbying and pressure groups.[14] Nor will a complex of semicompetitive, autonomous jurisdictions be acceptable.[15] Instead, local services will be controlled more locally while only the truly general services will be operated at the larger regional or metropolitan level.

There are three primary components to this alternative view: the future population distribution of large urbanized regions, their income distributions, and the political response to the social mosaic of this population pattern.

POPULATION DENSITY AND INCOME DISTRIBUTIONS

Likely urban population density distributions are suggested by the extension of a generally accepted model. Newling's development of Clark's idea indicates that the highest urban residential densities are located at some distance from the city center and decline away from this peak both toward and away from the city center.[16] The location of the zone of peak densities is a function of the age of the city, with greatest densities more distant from city center among older cities. Empirical tests by both men indicated that the urban population density profiles appear to be flattening over time even as their wave crests move outward from the city center, an observation often ignored by those commenting on urban prospects.[17]

In most of our older large cities, therefore, we can expect much smaller differences in population density between suburb and central city, perhaps before the end of this century (Fig. 29). The general density sequence outward from city center may remain about the same but the densities will be different. During the decade or so prior to 1970, older cities experienced rapid central city population decline and growth in the suburban ring. Since 1970, nonmetropolitan areas have been growing faster than metropolitan areas as a whole. The population of the city of St. Louis, for example, dropped 17% between 1960 and 1970 while that city's large ring of suburban communities grew in population by more than 28%. Since 1970, the total metropolitan population of St. Louis has declined by more than 30,000. By extension and interpolation, we can anticipate that the overall population density in the largest old urban areas, suburb and central city alike, will be lower than the present uneven but still rather high densities might suggest.

The income composition of the urban population is as important as the number and concentration of people because it is related to the financial underpinnings of metropolitan administration. We can expect, and in many cases can already see, a reversal of immediate post-World War II trends and an eventual return to central cities by families and individuals with substantial personal resources. The Capitol Hill and Southwest neighborhoods in Washington, D.C., and Society Hill and Queen Village in Philadelphia are examples that can be found repeated across the country. Partly because neighborhood "revitalization" can have undesirable effects on previous residents,[18] persistence of this flow and the length of time before it is significant will depend to some degree on governmental policies adopted.

With some notable exceptions, selection of residential location in American society is governed largely by individual choice within the constraints of available personal resources and housing availability. Racial discrimination is probably the major exception to this relative freedom. A gradual movement of substantial numbers of low income people toward the suburbs and the infiltration of interior

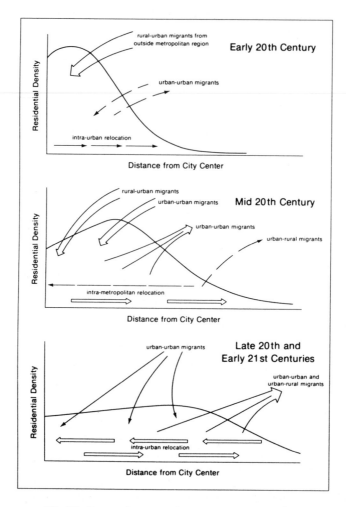

Fig. 29. Stage of metropolitan residential density.

areas by those of middle income will occur because the older suburbs will become less desirable and the inner city areas more attractive. For many, Manhattan *is* the Big Apple and a most appealing residential location if housing costs are "manageable."

There are several more substantial reasons to expect greater inward relocation by higher income persons. First, suburbs age one year at a time just like the inner city. Older suburbs are structurally similar to many sections of their primary cities. Urbanists often recognize this by distinguishing between "inner" and "outer" suburbs. Such inner suburbs as Alexandria, Jersey City, and Cicero have not been *sub*-urban for decades. Consequences of this aging will be resisted more effectively by some suburbs than others, but New York's close-in neighbor of Newark—now a major central city in its own right—holds the dubious honor of a first place ranking in terms of the "hardship experienced by its population" in a recent Brookings Institution study.[19]

Second, urban areas have spread outward partly because that was where land was available and partly because private personal transportation was so cheap relative to other expenditures. The long trip into the city, when necessary, was no more a burden than the shorter trip within the city had been decades before. Both of these conditions are changing. While our national travel behavior in the face of a doubling of gasoline prices in the half decade prior to 1979 is testimony to resilient budgets and an unwillingness to accept personal mobility restrictions, it remains to be seen whether another price doubling in a shorter time period will bring to the surface greater acceptance of alternative modes of travel and shorter trips. If it does, the far margins of suburban settlement will appear somewhat less attractive.

More clearly for the long run, alternative land for expansion has begun to appear within the larger metropolitan areas much as it was predicted by the Clark-Newling model.[20] This land, as "empty" as that on the outer fringes of exurbia, is deep within the central cities themselves. Some of this land is occupied by old structures, but many of the structures are also empty, abandoned by their owners as taxes, vandalism, and the costs of rehabilitation take their toll. In a few cases, residents of old apartment buildings remain to attempt the rehabilitation themselves, but more often the structures are reduced to rubble or stand gutted and empty as mute testimony to a policy of "benign neglect." In 1970, for example, the U.S. Census Bureau counted 3,000 vacant units in Baltimore not for sale or rent, nearly 5,000 in Los Angeles, and more than 15,000 in New York City.

In some cases, reoccupation of empty inner city land may come about through private efforts. An example of an unorthodox approach to such reoccupation is available in New York's South Bronx. There, the Bronx Frontier Development Corporation was formed to use cleared land to produce compost from local wastes. One use for the compost is to rehabilitate additional South Bronx land for gardens and parks where abandoned structures have been cleared away. Governmental programs could also ease the transition by assisting resident rehabilitation where it is feasible or demolishing abandoned structures where it is not and banking the land until large enough contiguous areas are accumulated to attract new housing— probably at lower density than before but still multi-family dwellings.

Anticipation of the residential distribution of specific income groups, such as those earning relatively little, is more difficult. Even independent of such injustices as discrimination and arbitrary restrictions on opportunity, our society is formally egalitarian of purpose but not egalitarian of resource distribution. Thus, significant individual income differences will remain. Variation in strength of purpose or ability, familial or peer support, random happenstance, and probably inheritance will lead some to gain more personal income than others.

Those who have disposable income above some socially established minimum (however imperfectly that minimum may be set or administered) may choose to spend all or part of it on residence-based consumption. Examples would be landscaping, a location requiring longer social or work trips, and the structure itself. However, there seems to be an increasing minority with income above this minimum who are choosing to spend it on nonresidential items and activities such as recreation, education, and self-actualizing experimentation. The poor may live most easily among congregate communities of this latter group.

What ever the resultant income pattern, the large monolithic and overwhelming central city is disappearing and is unlikely to reappear. Instead, the political city will slowly dissolve during future decades into smaller congregate communities similar in many respects to our current suburbs. Each community will need to have jurisdiction over many of the local services, such as recreation, some health care, and possibly primary education. Higher political jurisdictions will exist primarily for their coordinative function and to collect and redistribute taxes. Because of the significant fiscal disparities that will remain between a metropolitan region's communities, this higher jurisdiction should encompass the entire metropolitan region. Thus, metropolitan governments would be able to operate in much the same hierarchical fashion as county, state, and federal governments currently do but still with a purely urban constituency.

URBAN SERVICES AND ADMINISTRATIVE STRUCTURE

Many of the problems often seen as endemic to the older, large urban areas are aggravated by the metropolitan administrative structures' resistance to change in the face of new organizational needs. Most cities' administrative support systems were initially designed for multidimensional service: to maintain the urban economic base and facilitate its growth, and to serve the resident and working population. However, the political-administrative requirements of cities and towns are best met when they are in proper balance with the functional priorities of those communities. Thus, an industrial community has different governmental priorities than a recreational community, for example, and both will be different from the administrative emphases of a settlement dominated by retirees. There are similarities, of course, but the differences suggest alternative local administrative structures and a correlative hierarchy of public services.

Public services may be aligned generally along a continuum (Fig. 30). At one extreme are the *fundamental* services that everyone accepts as essential and even

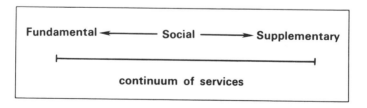

Fig. 30. Public service continuum.

obligatory for safe and healthy community living. Examples are a pure water supply, effective waste disposal, and adequate fire and police protection. At the other end of the continuum are what may be called *supplementary* services. These tend to be purchased privately and only supplemented by governmental agencies. The best example may be recreation, but personal transportation also comes close. In between these extremes is a broad range of *social* services that nearly everyone accepts as desirable but may not be viewed as possessing sufficient social value to consider them truly essential. Thus, there is considerable disagreement among members of society over the amount of public support to provide for such social services as assistance to the handicapped, youth involvement programs, environmental monitoring, and even many levels of medical care and education. As there are short-term fluctuations in the local public fiscal balance, governmental budgets tip toward the fundamental services. And long-term gradual changes in social attitudes may also shift specific social services toward one end of the continuum or the other, rendering them more or less liable to permanent public support.

Independent of whatever short- or long-term fluctuations affect characterization of specific public services, metropolitan administrative structures will have to be redesigned to permit the broadest jurisdiction to operate the fundamental services and those aspects of social services consistent with national social goals. Local communities, on the other hand, would be granted the jurisdiction to choose and operate the degree and types of the remaining social and almost all supplementary services believed appropriate by the local populace. In the redefinition of jurisdictions required by this two-level hierarchical organization, the most difficult decisions will involve identification of services truly essential to all.

Within such an alternative urban future, the tax base for all essential services would have to encompass the entire metropolitan region or communities would come to be defined by their residents' income. Without this, nationally valued social services might be privately purchased by individuals able to do so with subsequent attempts to escape the zone of taxation. The consequent central city/suburb fiscal disparity would be little different from the pattern that currently exists. Needed is direct and moderately progressive regional taxation—a metropolitan income tax—instead of the existing mixture of property, sales, and income taxes scattered among the fragmented jurisdictions. These metropolitan taxes would be seen by all to pay for essential services only. Additional local services could be financed by limited, local taxation, or by grants from state or federal agencies if such services are sufficiently valued by the local community.

As sections of our central cities are emptied, those who might otherwise seek relocation further outward will be encouraged to reenter the urban interior by the opportunity to move to congregate communities with public services appropriate to their life cycle stage and personal value structure. With all essential services equivalently supplied and tax levels based on income rather than residential location, these other factors will be even more important than they presently are when considering where in the metropolitan region to live.

If urban America still wants and can afford low density communities for much of its citizenry, a socially and economically multi-nucleated, low density city may be this country's most probable future urban form.[21] Central cities will have to dissolve into a diverse patchwork of interior suburban-like communities. Businesses will also have to be more widely scattered throughout the region. The essential administrative functions of government will have to encompass the entire metropolitan region, but nonessential services in their turn will have to be locally determined and locally controlled. Many of the urban ills perceived by observers are expressions of transformation and the resistance of existing patterns and institutions to the developing form. The outcome of this transformation will be an urban structure rather different from what has existed and may be, in many ways, better than what we have.

NOTES

[1] Two examples with divergent explanations for the conclusions are: Edward C. Banfield, *The Unheavenly City Revisited* (Boston: Little Brown, 1974) and R. J. Colenutt, "Do Alternatives Exist for Central Cities?" in *Geography of the Ghetto: Perspectives in Geography*, 2, H. M. Rose, ed., (DeKalb, Ill.: Northern Illinois University Press, 1972), pp. 87–109.

[2] *Consequences of Changing U.S. Population: Population Movement and Planning*, Vol. III, Hearings before the Select Committee on Population, U.S. House of Representatives, 95th Congress, 2nd Session (Washington, D.C.: U.S. Government Printing Office, 1978), p. 23.

[3] Wilbur Zelinsky, "The Demigod's Dilemma," *Annals*, Association of American Geographers, Vol. 65 (1975), pp. 123–43 and Wilbur Zelinsky, "Beyond the Exponentials: The Role of Geography in the Great Transition," *Economic Geography*, Vol. 46 (1970), pp. 498–535.

[4] Brian J. L. Berry, "The Decline of the Aging Metropolis: Cultural Bases and Social Process," in *Post-Industrial America: Metropolitan Decline and Inter-regional Job Shifts*, George Sternlieb and James W. Hughes, eds., (New Brunswick, N.J.: The Center for Urban Policy Research, 1975), pp. 175–85.

[5] E. W. Burgess, "The Growth of the City," in *The City*, Robert G. Park, Ernest W. Burgess, and Roderick D. McKenzie, eds. (Chicago: University of Chicago Press, 1925), pp. 47–62.

[6] Homer Hoyt, *The Structure and Growth of Residential Neighborhoods in American Cities* (Washington, D.C.: U.S. Federal Housing Administration, 1939).

[7] Chauncy D. Harris and Edward L. Ullman, "The Nature of Cities," *Annals*, American Academy of Political and Social Science, No. 242 (1945), pp. 7–17.

[8] Kevin R. Cox, *Conflict, Power and Politics in the City* (N.Y.: McGraw-Hill, 1973) and David T. Stanley, *Cities in Trouble* (Columbus, Ohio: Academy for Contemporary Problems, 1976).

[9] Peter O. Muller, "The Outer City: Geographical Consequences of the Urbanization of the Suburbs," Association of American Geographers, *Resource Paper*, No. 75-2 (1976), p. 37.

[10] James D. Williams and Andrew J. Sofranko, "Motivations for the Immigration Component of Population Turnaround in Nonmetropolitan Areas," *Demography*, Vol. 16 (1979), pp. 239–55.

[11] Peter A. Morrison and Judith P. Wheeler, "Rural Renaissance in America?" *Population Bulletin*, Vol. 31 (1976) and Kevin F. McCarthy and Peter A. Morrison, *The Changing Demographic and Economic Structure of Nonmetropolitan Areas in the United States*, Paper No. R-2389, The Rand Corporation (Jan. 1979).

[12] Harold M. Rose, "The All Black Town: Suburban Prototype or Rural Slum?" in *People and Politics in Urban Society*, H. Hahn, ed. (Beverly Hills: Sage Publications, 1972), pp. 397–431.

[13] James E. Vance, Jr., "The American City: Workshop for a National Culture," in *Contemporary Metropolitan America*, Vol. 1, John S. Adams, ed. (Cambridge, Mass.: Ballinger, 1976), pp. 1–49.

[14] Kevin R. Cox, op. cit., note 8.

[15] Robert C. Wood, *1400 Governments* (Cambridge, Mass.: Harvard University Press, 1961).

[16] Colin Clark, "Urban Population Densities," *Journal of the Royal Statistical Society*, Series A., Vol. 114 (1951), pp. 490–96 and Bruce E. Newling, "The Spatial Variation of Urban Population Densities," *Geographical Review*, Vol. 59 (1969), pp. 242–52.

[17] A recent exception is: John S. Adams, "A Geographical Basis for Urban Public Policy," *Professional Geographer*, Vol. 31 (1979), pp. 135–45.

[18] Roman A. Cybriwsky and Paul R. Levy, "Neighborhood Revitalization: Worthy Accomplishment–But What About the Side Effects," *Vital Issues*, Vol. 28 (1979) and Paul R. Levy, *Queen Village: The Eclipse of Community* (Philadelphia: Institute for the Study of Civic Values, 1978).

[19] Richard P. Nathan and Charles Adams, "Understanding Central City Hardship," *Political Science Quarterly*, Vol. 91 (1976), pp. 47–62.

[20] Colin Clark, op. cit., note 16 and Bruce E. Newling, op. cit., note 16.

[21] A similar conclusion regarding our future urban form was reached via a slightly different route by: Charles L. Leven, "Growth and Nongrowth in Metropolitan Areas and the Emergence of Polycentric Metropolitan Form," *Papers*, The Regional Science Association, Vol. 41 (1978), pp. 101–12.

Contributors

Stephen S. Birdsall, University of North Carolina, Chapel Hill
Susan R. Brooker-Gross, Virginia Polytechnic Institute and State University
Stanley D. Brunn, University of Kentucky
Frank J. Calzonetti, West Virginia University
Thomas A. Clark, Rutgers University
Roman A. Cybriwsky, Temple University
Joe T. Darden, Michigan State University
Brian P. Holly, Kent State University
James H. Johnson Jr., Michigan State University
Edward J. Malecki, University of Oklahoma
Peter O. Muller, Temple University
Philip D. Phillips, WAPORA, Chicago, Illinois
Curtis C. Roseman, University of Illinois
John D. Stephens, University of California, Los Angeles
Donald J. Zeigler, Michigan State University

Index

Albuquerque, 24, 137, 138
Arizona, 4, 10, 70, 72, 79, 138
Atlanta, 12, 24, 26, 27, 28, 59, 63, 65, 79,
    80, 139, 172
Austin, TX, 39, 63, 137, 140
Automatic Interaction Detector (AID), 51

Baltimore, 24, 37, 44, 63, 82, 207
Boston, 24, 27, 38, 86

California, 4, 59, 62, 70, 72, 79, 101, 133,
    139, 140
Central business district, 22
Central cities, 37, 44, 90, 203, 204
 tax base, 203
Chicago, 13, 24, 25, 60, 122, 161, 172
City
 back to city movement, 28
Commission on Population Growth and the
    American Future, 9
Communication systems, 144-159
 costs/marketability, 149, 150, 154, 155
 diffusion/adoption, 146, 149, 153, 154
 impact on travel, 153, 155, 156
 mobile systems, 156

related to city size, 149, 152
supply, 145, 146, 147, 148, 149, 152
technologies, 12
urban vs. rural, 154
Community needs, 78
Corporate control, 168
Corporate Headquarter Offices (CHO), 161
 external/internal linkages, 163, 164
 linkages to cities, 163
 relocation, 165
 role of mergers, 166, 167
Cost of living index, 69
County
 business patterns, 44

Dallas, Dallas/Ft. Worth, 39, 59, 65, 136,
    140, 161
Denver, 39, 44, 46, 137, 138, 140, 165
Detroit, 25, 60, 88, 90, 132, 161, 172, 193
District of Columbia (Washington, DC), 8, 24,
    27, 28, 30, 44, 46, 63, 127, 133, 137,
    193, 205
Downtown areas, revitalization, 21, 22

Economy, no growth/slow growth, 5, 16, 17,
    18, 19

Employment trends, 13, 44, 45, 46, 47, 113, 114, 115
Energy availability, 8, 182, 183
  regional variations, 184-190
Energy crisis, 182
Energy, impact of, 26, 181, 182, 190, 191, 192, 193
Energy pricing, 187, 188
Energy producing and consuming states, 185, 186, 187
Exurbia growth, 51, 55, 56
  migration, 54, 55, 57
  model for development (tree graph), 54
  problems, 51
  variables related to, 53

Florida, 4, 10, 13, 53, 54, 62, 70, 72, 79, 89, 101
Fortune 500, 168, 169, 173
Fossil fuels, 184, 185
Fragmented metropolitan areas, 77

Gentrified areas, 22
  problems of, 29, 30
Geopolitical fragmentation, 78, 81
  cities, 80, 81
  city-county consolidation, 86
  consequences, 90
  index (IGF), 77, 80, 82
  revision/changes, 82, 84, 85

Home ownership, 106
Housing, 17, 26, 30
Houston, 39, 59, 63, 65, 86, 90, 132, 136, 139, 161, 168, 172, 173, 192
Human services, 112

Land, cost, 207
Lending, related to, 93
  discrimination, 94, 98, 99, 100
  geographic and social variations, 92, 93
Loan available, 94
Los Angeles, 4, 25, 62, 65, 70, 72, 122, 127, 139, 140, 172, 181, 187, 188, 193

Manufacturing, 9, 112
Memphis, 63, 90, 139
Metropolitan decline, 51, 52, 77, 78, 79
Metropolitan deconcentration, 168
Metropolitan growth, 2, 4, 78, 111, 170
  energy, 190-193

future, 201
regions, 78, 79, 80
Miami, 63, 139, 193
Middle Atlantic region, 4, 39, 60, 61, 62, 114, 139, 172
Middle West (Midwest) region, 39, 59, 72, 89, 137, 182, 185, 193
Migration, black, 59
  direction, 59, 65
  history of, 60, 61
  regional/state patterns, 61, 62, 63, 65
  variables related to, 67, 68, 69
Mortgage loans, 94, 99, 100
  bias involved, 99, 100, 101
  government involvement, 100, 101, 107
  policy recommendations, 107, 108

National office headquarters, 162, 163
Needy cities, 87, 88, 89
Neighborhoods
  decay, 22
  revitalization, 21, 22, 23, 24, 25, 27, 74
New England, 10, 13, 38, 62, 70, 81, 82, 90, 101, 114, 139, 172
New Orleans, 24, 27, 39, 44, 46, 63, 68, 139
New York, 8, 11, 13, 62, 70, 99, 133, 161, 165, 202
New York City, 24, 27, 30, 37, 39, 44, 60, 97, 122, 127, 161, 165, 172, 207
North Central region, 4, 17, 77, 78, 79, 81, 84, 85, 88, 89, 113, 114, 119, 121, 122
Northeast region, 4, 12, 13, 17, 59, 77, 78, 79, 81, 82, 85, 86, 88, 89, 94, 111, 112, 114, 117, 119, 121, 122, 138, 139, 161, 165, 182, 185, 193

Pacific region, 38, 61, 62, 104, 172
Philadelphia, 24, 25, 27, 28, 30, 37, 44, 46, 60, 193, 205
Phoenix, 39, 86, 139
Pittsburgh, 25, 60, 136, 161, 172
Population changes, 1, 4, 13
  birthrate/trends, 5, 8, 25
  density, 205
  future, 202
  impact on employment, 113
Post-city age, 11, 12
Post-industrial society, 112
Propagator
  mononuclear, 150
  polynuclear, 149

Rank-size function, 170
Redlining, 93, 94, 95, 96, 97, 98
Regional growth patterns, 3, 4, 11
Research and development, 127, 128, 130,
    131, 133, 134, 136, 137
Retirement developments, 10
Rural mystique, 10
Rural renaissance, 9, 51, 55

St. Louis, 24, 37, 44, 46, 89, 165, 205
San Francisco, 24, 27, 30, 37, 44, 46, 86,
    88, 132, 140, 147
Science and technology, 126, 128, 132, 136,
    140
Seattle, 4, 24, 139, 147
Second home developments, 10
Service occupations, 111, 112, 113, 124, 208
Shift-share analysis, 117, 119, 120
South, 4, 13, 17, 39, 59, 60, 61, 62, 65, 67,
    68, 69, 70, 72, 77, 79, 82, 84, 85, 86, 88,
    89, 91, 94, 100, 102, 104, 107, 113, 114,
    117, 119, 121, 122, 137, 139, 185, 191,
    192
South Carolina, 62, 70, 72
Southwest region, 4, 10, 53, 54, 80, 191

Suburbia, 37, 39, 40, 203, 204
  aging, 207
  economic/racial changes, 42, 43
  impact of automobile, 192
  independence, 37
  migration, 28, 29
  multiple dwelling units, 47
  population growth, 37, 38, 43

Tax base, 209
Television, cable, 147, 150, 152
Territorial annexation and detachment, 77, 84,
    85
Texas, 39, 55, 59, 62, 65, 70, 72, 79, 89, 101,
    138, 181, 187, 188, 190
Transportation costs, 191

Urban development models, 202, 203

Videotelephone, 148

West, 60, 61, 65, 79, 82, 84, 85, 86, 88, 91,
    94, 100, 102, 104, 107, 113, 114, 117,
    119, 121, 122, 139, 172
Working class communities, 31